50

Dates with the Lord

50

Dates with the Lord

A BROKEN WOMAN'S JOURNEY TO FINDING
THE MAN WHO COULD FIX HER

Caren Bright

Fedd Books
P.O. Box 341973
Austin, TX 78734
www.thefeddagency.com

Published in association with The Fedd Agency, Inc., a literary agency.

ISBN: 978-1-943217-45-8
eISBN: 978-1-943217-46-5

Printed in the United States of America
First Edition 15 14 13 10 09 / 10 9 8 7 6 5 4 3 2

For Lori.

PROLOGUE

My first memory is of my mother attempting to drown me in our bathtub. I was three years old and flushing toilet paper, watching it spin and disappear—an innocent act that caused the toilet to overflow. My mother exploded in a fit of rage, and her anger only got worse as she waited for the bathtub to fill. When the water level was high enough, she submerged my little body and pinned me down underneath. My thrashing and screaming—"Mommy, Mommy, please help me!"—made no difference. Nothing could diffuse her hate for me.

Passing out from lack of oxygen and sheer terror saved my life that day. But it didn't protect me from abuse, neglect, and lack of love in the years to come, nor did it shield me from her poor example of how to live. My mother suffered from eating disorders, body image issues, personality and mood disorders, suicide attempts, self-hate, and addictions. She was married and divorced eight times. No one she chose could save her.

I learned well. My mother regularly shouted at me, "Who do you think you are?" and I always responded correctly and sincerely, "I'm nobody, Mommy. I'm nobody." I grew to become a troubled teen and an even more troubled adult as I battled the same issues and made the same mistakes as my mother. I thought that if I could just find a man to love me, I would finally be worthy of love and happiness. I spent years searching, allowing men to use me, trying to make abusive relationships work, failing, and looking in the wrong direction again and again. I never could find the man who would complete me.

It wasn't long after I left home that I had a child out of wedlock. My son and I lived on friends' couches and in a homeless shelter for a while. I got pregnant again with a different man and, though he was abusive, stayed with him out of a misguided attempt to "do the right thing." Eventually we moved to Texas, had another child together, and married. For thirteen years I tried to make that destructive, unhealthy relationship work. I finally gave up and, after my husband left, went right back to my wild ways with a vengeance.

I regularly entertained thoughts of suicide, but as a mother of three resisted the urge to give up on life. Though I followed in my mother's footsteps in most ways, I took a different path in one critical way. I adored my children and loved them to the best of my ability. This love prompted me to make one last desperate attempt: I called out to God to save me.

He answered my cry in a most unusual way. Thus began the greatest love story of my life.

PART ONE

"In a desert land he found him, in a barren and howling waste. He shielded him and cared for him; he guarded him as the apple of his eye."

—Deuteronomy 32:10 NIV

DATE 1
Paddle Boarding

As I lie in my bed in the fetal position, sobbing, I yearn to die. I live in constant emotional pain and long for someone to save me from my fears of life, rejection, this constant feeling of loneliness and abandonment. I need someone to rescue me from the enemy I have found within myself. I do everything wrong. Though I have seen a therapist for six years, and several months ago started seeing a new therapist, I still loathe myself for the many horrible decisions and mistakes I've made. I cannot undo them, so I live with constant guilt, shame, and regret. I am unlovable—so unlovable that I can't even find a way to love myself. At this point, I have only two choices: I can remove myself from this painful existence, or I can turn to the Maker I used to believe in as a child and give Him a chance to save me. If there is a God, and if He truly has a plan for me, He will come to my rescue. If He doesn't, I am ending my life.

"God, if you are real, I'm begging you to please answer me!" I say to Him. "I can't take this pain anymore. Why did you make me like this? Why am I so unlovable? Everyone wants to leave me. This pain is too big to handle anymore. I am begging you on my knees. Please fix me. I can't do this anymore. *Please!* Take this emptiness and comfort me like you did when I was a little girl. Please God, come back to me."

At that moment I feel His voice within me. It isn't an audible voice, but an internal voice that is not my own; it is powerful, yet gentle and comforting. *Caren, I never left you. I have been right beside you all along, longing for you to turn to me.*

I feel a sense of peace, as if He is wrapping His arms around me. I haven't felt this comforted since I was a child so many years ago, when I once knew God and walked beside Him. At the same time, I feel myself withdraw. How can that be true? If I were God, and a child I created was suffering the kind of pain I've suffered, I would rescue her. I would do something to ease her pain.

I reply angrily, "No, that's not possible! If you have been right beside me, then you must hate me! Why else would you have made me so unlovable and let me suffer so much pain?"

I hear the internal voice again. *Sweet child, I love you more than you could ever know.*

"If you love me, then why won't you send someone to fix my brokenness? A man who will love me and stay by my side?"

I have, but you won't accept him.

I feel His answer, but I try to push it out of my mind. None of that "Jesus stuff" makes sense to me anymore. Yet I still have that unfamiliar sense of peace, and as I kneel, I begin to understand. I can't accept Jesus because my wounds run too deeply. I feel God's speak again.

Caren, you called out and asked me to mend your brokenness. I have been longing for this moment for many years. I have a special plan for you and your life. Give me fifty dates with you, and I will mend you and lead you to the man who will heal your brokenness.

I start to question my sanity. Can this really be the voice of God, or am I delusional? It seems crazy, but at the same time . . . this voice, a voice I've never heard before, is nothing like my normal internal voice. I have no capacity for self-comfort, and these thoughts go directly against my usual thought process. I am filled with self-contempt and shame; I certainly don't use terms of endearment to refer to myself.

I sense that what I've been chasing isn't love but a misconception of what I've experienced as love. It dawns on me that I have a very romantic soul and have longed my whole life for the man of my dreams to make me happy. Maybe this *is* the voice of God, and maybe He knows that "dating" me is the best way to reach me. And quite frankly, what have I got to lose by believing? Moments ago I was in bed contemplating suicide. Every other path I've chosen leads me right back to this same dead end. I find myself reluctantly agreeing.

"Okay, Lord. This seems crazy, but I will accept your offer . . . if this is real."

Good decision. I want you to take notes after all our dates. Write down what happens—your thoughts, your feelings—everything. One day we will turn your notes into our first book together. Now wipe your nose, rinse off your face, and let's go paddle boarding.

***

As I get into the car and head to the lake, I am excited. I have never been paddle boarding before! It's something I have always wanted to do, but I've never felt good enough to participate in outdoor activities. In my mind, fun things like paddle boarding are reserved for people better than I am.

BRIGHT

I pull up to the lake and notice how beautiful the water looks. The sun is shining brightly, and a heavy wind blows from the west. I look to the left at the center of the lake and admire miles of vast openness where the water is clean and stirred by the wind. It looks so fun! I imagine myself out there standing in the waves. I look to the right and see that the lake turns into a creek lined by a wall of trees on each side. The trees shield the water from the wind, so the water is stagnant. I eagerly anticipate heading to the left.

But I feel the voice calling me to go right. I think, "But it looks so boring and dirty over there! God, I want to go to the pretty part." I feel His answer.

Not yet. You must first build your skill. You need to learn how to stand up and balance in order to steer in the deep. If you go out there now, you will fall off your board.

The attendant briefly instructs me on how and when to stand up, makes sure the safety cord is safely strapped around my ankle, and gives me a gentle push into the water. I slowly stand, steady myself, and begin to paddle. I head, resignedly, toward the right side of the lake.

After a few minutes, I stop to marvel and take in the moment. I can't believe I am really on this paddle board! How many years have I been telling myself that I would like to do this one day? I was in bed wanting to die an hour ago, and now here I am, in the middle of the lake, surrounded by God's presence! The wind blows, and the leaves begin to dance. With a childlike fascination, I put aside my desire to control this moment and decide to let God lead me.

I spy a turtle resting on a log. A smile spreads across my face. The turtle sees me approaching and quickly plummets into the water.

A sense of peace settles over me. I realize God created me just like He created that turtle on the log, the birds in the trees, and those ducks in the brush. They simply exist, living in the present and enjoying the life God created for them, content in the moment.

You are just as much a part of my plan as they are. It is safe for you to exist in this beautiful place I've created for you, step away from the world in your head, and experience what I've given you.

His words ring true. I spend so much time in my head that I usually don't even notice the world around me. I decide to take this time to really focus. Sun is shining through the clearing. A crane stands on one leg as still as a statue, and a duck rests on a fallen tree. No, make that two ducks . . . three, four, five . . . six ducks! I almost looked right past them. Another turtle flops into the water. All of this is so beautiful! And if *this* is beautiful, *I* must be beautiful, as I was made by the same artist. Why is that so hard for me to believe?

The creek ahead looks dingy and creepy. An oily film covers the top of the water, litter is trapped in the brush, and broken branches and fallen trees dot the water. I pray, "Lord, can I turn around now and go to the nicer part of the lake? I have my balance now, and I can steer just fine."

I don't feel confirmation within, so I reluctantly keep going. Soon I see a family of turtles resting on a log. I chuckle as they jump into the water, one after the other. Plop, plop, plop, plop! Even surrounded by the mess in the creek, they seem content and are living in the moment.

Caren, there are pockets of mess and brokenness in every journey. It is finding the beauty and the message within the brokenness that provides you contentment. The less favorable areas teach you to be more appreciative in the midst of your next clearing. Keep going.

I respond with frustration. "I hear what you're saying, Lord, but it's easier said than done. I just want to be loved. I want to be treasured by a man who won't leave me. I want to feel safe to speak what's on my mind and in my heart. What's wrong with that?"

I become overwhelmed by sadness and loneliness. Except for my children, everybody leaves me. God says we are all perfectly made and beautiful, but then why does nobody see my beauty? How can I believe I'm beautiful and lovable if nobody else does? I think about the various men in my life. Andy says he'll get a hotel and spend the afternoon with me, but I know what that means. And I miss Wallace so much. I wish he would look at me the way he did before the "mistake." But above all, it is Stewart who hurts the most. Why can't he love me the way I love him? We just started talking again, and now he's moving to California for good. Should I wait to see if he'll come back for me someday? God's voice interrupts my ruminations.

Get out of your head, dear. It no longer keeps you safe. Become part of what I have created. Living in your head resurrects unnecessary pain. There is no pain in this moment. You are in the middle of a lake with me on a paddle board. Enjoy what I am giving you. I have made you ruler over all of this.

He is right. I *am* living in my head instead of being present . . . as usual. In fact, if I had been paying more attention to this moment, I would have spotted the low bridge in front of me and realized sooner that I am too tall to pass under it! I panic. "God, should I turn around?"

No, keep going

I duck and manage to pass under the bridge without losing my balance. I float into a clearing. The warm sun shines on my face. A red cardinal flies through the opening. A few ducks float past me, and turtles rest on a log to my right. Wow, this is so beautiful! Had I turned around, I would have missed this majestic moment.

My feeling of joy is short-lived. The clearing disappears. Trees umbrella over me, blocking the sun. Mosquitoes abound. Residue covers the water again. Trash, broken branches, and rotted logs litter the water, which is becoming shallower. A fallen tree blocks the path ahead. "God, I think it's apparent we should turn around now! Don't you agree?"

Not yet. There is something I want you to see.

The only way to pass the fallen log is through a small space cluttered with twigs sticking out of the shallow water. I won't be able to get through. I'm going to fall, and what if there are water snakes? Dammit! The safety cord on my ankle is stuck on a twig! If I bend down to free it, I'll lose my balance and fall in. I knew I should have turned around! How will I get my cord unstuck? I'm going to fall! My anxiety lessens as I hear the inner voice once again.

Stay present, and keep going. Don't let fear get in your way. If you stay focused and believe in yourself, you won't fall.

I concentrate on how to free the cord. I determine that if I keep my body steady enough, face forward, and blindly reach my paddle behind me, then perhaps I can break the branch that snagged my cord. It works! The cord is free, and I can move forward. What a rush! I don't have any space to turn this thing around anyway, so I keep going.

The farther I paddle, the darker and drearier the creek becomes. Soon I reach a dead end. Why, after going all that way, did I end up in this eerie place? I have reached an island of trash and pollution. All the trees are dead. It is lifeless—no sunlight, no birds, no ducks, no turtles—except for the blood-sucking mosquitoes. It is scary, dark, and lonely like a scene from a horror movie.

Sweet Caren, do not fear. I am with you. We do not have to stay here. I have taken you this way to paint a clear picture of where you have been and where you are now. A long journey lies ahead of us. To gain the ability to stand and steer in the deep, where the water is beautiful and the waves ebb and flow, you have to understand where you came from.

As I stand there, confused, understanding slowly begins to creep in. I was born into a land of lifelessness by a mother who chose to reside there. She did not choose a life with God. She chose to live in brokenness and despair. It's not that I am unlovable; it's that my mother didn't choose to love herself enough to embrace a life filled with God's love and truth. Because of this, I was completely misguided. My mother hated herself, and she resided in the misery and pain that I am in now.

I realize that God is offering me a freedom that no one in my family's past generations chose. They never sought God. But I have faith! I've carried it since I was a child. I remember a time when even amidst pain, abandonment, neglect, physical abuse, and sexual abuse, I trusted God. I knew He had a plan for me, and I was confident and secure in my love for Him. I remember skipping up and down the street singing "Jesus Loves Me" and telling everyone I could about the love of Christ. God is offering me the opportunity to break a generational curse and find the peace I once felt knowing His Son Jesus Christ. I hear His voice confirm.

Yes, in order to free you, I need to completely reprogram you. I will re-teach you and rewire the way you think and act. I will change what you believe about yourself, the people around you, and the world in which you live. Success requires a complete act of faith on your part. Letting go of what you have always believed to be true—those beliefs that come from the lies fed to you as a little girl—will be difficult. But I will never leave you or forsake you. When the weight seems too heavy to bear, I will bear it for you. So what do you say, dear? Will you choose this freedom? Will you give me forty-nine more dates?

My heart swells with hope, joy, and peace. "Lord, this may sound crazy to the rest of the world, and even to myself, but I believe you. I don't want to live in pain and misery anymore. I can't! I will give you what you ask of me." I turn my board around and start paddling back to our starting point.

DATE 2
Scruffy Duffies

My heart is broken. I just received a text from Stewart, a man I met a year ago who became my close friend and mentor. I am hopelessly in love with him. I hope one day he will see me as more than a friend. He travels between Dallas and other cities for business, but we communicate regularly. His text informs me that his company is moving him to San Diego. He is headed back to Dallas to pack up his apartment before the movers arrive. I ask him if he can make time to visit me before he goes, but he is noncommittal. He explains that he has only three days to pack all his belongings, take his work team to dinner, go to an important appointment, and catch a flight to San Diego.

When I read his response, I begin sobbing. Clearly seeing me before he leaves town is not important to him. He is trying to be nice so he doesn't hurt my feelings, but I know that if he truly wanted to see me, he would make time for me. I feel terrified and defeated. How can I win him over if he is in another city? I won't even be able to see him!

I truly love Stewart. I have seen other men in the last year, but those relationships have been fillers until Stewart decides he wants to take our relationship to the next level. All I want is time for him to get to know me better, time for him to fall in love with me, time to become his romantic interest. I have never desired anything as much as I desire a relationship with Stewart. Why can't I ever have what I want? I finally find a nice guy who treats me with respect, and now he is gone. *Gone forever.* And he won't even take thirty minutes of his time to say goodbye to me.

My self-pitying sobs turn into child-like rage. I hate myself. I *hate* myself! I am not beautiful or lovable enough for someone like Stewart—for anyone! Sex is the only thing I have to offer a man, and Stewart doesn't even want that. Why won't anybody love me? Why am I not worthy of getting anything I want in life? I am tired, so very tired, of trying to make people love me. It would be easier to die!

At this last thought, I calm down a bit. I know that's a silly, hysterical thing to think. I don't know why I feel like I want to die every time I am rejected and feeling unloved. As I try to calm down, I feel the same presence around me that I did yesterday at the lake. I wonder if it is God again. I call out, "God, is that you? Can you hear me?"

Yes, child, I am here.

My voice chokes with tears as I plead, "God, Stewart is in Dallas for three days before he goes to San Diego. He said he will probably be too busy to see me before he goes. But I love him, God. Will you please make him want to see me before he goes? Please? I'm sorry I said I want to die. I'm sorry I am acting as if I have nothing good in my life. I know my children are beautiful, and they love me. They are everything to me. When I said nobody loves me, I didn't mean them. I meant that nobody *but* them loves me."

Caren, when you are hurting, your default emotion is the desire to die. I want you to think about the reasons behind that emotion.

"I don't know. When people reject me, I feel completely unloved and worthless. I have an intense feeling that goes beyond sadness, Lord. I suffer so much that I desperately yearn for the misery to end. The pain feels like a heavy burden that can't possibly go away unless I cease to exist. It's not so much that I want to die as that I don't want to continue living."

The depth of agony I feel is hard to adequately explain. I imagine my emotional pain would seem like a gross overreaction to a "normal" person, but these crushing, hopeless feelings are starkly real to me.

Do you remember what your therapist told you about pain coming in waves?

I am startled that God knows about that. I guess He truly is all-knowing. I answer, "Yes. She said that pain comes in waves, and when I think the pain can't get any bigger, it will start to ebb."

She is right. Keep that in mind. Now, try to step back and look at your situation more objectively. What emotions do you feel? Why?

My tears ease. I analyze my reaction to Stewart's texts. I feel abandoned because Stewart is leaving. I feel rejected because he didn't say he will make time for me. I feel alone because he is leaving. I feel unlovable because he doesn't love me in the way that I love him.

Very good. All those emotions and feelings frighten you. But can you recognize that they are exactly that: feelings and emotions, no more, no less? A feeling is not a fact. A feeling does not define the truth of who you are.

I kind of know what He means, but . . .

Stay with me, Caren. I want you to examine the facts of the situation. Stewart is moving to another state. He is not abandoning you personally. His decision to take this course in his career is separate from you.

"Well, true, but…"

Another fact: Stewart said he is extremely busy and does not know if he has time to see you. He never said he does not want to see you. Because of your past experiences, you jumped to the conclusion that he is politely rejecting you. You do not know if that is true. Viewing conjecture as reality is unnecessary and adds to your pain.

"That makes sense, Lord."

Good. Now, Stewart is leaving, true. He does not love you romantically, also true. But is he the only person in the world?

"No, of course not."

Correct. Stewart is one person in a world full of people. Assuming you are alone because a particular person is leaving town is a false conclusion. Assuming you are unlovable because a particular person does not return your love is also false logic.

Wow, the Lord's reasoning rings true and makes me feel a little better. I am reading a lot more into Stewart's words and actions than I should.

Caren, when you feel low, I want you to start paying attention to your feelings and the meanings you assign to them. Then use logic to separate your feelings from the facts, like I did for you today. You will learn to be more aware of what you tell yourself. Doing this will take a lot of practice and won't be an easy fix, but it will slowly ease your suffering.

***

I've been trying to use God's "being aware" technique for the last two days as I grieve for Stewart. I have cried a lot anyway,

24

and I've been on the edge of my seat anxiously waiting for a text from him. I fervently hope he saves a small window of time to see me before he leaves tomorrow morning. I have pleaded with God repeatedly to make this happen, but now that the window of opportunity to see Stewart is closing, I have almost lost hope. I wonder for the umpteenth time whether the voice I heard was truly God speaking to me or whether it was an idea gleaned from my many years of therapy, tucked away in my subconscious. I decide that if God's voice being real is even a slight possibility, I can't give up. I pray yet again to see Stewart before he leaves.

Around five o'clock I wipe my tears and force myself to do something other than moping and checking my phone. I remember tonight is the NBA Playoffs. I'm a big basketball fan, and my favorite player is LeBron James. During the finals I've been going to different sports bars in Dallas to watch the games on big screens. Even though I am not connected to others, when I watch a game at a bar, I feel like I'm celebrating with a bunch of "friends." I enjoy going to a different bar every time so I can explore new places in Dallas and find fun places to hang out. I decide I'll watch the play-offs tonight to take my mind off Stewart. I'll figure out which bar to go to after I buy some game snacks for the boys at Tom Thumb.

Before I start the car to drive home from the store, I text Stewart one last time. I ask if he has time to see me before he leaves. His reply breaks my heart again. "Sorry, I am still packing and have a lot more to do. I have to head to the airport immediately after my meeting in the morning."

I sit in my car, sobbing. I had so wanted to tell him good-bye. Perhaps "God" not answering my prayer to see Stewart is proof that He is not real. But if God is real and truly has specific plans for His people, then maybe I am not meant to see Stewart again for reasons I don't understand. My heart feels more open to the latter scenario, so I say a different kind of prayer.

"God, will you please let me see Stewart before he leaves . . . if visiting with him one last time won't get in the way of any of your plans? I will understand if it isn't meant to be. But will you please let me see him?"

Somehow I feel as if God is smiling at the innocence of my prayer. I hear Him answer, Caren, go home and get yourself ready to go out. We will go to the game together. I think we should go to that sports bar you heard about, Scruffy Duffies.

His words give me a glimmer of hope. I am not sure, but I sense that God means Stewart is at Scruffy Duffies, a bar north of Dallas someone told me about recently. I don't know why Stewart would be there. He has never mentioned it to me before, but I hurry home in case I am right. I wonder if this is another fantasy of mine. How can I differentiate between the voice of God and my own thoughts? The voice I hear is exactly the same voice I heard when paddle boarding on Wednesday. It is not audible. I hear it inside my head, like I hear my own inner voice, but it has a different quality than mine. It is still and comforting.

I begin to waver again when I get home. This is silly. I should go to Humperdinks on Greenville. It is much closer to my house. According to Google, Scruffy Duffies is a twenty-five -minute drive from here, not including possible traffic delays. But . . . if I am right that God implied Stewart is at Scruffy Duffies, I have to go! I can't miss a chance to see him. My heart wants nothing more than to tell him in person before he moves that I love him and will miss him. I want to sit next to him and hug him. Could God actually be arranging the universe so that

Stewart's and my paths will intersect before he leaves town? Is it possible that I am about to see Stewart? The thought is ludicrous! But I have to see for myself.

I excitedly get dressed and put on makeup, feeling fearful at the same time. If Stewart isn't there, then I will have to acknowledge that the "voice of God" I've been hearing is my mind playing tricks on me? That is a scary thought. I know I've had only one "date with God" so far, but I like the idea that He is real, that He loves me, and that my life will have purpose if I follow Him.

I put on my prettiest light green skirt, a feminine light floral spaghetti strap top, and one of my favorite pairs of shoes. I wore these shoes when Stewart helped me make a personal budget once, and he noticed and admired them.

I say good-bye to the children, get in my car, and begin driving north. "God, are we really going to see Stewart?" I ask tentatively. "He said he will be packing. Why would he be out? And of the hundreds of sports bars within a thirty-mile radius of his apartment, why would he be at Scruffy Duffies?"

Caren, I love you.

"I love you too . . ." Immediately following my reply comes the thought "if you are real." I feel guilty for thinking it. I love God. I believe He created the earth and everything in it, and I love Him for that. I love Him for my children and everything else He has given me. But believing God personally oversees the details of my life seems like a stretch.

I follow Google's directions and take the Legacy Drive exit. I stay in the right lane and make another right. There it is on my left! I am giddy with anticipation. I try to calm down in case I am wrong. I pull into the parking garage, take a deep breath, and walk toward the parking garage exit. I hear the Lord tell me to turn right and enter the first door I see. I turn right and see the main entrance to the bar ahead, but the voice insists I go in the set of doors before the main entrance. I can't tame the jitters swarming my gut as I place my hand on the door. I take another deep breath, swing it open, and walk in to a direct view of the back section of the outside patio.

Sitting on a bar stool at a high top table with three other people is my dear and beloved friend, Stewart.

I can't believe it. I say a silent prayer of sorts. "Oh, my God! Are you serious? You have really sent me to say good-bye to Stewart?"

Stewart notices me right away. He stands up and invites me over. He looks puzzled as he says with his usual witty, dry sense of humor, "Are you stalking me?"

I smile broadly and reply jokingly, "I put you in God's GPS."

He smirks. "Well then, it must be fate that we see each other before I go. Have a seat! Are you here with anybody?"

I tell him that I am here alone, and I explain my routine of watching each game of the Finals at a different sports bar.

"You came all the way over here because there aren't any sports bars closer to your house?" he asks sarcastically.

I can almost see his brain processing the situation. He is trying to figure out how I came to be at the same sports bar as he is. I am wondering the same thing! I don't feel comfortable sharing that God really told me to come here, so I don't say anything else on the subject.

He introduces me to the man beside him. "This is Coach Holmes. He came all the way down from Cali to help me pack."

Wow, what a nice friend! He then says to Coach Holmes, "This is my friend Caren. She is the one I told you about, the one who sent me flowers at the office."

When Stewart's grandmother passed away a couple of months ago, I sent him flowers potted in soil. He really appreciated the gesture, and the flowers are still alive.

Stewart explains, "We needed a break from packing, so we decided to have dinner and catch some of the game. We're leaving at half-time to finish packing."

As we watch the game and they chat, I sit in awe and talk to God in my head. "You are real! You must be! What does this mean?"

Caren, I needed to show you that the voice you hear is indeed my voice. Seeing Stewart was your heart's desire. Giving you this moment does not interfere with the plans I have for you. Remember this time when you doubt me in the future.

Stewart's voice brings me out of my reverie. "I'm sorry. What did you say?"

He points to the couple sitting on the other side of the table. "They asked us where we work." Stewart is about six-and-a-half feet tall and very athletic. Coach Holmes is quite fit as well. I bet the couple thinks Stewart is a professional athlete, but I'm not sure because I was busy talking to God. I am saved from replying when LeBron makes a shot, and everyone erupts into cheers.

For the next ten minutes I soak up everything Stewart says and does. I am overjoyed to have this time with him. I am thankful to God for giving me this moment. At one minute to half-time, my heart saddens. Our time is coming to an end. I notice a rubber bracelet on Stewart's wrist. I can't quite see the words on the bracelet, so I reach out and begin to turn it toward me. Stewart pulls his hand away and says, "Don't snap it. That would hurt."

I am wounded by his words. I would never hurt Stewart. I

simply wanted an excuse to touch him.

Half-time arrives. Stewart stands up and says, "Well, we've gotta finish packing. You ready, Coach?"

Coach Holmes says it was nice to meet me. Stewart asks me for a hug. I want nothing more. I reach up and wrap my arms around him. He hugs me and lets me go, but I continue to hold on. He chuckles and says, "Well, okay, one more hug." He gives me another quick hug, and I finally let go. I am a little embarrassed that I might appear too clingy.

I say, "It was nice to see you again. Be safe and enjoy San Diego."

"You too, Caren. Take care," he replies. Then he and his friend walk out the door.

My heart sinks. I want to run after him. I could offer to help him pack! But I hear God's voice again. *Let him go, dear.*

"I don't want to let him go! I love him too much. I want him to love me too."

But I stop. I am ashamed at feeling this way. I know God allowed me this experience to confirm that His voice is real and that He loves me. I am being ungrateful to want more. "God, thank you for all you did for me tonight. I am sad that I won't get to see Stewart anymore, but I am also very happy and thankful that you arranged for me to see him one last time."

You are welcome, Caren. It is indeed I, and I want to continue our journey together. Do you?

I am humbled. "Yes, Lord. I do."

DATE 3
Massage

All morning I've been struggling with sadness and feeling guilty for being sad. I am a horrible person. I'm so unappreciative! Despite the hope I felt after my paddle board outing and seeing Stewart a few weeks ago, I shut myself in my bedroom and cry for hours every day, absorbed in self-pity and dissociated from the world around me. Even worse, I am dissociated from my own children. How can I behave this way?

When I examine my life as it truly is in this moment, I recognize it is a good life. The tragedy and trauma of my past has ended. I love my three amazing children, and they love me. We are all healthy. We have a roof over our heads and food on the table. Yet I feel so much shame and unhappiness. Life seems meaningless. Loneliness is my constant companion, and I can't think of anything but my aching desire for Stewart to rescue me from it.

Andy texted me and asked if I want to "hang out" today. Escaping with him for a few hours would distract me from my constant suffering and the sadness I feel about Stewart leaving.

I feel safe and sexy and adored when I'm in Andy's arms. Even though I know this empty feeling will increase ten-fold when he leaves, as it always does, I'm going to say yes. At least I'll have physical pleasure and a few hours' break from this suffocating loneliness.

But something makes me hesitate before texting him back. I debate a few moments and then begin talking to God . . . if He's real and listening, that is. I voice my feelings of shame and depression and my desire to see Andy. "Lord, I believed in you until I was ten years old. Though young, I learned a lot in those ten years, and I know you wouldn't condone an afternoon liaison with Andy. But is denying myself male companionship really that important? I mean, do you really want me to be an abstinent, single, lonely lady who spends all her free time baking for the church?"

I hear that same internal voice—the gentle authority, the odd sense of comfort. The voice, or God, or whatever it is, tells me I'm letting my emotions and imagination distort the vision the Lord has for my life. His plan for me involves a future filled with hope. Rather than predicting depressing scenarios, I need to trust Him and follow His process.

Sweet Caren, the things that put you where you are today—in bed feeling shameful, abandoned, and lost—are the things you need to let go of. Your choices prevent you from reaching your potential. Our first step must be a period of solitude.

A period of solitude? Outrageous! I only have a couple of people in my life as it is. Since my husband left two years ago, I've kept distant from others because I know someone like me doesn't deserve real friendships. And the few people I haven't pushed away inevitably leave me. As my indignant thoughts wind down, the voice explains that living in solitude with God is different than alienating myself from others out of fear and shame. And the reason I've reached out to God today is because I know in my heart that my lifestyle doesn't please Him or me.

Caren, right now you don't have a strong sense of self. What others think about you influences you too much. I want time alone with you to fix your distorted self-perception. I want to teach you who I, your Creator, your Father, designed you to be. So tell me, what keeps you in bondage today? What can you give up that will make you feel better about yourself?

He is right. I have to do something about this almost-constant paralyzing shame. Even though God is supposedly all-knowing, I tell Him (and admit to myself) one of my biggest and most recent sources of shame. As a massage therapist, I have been giving men sensual massages. This was never my intention, but somehow . . .

It all started when an acquaintance who knew how much I needed money suggested I list my massage practice on a particular classified advertising website. She explained that although the website is known for its adult-oriented listings, not everyone on the site provides adult entertainment. By listing myself under the massage services section (versus the adult section) with an attractive picture, I could get a lot of customers who might be hoping for something more, but it was up to me what I did or did not do in the massage room. The lure of good money was too much to resist. I posted an ad, and it was very effective.

At first I gave standard massages, but I flirted and wore sexy dresses and heels to get better tips. Then that led to more, and now most of my clients are male and being seductive is expected. Though I feel trapped in the situation, I've been rationalizing my actions. "Lord, if I return to wearing scrubs and giving strictly therapeutic massages, I'll lose most of my clientele. I'm a single mom of three. For the first time in my life, I'm making good money. I can finally provide for my children comfortably.

I'm able to give them things they want like other parents do. I don't want to go back to a life of poverty, barely making ends meet!"

My heart lightens a little after my confession. And though I have three good reasons to continue my lucrative practice, I start to view the situation differently. At what cost am I maintaining my lifestyle? Putting a price on my sensuality and compromising my dignity is not the life God intends for me. Wants are not needs, and certainly not worth my dignity. And why am I worrying about having enough food and clothes anyway? God has always provided for me.

Caren, my child, look at the birds in the sky. They don't plant or harvest or store food in barns. I feed them. You are far more valuable to me than they are. If you turn over your worries to me, I will take care of you and restore the joy you once knew as a child. I ask again, What are you willing to surrender?

When I envision giving up the sensual massage part of my practice, even knowing my income will drop at least fifty percent, I feel the rightness of the decision. My mind quickly turns to another source of shame: the less-than-wholesome relationships I have with a few men. But if I end them, how can I meet my need to feel connected, to love and be loved, to be touched with affection? After all, God made me with these needs. Why does He expect me to stifle them?

Again the voice urges me to view things from a different angle. Yes, God created humans with the desire to be connected to others, and physical touch is part of His design. That's what drives us to pursue relationships with one another. But my past experiences have distorted my perception of relationships.

I would like to begin rewiring you today. Will you allow me that opportunity? Will you go on a third date with me?

My head spins at this strange, yet comforting, experience. Am I really having a conversation with God, or have I lost touch with reality? But I succumb. "Okay, Lord. Where to?"

***

As I sit back in a massage reflexology chair, I take a deep breath and relax. I feel an unfamiliar sense of pride. Today I made two very difficult decisions that go against my nature: giving up income to regain my dignity and choosing to go on a date with the Lord over meeting Andy at a hotel. The feeling that comes from making choices that won't cause future regret is so amazing that I wonder why I was tempted to do otherwise. After all, God, the Maker of the Universe, wants to spend time with me and heal me! I wonder if He is angry or disappointed that the choice was such a struggle for me. I hear His assurance.

I accept you as you are. Your mind leads you to believe you will find more fulfillment in other things, but I give you grace, and I am patient. My love for you is not conditional. I give you free will to choose what you want for yourself, but I cannot be present in the midst of sin. So when you knowingly choose a life of sin, you feel separated from me. That is the emptiness you describe. Conversely, the more you let go of sin, the closer we become.

God's idea of love is much different than mine. I have a lot to learn, but I feel at peace. For now, I will lie back, relax, and feel His presence as He wants me to. I haven't had healthy physical attention in a very long time. Being pampered feels delightful. I marvel at the warmth of hot rocks on my feet. And then . . . I'm being awoken by a whisper. "Your forty-five minutes are up, ma'am."

What a fabulous foot massage and rejuvenating nap! I'm so thankful for this experience. Thank you, Lord, thank you! I am calm and relaxed and simply feel *good*.

You looked peaceful as you slept. Notice how healthy, appropriate physical touch fills the void you feel but does not leave you feeling ashamed? This is what I want for you. I want you to know a peace that surpasses all understanding in all areas of your life. If you continue to walk with me, I will lead you there.

I want nothing more than what my Lord is offering. I need to give my children more attention. If I were at peace, not consumed with my own emotional struggles, I could be more supportive. I feel guilty that even though I love my kids fiercely, I am not allowing their love to be enough for me. God's compassionate response lifts my spirits.

Sweetheart, you do a beautiful job parenting your children with the limited skills you currently possess. You refuse to treat them the way you were treated. Work at shaming yourself less and giving yourself grace. They do need more of your love and wisdom, and we will get there. For now, tell them a little about your emotional struggle. They notice your sadness and withdrawal. They need to know you are broken and have turned to me for help. Otherwise they will be confused and scared. Keep trusting me, my precious daughter. Let me love you, and together we will rewire and re-parent you so you can be a joyful woman of God for your children.

Re-parent. I love the way that sounds. Full of hope and possibility. "Thank you, Lord. You have my attention. I will continue this walk with you."

DATE 4
Painting

The euphoria I felt slowly dwindled over the days following my massage experience. Now, almost a week later, I'm haunted by a deep longing for companionship. I wish I had a true friend to spend time with. I fantasize that I'm like everyone else—a normal person who has close friends and doesn't struggle with her mind. I envision sitting on my bed with a friend, sharing laughter and tears, life experiences, goals, dreams.

Then reality rears its ugly head. I can't maintain the facade of being normal long enough to make a friend. The only person I can be myself around—fully exposing the mess that I am—is Stewart. He sympathizes with me about my emotional issues and wants to help by being my confidant, but he doesn't want to mislead me. We communicate through texting only because he worries having more personal phone conversations will confuse me about his feelings toward me . . . and mine toward him.

He is right. I love him, even though the feeling isn't mutual. On one hand, I want him to whisk me away and take me around the world with him, and on the other, it hurts to be near him. If only he were in love with me!

Ugh. Here I go again. This is *exactly* why he doesn't call. I live in a "someday my prince will come" fantasy world. I want to accept Stewart as a platonic and helpful friend, but I struggle; my feelings are my feelings, and I can't control them. Relationships of this nature are a pattern in my life. Why is it that I desire closeness only with people who aren't interested? I recall the poem I wrote in seventh grade.

A love not loved but only one-way.
Why must I feel this from day to day?
Hardly known, but the gleam in his eye,
One look, and I'm trapped—should I laugh or cry?
Not understood are the tears I shed . . .
maybe it's the knowing my love is only one-way.

Since youth I have chased unobtainable love and run away from people who want to get close to me. I want nothing more than closeness, but I fear nothing more than closeness. I wonder if God can really erase my constant loneliness. The only way to find out is to continue this journey with Him. I have nothing to lose. I may be losing my mind, but these recent conversations and "dates" with God have been warm, bright spots in years of suffering.

I reach out to Him, speaking of my desire to hang out with a friend today and my sadness that I'm too messed up to have a friend. Sure, some of my acquaintances would probably be open to getting to know me better, but I'm too damaged to be a good friend; I have nothing to offer. I would scare away people if I admitted I suffer from deep depression, have lingering thoughts of suicide, experience constant mood fluctuations so

I never know how I'll feel from one moment to the next, am recovering from sex addiction, and can't focus on what others are saying because I'm consumed with my own racing thoughts.

"Lord, I feel so alone stuck in this purgatory between wanting, yet fearing, closeness. Why is obtaining and maintaining relationships so difficult for me? Why did you make me this way? You said I'd get better if I walk with you. But these feeling aren't going away!"

What I'm hesitantly coming to accept as God's voice reassures me that He did not design me to be broken. He created me with joy and purpose, to soar high above the clouds like a bird. Nothing is wrong with me; anyone with a childhood and upbringing like mine would develop in a similar way. He urges me to keep my faith in Him and His plan for me.

He also reminds me that I've lived this way for thirty-eight years. My psyche has been embedded with layers of wrong messages since my developmental years. I'm not going to become a new person overnight. But I *will* get a little better each day. He tells me healing will be hard work, and I am worth the effort. He asks for patience.

You wouldn't rescue an injured bird only to throw it immediately back into the wild and expect it to be able to survive—let alone fly—would you? No; you would keep it in a safe place and nurture it until its wounds heal. Like an injured bird, you must be in a safe place while I nurture you until you are healed. That is why I have called you to be in solitude with me. We have internal work to do before you are ready for relationships. Sweetheart, you are right; most people won't understand the depth of your brokenness. Until you have done some healing, give your burdens to me, and share your struggles with Audrey. She is a skilled therapist; you can trust her.

I feel disappointed that God is not going to send me a friend, at least not now. But His explanation makes sense. I hear Him speak even more encouraging words.

If you choose to continue walking with me, not only will you become the person I originally designed you to be, but I will also use your life to inspire others. You will be part of a beautiful story that can be used to bring others to a place of freedom.

This is unbelievable. God is telling me that my complicated, hurt-filled life can be used for great things. I might have my own purpose in life, beyond being a mother. But before I can get too excited about the prospect, He tells me to slow down and focus on what needs to be done *now*. He suggests spending time with Him this evening doing something I've often thought about but never had the self-confidence to try: painting. I like the idea, but . . . "Lord, doesn't that cost a lot?"

His response: *Check Groupon.*

I pull up the popular discount website and search for a painting-related offer. What pops up on my screen? Fifty percent off a painting class at Pinot's Palette. I laugh aloud. Hilarious! The Lord continues to amaze me.

***

I'm excited to be here. I seem to be the only one without a group of friends, yet it doesn't bother me a bit. I'm here with the Lord! But I suspect painting alone is not the norm. The instructor confirms my suspicion when he asks me about saving seats for the rest of my party.

The paint brush feels good in my hand, and creating a beautiful display of color and design on the palette is invigorating! The instructor gives step-by-step instructions, but I feel drawn to paint mine somewhat differently. The class is painting lampposts in a park; I think trees full of summertime leaves would be beautiful.

As I paint my first masterpiece, I listen to the group of women nearby. They clearly work together, and they are gossiping about a co-worker who hasn't arrived yet. I feel empathy for the woman who is running late. She believes these women are her friends, yet they are insulting her. They are discussing her personal business and questioning her life decisions. I have been in her shoes, and I recall the feeling of betrayal vividly. Avoiding mean-spirited people is yet another reason I have removed myself from social situations. I feel safer running solo.

Perhaps because "friends" have gossiped about my poor choices before, I passionately believe that friends should never talk negatively about each other. Women should build each other up, not tear each other down. I'm confident I would never gossip about or betray the secrets of a friend. I feel proud about that. I wish the negative talk would stop. I have an idea.

"Excuse me, ladies, I don't mean to interfere, but I can't help but notice how nicely your paintings are coming along! You're doing great work. And what fun to paint with girlfriends!"

The ladies smile, and the conversation turns. They ask to see my painting. They admire it, impressed that I didn't follow the instructions exactly but instead added a twist to my painting. Soon they are getting creative with their own paintings, giving each other helpful suggestions, and speaking about happier things. Mission accomplished.

As I look at my picture, I smile. I'm proud of my art work. I've impressed myself with my first run at painting! Deeply satisfied, I say, "Thank you, Lord! That was fun!"

You did a beautiful job! So tell me what you learned about yourself this evening. I want you to notice the great qualities and gifts you have, tools you can build upon, and draw strength from during low times.

I reflect upon my experience. I realize I am the only person holding myself back from discovering my talents. Because
I never tried, I didn't know I have a talent for painting. The
thought of pursuing my artistic side excites me. I also take pride
that I risked rejection from a group of ladies, but successfully and discreetly brought light to their evening. I learned that
positive energy is just as contagious as negative energy. Finally,
I learned I have some qualities that would make for a good
friend. I recognize that gossip is unkind and hurtful and am
unwilling to participate in it.

*You did a great job, Caren. I am proud of you. The next time you feel
insecure, unworthy, or simply "not good enough," focus on these wonderful
qualities you've discovered in yourself.*

DATE 5
A Picnic at the Lake

I lie in bed with my covers curled over my head, crying softly. What am I doing? I believe I hear the voice of the Lord. I must be insane!

And why? I ask myself. What miracle has happened? I haven't been delivered from my problems. Four dates and three weeks later, I am still just as broken, but now I have only half my income. I never planned for this sudden switch in lifestyle, and I'm running out of money. I need to fire my nanny and housekeeper and pull my children out of extra activities. I don't have money to shop anymore. I can't afford new clothes or shoes, my perfume bottles are running low, and I had to cancel my regular tanning bed sessions. I am losing all the things that make me feel beautiful.

Do I feel better? Hardly. My pain and sadness has intensified without my usual distractions—men and acquiring material possessions. Daily I fight the urge to take my life. The same thoughts play in my head like a broken record:

I just want to feel loved and safe.
I want to see Andy.
No, I really want Stewart to love me. Why won't he love me?
Why won't anyone love me?
I know why. I am simply unlovable.

I abruptly sit up and bang my fists on the mattress beside me, kicking off the covers. I glare at the ceiling, as if searching for an invisible God above me, and whisper-scream, "God, this isn't working! You ask too much of me. Don't you see that life as I know it is falling apart? Are you even real, or have I conjured a fantasy? I hate myself! I hate my mind. If you are real, you must hate me too! Why else would my life be so full of tragedy and pain? Aren't you *God*, the Creator of the universe—omnipotent, omniscient, omnibenevolent? You could have saved me from the hands of my mother, but instead you let her destroy me! You let her spit in my face. You stood by while I gagged and cried, and my lungs burned as she angrily poured bleach over my head because I had lice. When our dog peed on the floor, you let her rub my face in the urine. You allowed one of my stepfathers to beat me and my brother every single day that he lived with us, with mother's permission. You didn't stop her from hitting me so hard with our rotary phone receiver that my head cracked open and required stitches, all because she thought I said the "F word" when I muttered "Fudge!" My God, the horrible, horrible things my mother put me through . . . and she didn't even protect me after witnessing with her own eyes my flesh-and-blood brother molesting me! How could you allow me to have my first sexual experiences with my own brother at age three? I had countless other equally horrifying experiences. You let me suffer while my mother ruined me, and now I am broken beyond repair."

My crying builds to sobbing, and I continue ranting, my thoughts scattered. "The *only* thing that helps ease this pain is the pleasure I get from sex and money, and *you* ask me to give up both of them! I hate you! If you weren't going to protect me from my mother, you shouldn't have let my dad stop her from aborting me when she tried! You supposedly know everything. Ha! How could a perfect and loving God allow this kind of existence? My whole life everyone has used me and abused me. Nobody has ever chosen to love me, except my children. I couldn't even inspire my own mother to love me. My one prayer to you was to please send someone to love me, and you didn't! I wish I had died when my mother tried to drown me. *I hate you for keeping me alive!*"

My rage begins to subside as I weep. I feel a warm presence surround me, as if God is patting me on the back and telling me to go ahead and let out all my anger. I feel like He is just as sad as I am at what I have been through. I hear His strong voice in my head, telling me He loves me more than I can fathom.

Darling, I have been beside you, protecting you, always. Your mother was a broken woman who did horrible things to you, which caused you to treat yourself poorly. Without interrupting the balance of free will, I kept you safe, Caren. How do you think you survived your mother's numerous attempts on your life and your three suicide attempts, much less your reckless lifestyle? When you ran out of breath in that bath tub, I breathed life into you. I love you more than you can understand. You are my precious child, and you have a great purpose. I can't promise you'll never experience pain; that's not how my love works because I've given everyone free will. I do promise, however, that I'll teach you to overcome your past injuries and use them as a blessing in the beautiful story of your life—a story of overcoming pain and experiencing freedom, love, redemption, forgiveness, peace, joy, and grace. IF you let me.

All of it is so tragic and exhausting. My mother hated me.

I hate myself. I am nobody to everybody. After seven years of therapy, my life experiences still traumatize me so much that I believe I don't deserve to live. And then . . . with a whoosh of clarity, I realize I can go only so far through the healing process on my own. Now that I have invited God in, I can truly heal. But I have to do the work to get there.

Precious child, your continued determination to get better makes me very proud. I want you to move past this painful phase of your healing, but the only way is to work through every single issue. Each experience helps a part of you become whole again. Imagine a jigsaw puzzle in a box. The puzzle was once a whole picture, but it was broken into pieces and needs to be reassembled. Caren, you are like a beautiful puzzle. Let's take the time to put you back together. The hard work and dedication required to do so, and remembering what it was like to be broken into pieces, will give you a much greater appreciation of your wholeness.

I understand on some level, but I want to feel protected and safe *now*. I know the empty feeling would go away if someone held me in his arms. "Lord, I just want to be loved, embraced, and provided for. I am tired, Father. I am tired of trying to make the pain go away. Please fix me, *please!*"

God tells me I am in the first phase of my healing. This emptiness I feel comes from fully releasing the feelings of abandonment, fear, and hurt I spent my whole life suppressing. I can't be truly happy until I deal with these feelings. He wants me to work through my pain with Him, while He protects me.

I certainly *want* to stop reliving the hurts of my past. People say happiness is a choice, but something deep inside prevents me from choosing happiness. The emotional pain I feel is so big that I can't breathe. I'm afraid the only way the pain will go away is for *me* to go away. Maybe the pain would be easier to bear if I knew how long it will take to get past it?

Caren, the length of your journey depends on you. We have a lot of healing to do. If you continue to lay your troubles at my feet, I will comfort you through the process. When your burdens get too heavy, bring them to me. Now, let's get your mind off your worries. How does a picnic at the lake sound for our fifth date?

Of course the Lord knows I've often dreamt of a sweet picnic at the lake with someone special. I've imagined it many times—lounging under a large tree on a big comfy blanket, a small vase holding a single red rose, a lit candle, fresh fruit and vegetables to nibble on. And, of course, a little dark chocolate! Now He wants to make my fantasy a reality. I regret my anger, and I am sorry for saying I hate Him.

I know, Caren. Do not worry. I can handle it.

***

As I lie on the big red comforter and look up at the sky, gratitude wells up within me. The sky is so blue, and the wind is perfect. This is better than I expected. I hear the Lord's voice again.

I'd like to teach you something. Focus on taking deep breaths, breathing out slowly, and watching the rise and fall of your chest. Connect with your ability to smell the air. Try to identify familiar fragrances.

I focus on smelling the soft breeze. The water smells damp. It exudes a slightly fishy, yet fresh and earthy, odor. Then I detect a hint of the candle scent as the wind blows toward me.

Good job, dear. Now observe your surroundings. Focus on colors and shapes, what lives and moves.

I look—*really* look—at the ground. An ant carries a tiny piece of food. A small yellow butterfly flutters past and rests on a blade of wheat. Suddenly I spy a dragonfly camouflaged in the grass. I almost missed it, with its black and green body and a small blue spot at the tip of its tail. I am moved. I have never observed this intensely the depth and multitude of color that surrounds me. I wouldn't have even noticed the dragonfly had the Lord not asked me to look at my surroundings. This experience parallels my life. My constant barrage of thoughts prevents me from noticing the world around me. My mind wanders even in the midst of conversations. When my children speak to me, I respond on autopilot: "Uh huh. Yeah. Really? That's great." I doubt I could repeat what they said if asked. I am completely disconnected from the world, from other people . . . from myself.

That is exactly why I asked you to do this exercise. Emotional pain is excruciating and can be all-consuming. When you disengage from addictions that dull the pain, like sex and shopping, the pain initially intensifies. To get past it, you must learn to feel it. But you need a healthy way to take a break from it as well. When your emotional pain becomes too much to bear, remember how focusing on what you see, hear, and feel can bring you out of your head and into the present moment.

I am relieved that feeling this incredible pain after all these years is not crazy or strange; it is simply part of the healing process. I must allow myself to feel the pain in order to purge the emotions I've stuffed down so deeply for so long. I feel remorse again at telling the Lord I hate Him. I lashed out at Him only because I felt broken, unloved, and worthless.

Caren, you are priceless, and soon enough you will understand this. For now, be in the moment. Lie down, close your eyes, and let me embrace you. Listen to my lullaby of chirping birds, whispering winds, and crashing waves. Rest your mind while I brush back your hair with my breeze. I love you.

I comply and feel supremely content and peaceful, even loved. My eyes are open to the world around me, full of people and places to enjoy. I believe what the Lord is saying. I can choose to live in my head replaying the past and imagining the future, or I can embrace the moment and enjoy the amazing world He has given me. I may not be able to fully practice doing so yet, but I can at least focus on the children He has blessed me with. I have two amazing sons who love me unconditionally and a sweet daughter who thinks I am the most beautiful woman on earth. I don't have a male partner or many friends, but I am not alone. My children and I love each other. Instead of longing for what I do not have, I vow to start appreciating and embracing my children more, as God appreciates and embraces me.

DATE 6
Art Museum

In the few days since my picnic with the Lord, my emotional pain has continued to deepen, just as God told me it would. Without the distraction of men and the comforts of money from my previous massage clientele, I walk the world feeling disconnected from everyone else, in a constant state of unrest, with the sense of being trapped in a prison that is my life. I want to break out of my skin, flee my circumstances. The fervent desire to be someone else—*anyone* but the woman I am—overwhelms me. I have plenty of dreams and ideas, but I don't know how to make them a reality.

And I am mostly alone. I have my children, but the rest of my family, whom I have no connection to anyway, lives up north. I have no close friends other than my texting friendship with Stewart, which speaks volumes. My mother poisoned my thought process, and now my brain is broken. I haven't succumbed to suicide because I love my children, yet what good am I to them? I cry all the time, I provide no examples of healthy relationships or living life to the fullest . . . I am a wreck who is going to ruin my children's lives. The thought of passing my emotional pain on to them is torturous. I have to leave this house before I lose my mind.

I wander the city in my car feeling lost and scared. The years of abuse and oppression have taken a toll, and now I must be losing my sanity. I am either listening to the voice whispering in my head that says, "I don't deserve to live, and the pain won't go away until I cease to exist," or I'm calling out to God, believing that I have a personal relationship with Him, and He speaks to me as a comforting voice in my head. Is any of it true? I hear the familiar disdainful whisper, and it takes all my strength to resist driving into the freeway side rail. "Caren, you are as crazy as your mother. Life is pain. You'll never know anything different. You are going to ruin your children. They will end up sick like you. Unless . . ."

No. Not true! My children need me! I refuse to listen to these lies. I must get a grip and rebuke these thoughts. God loves me, and He is here with me. I cry out in desperation, "Lord, please say you're beside me. These poisonous thoughts are seeping into my brain again. I can't bear feeling this sadness and suffering today. I want to feel happy, safe, and comforted, like I do when we are together."

Sweet daughter, I am here. You chose to ignore the lies you tell yourself and instead called for me in the midst of your pain. I am proud of you. I am always here and will never forsake you. All you have to do is acknowledge my presence. Now, examine this moment and tell me how you feel.

Okay. I already feel better than I had moments before. I recognize that as soon as I became mindful of what was happening—that my self-destructive thoughts were taking over—I found the strength to take charge of my emotions and call upon the Lord. I had an "aha" moment. It was a *choice*, and the more

I choose to interrupt toxic thoughts and turn to God, the easier it will become. But why can't I choose not to have the toxic thoughts in the first place?

Caren, for most of your life you have been either told or showed you are unloved and worthless. This idea is branded so deeply into your psyche that it masquerades as truth. Imagine your mind as a garden and your destructive thoughts as weeds. If the weeds are not pulled, they will eventually take over the garden and prevent flowers from growing. You and I have just begun the process of cleaning out the garden. A season or two will pass before we see the beautiful display of flowers hiding under the weeds. Though there is much work to do, together we can bring the garden back to life.

This certainly makes sense but . . . "Lord, my first suicide attempt was at age ten. I don't even know how to explain the kind of horrible pain that causes a ten-year-old to want to die. That kind of sorrow always surrounds me, bigger than any room I'm in. Is it possible that much anguish can ever go away completely?"

God assures me that if I keep following Him, He will lead me to a life filled with peace and joy. I so want to believe it, but I can't let go of my fear. While part of my brain believes, a large part suspects I have a mental disorder, and symptoms include delusions of speaking to and dating God.

He gently suggests that I continue to follow Him, and if ever He is proven false, or His words don't ring true, I can turn back to life as I knew it. He has a point. I have been following this voice for close to a month. If one part isn't true, then none is true. All of my recent actions are based on hearing and believing in God's voice. If I determine this whole "God thing" is a hoax, a trick I've played on myself, I can always go back to dating random men and giving sensual massages to make good money.

Caren, would you like to go downtown together for our next date?

The prospect is enticing. Having lunch on the rooftop of the new NYLO Hotel immediately comes to mind.

Take the next exit.

I falter. That's the St. Paul exit, and I'm not sure how to get to the NYLO from there.

I am well aware. You better change lanes soon so you don't miss the exit.

Huh. I'm surprised God seems to be steering me away from the NYLO. Wouldn't He want me to go to the place topmost on my mind? Especially if "God" is a figment of my imagination?

Dear, you are welcome to go where you have suggested. Or, you can trust that I have something else planned for us by exiting now, turning left at the light, and driving a bit until you see what is on your left.

I chuckle and exit the freeway. Within a few minutes I see the Dallas Museum of Art. Amazing! This is another place I've always wanted to go to but never have. I forgot about it until now.

Caren, indulge in enriching experiences. Allow yourself to experience activities you want to enjoy. The only person who prevents you from doing so, darling, is you. I take great pleasure watching your joyful smile and childlike enthusiasm. More importantly, your children are watching you. If they observe you taking opportunities to enjoy the greater things in life, things that matter to you, they will learn to do the same.

I am ridiculously excited to see the works of art in this museum! I can't wait to admire the artistic ability some people are blessed with. God reminds me that all people are blessed with amazing abilities, but only some take advantage of the artist within. I remember our fourth date. I had never picked up a paint brush before, but as soon as I did, something I didn't know existed emerged from me onto the canvas.

Exactly. Abilities are within people to enjoy and be proud of. Whatever a person enjoys is there—singing, sewing, painting, drawing, writing, playing an instrument, dancing, pottery . . . the list goes on. The only thing preventing one from tapping into one's artistic abilities is choosing not to.

This is a "Big Idea" I've never considered. The only difference between great artists and myself is a personal choice? Quite a powerful concept. "Thank you, Father."

God explains there is freedom in choice. I can choose to get lost in my sorrow, or I can go to an art museum. I can choose to cry, or I can pick up a paint brush. While allowing myself to feel the hurts of my past is important, morbidly wallowing in those thoughts is not healthy. I have a choice in what I think about. I can choose to do something creative and fun in the midst of *any* feeling, be it sadness or joy, anger or love, restlessness or peace. I can enjoy who I am and what I am capable of.

I like the sound of that. A lot.

***

I spend hours strolling through the museum, soaking up the beauty and meaning of the many art pieces. Three pieces especially speak to me. The first to hit me in the heart is *Small Bound Goat* by Jack Zajac, 1962. The bronze sculpture depicts a goat held down by a board. The artist perfectly captures the goat's struggle to break free from its bondage. I empathize with the miserably desperate goat.

The next piece that engages me is *The Light of Coincidences* by René Magritte, 1933. The oil painting depicts a sculpted female torso (the Venus de Medici) illuminated by a lit candle. What catches my attention is how brightly the candle glows in his painting. I want to shine that bright. I'd like to be a light in every room I enter.

Then I see *Nature or Abundance* by Léon Frédéric, 1897. It is a larger oil painting of a woman covered in flowering plants and fruit, surrounded by children. She is nursing one and hugging others, while looking down at them serenely. The image is nurturing and loving, yet exudes strength and competence. It has many layers; the longer I stare at it, the more details I notice. The painting reminds me of God's love for us. It also reminds me a bit of myself and my nurturing side. Admiring it, I feel convicted I truly am made in His image.

DATE 7
Dinner

Something within me is subtly changing. I don't know if it's because I'm starting to let go of some of the atrocities of my past, I'm starting to recognize my positive qualities, my eyes are open to how my thoughts and actions are my choices, I've seen how stopping to deliberately observe the world around me can pull me out of myself, I've started talking to the Lord more consistently, or all of the above. But my step is a little lighter, and I am no longer getting stuck in the deep, deep sorrow I was experiencing since giving up my unhealthy coping mechanisms.

Something clicked for me yesterday. I realized that I have no problem admiring others for their accomplishments and positive qualities, but I have a hard time acknowledging, let alone admiring, my own. If I were to meet someone who had been through and overcome tragedies like mine, I would consider that person amazing. Yet though I can recognize my struggles, fights, and victories, I can't seem to connect them to me. It's as if I have no sense of self. In one way, I see myself only as others see me, because if someone criticizes me, I accept the words as true. Yet if someone compliments me, I dismiss the compliment as a bad judgment call.

This revelation was fresh on my mind when I texted Stewart last night. I asked him to describe me, to tell me what kind of person he thinks I am. He replied, "I think you are a woman who struggles with knowing who she is."

"Do you think I'll ever figure it out?"

"If you keep going in the direction you're going and keep doing the work required to get there, then yes, I think you will figure it out someday."

This conversation spurred me to discuss my missing sense of self with my therapist, Audrey, today. I tell her I feel disconnected and have no idea who I truly am. In the ten months I've been seeing Audrey, I've learned she is a wise, beautiful, confident woman who loves the Lord. I think highly of her and wish I were more like her. In our session, she recommends I read a scripture that she reads when she feels down about herself.

I return home, grab my Bible, and read her recommendation, Isaiah 62:1-5.

> For Zion's sake I will not keep silent,
> for Jerusalem's sake I will not remain quiet,
> till her vindication shines out like the dawn,
> her salvation like a blazing torch.
> The nations will see your vindication,
> and all kings your glory;
> you will be called by a new name
> that the mouth of the Lord will bestow.
> You will be a crown of splendor in the Lord's hand,
> a royal diadem in the hand of your God.
> No longer will they call you Deserted,

or name your land Desolate.
But you will be called Hephzibah,[1]
and your land Beulah[2]
for the Lord will take delight in you,
and your land will be married.
As a young man marries a young woman,
so will your Builder marry you;
as a bridegroom rejoices over his bride,
so will your God rejoice over you.
Hephzibah means My Delight Is In Her
Beulah means Married

The verse is so beautiful tears come to my eyes. I re-read it, hanging on each word. I want to believe it is true. I start to wonder how God and I can address my identity issue. He hears me. *Would you like to go out to dinner tonight to talk about it?*

***

As I enjoy the amazing South American cuisine at Nazca Kitchen, I carry on a conversation with the Lord in my head. I thank Him for pursuing me, for seeing something in me *worth* pursuing, even though I don't yet see it myself. He sees past my sins and shortcomings into my heart, soul, and mind, into the woman He created me to be. He reminds me that He sees all the good we have done and all the good we will accomplish together.

I am grateful He sees my goodness, and the thought of learning to see it myself excites me. I admit to Him, "Father, even when *you* say flattering things to me, I don't truly take them to heart. Instead I assume I subconsciously put words in your mouth because even you could not possibly see past all my flaws and still love the core of who I am. Why am I so disconnected from myself?"

My dear, you are smarter than you think. Reflect on your life for a moment. Think about possible reasons you are not in tune with who you are, what you like, and what you want.

I ruminate a bit, thinking about my childhood. Every time my mother hit me, she told me not to cry. If I cried anyway, the beatings increased in severity. Also, she and others consistently labeled me. "You are a horrible little girl . . . you are ungrateful . . . you filthy pig . . . you are fat . . . you are just like your mother (or father) . . . if you were more like your brother . . . I wish you were never born . . . you couldn't be hungry . . . you are fine, quit crying . . . what is wrong with you?" I was always told who I was (an awful person) and how I should feel (ashamed). I didn't have a chance to—and certainly wasn't *encouraged* to—figure out who I really was or what I was actually feeling. So I hesitantly borrowed the titles others gave me to define myself.

"Gosh, Lord, when I think about all the names people have used to describe me, I'm blown away. As you know, my mother's favorite question was 'Who do you think you are?' and my required reply was 'Nobody, Mommy. I'm nobody.' An ex-boyfriend frequently declared 'Nobody else would ever want you.' Throughout my years in therapy, hospitalizations, and doctor visits, I have been clinically diagnosed as having severe depression, borderline personality disorder, food and sex addictions, PTSD, OCD, social anxiety disorder, and obesity. And yet . . . deep down, especially in my adolescent years, I always believed I was created by a loving God, which makes me something greater than those derogatory labels. Maybe the disconnect between how I have been labeled and what I believe deep in my soul has been tormenting me on a subconscious level. Maybe I have been searching to redefine these labels, to connect to the child of God deep within me."

You have developed incredible insight, sweet daughter. Let go of all those labels. I am your Creator, and I have never given you any of those hurtful names. You are no other than whom I, your Creator, say you are.

I feel a powerful sense of healing in God's words. I fervently hope this conversation is real. The thought of being a child of God is beautiful. The idea that I no longer need to label myself with the titles others give me is freeing. "Father, *please* be real. Please say the time we spend together is genuine. To think I am a woman you created with love gives me hope for a greater life."

Caren, the words you hear are not your thoughts. They are promises I make to you. I am the truth, the way, and the light.

DATE 8
Reading on the Dock

Since my dinner date with the Lord last week, I have been in almost constant conversation with Him. I am in solitude except when I'm with my children, at work, talking to Audrey, or texting Stewart, so that leaves a lot of time to talk to God!

Today I am dreading going to work. Though I stopped giving sensual massages, my male customers still hope for more; after all, they found me through classified ads known for adult-oriented services. Because my ad is listed under a legitimate massage category, my customers know I am not a prostitute, but they assume that, like many other massage therapists listed, I will offer "sensual upgrades" to their massages. They make lewd, insulting comments and complain when I give only therapeutic massages. Though the men have always spoken to me this way, their attitudes have only begun to bother me in the last few weeks. I suppose as my self-esteem increases, and I have more experiences with God treating me in a loving way, I am less tolerant of male disrespect.

As I get ready for work, I think, "Lord, I really, *reeeeally* don't want to do massages today. I need a break from that atmosphere."

Take the day off. Take a break with me at White Rock Lake, on the dock near the spot we had our picnic.

I wish I could! But all the bills are due this week. "As much as I enjoy surrendering my life to you—it is so much easier than worrying about everything myself!—I can't afford to take the day off."

Trust me. Taking the day off will not hurt you.

"Going against my instinct and trusting you is still hard for me sometimes. I want to learn to fully trust you again, like I used to years ago."

I know, dear. We will work on trust issues as long as you are willing. But for today, would you like to go back to the lake with me to sit and relax?

I finally give in to temptation. "Yes, Lord! Thank you for loving me."

I cannot help but love you as you are my precious child. And do not forget your book!

***

With my blanket and book, I approach the dock. I notice two young boys fishing. They look so innocent and happy. I wish joy for them and whisper, "Lord, let them continue to smile and protect their hearts from hardening." I look around and take in the waves and birds and sunshine and think about how great my God is to create this splendor. I bake in the Texas sun, feeling nothing but gratitude and awe. I love the power and order in this moment, how nature works together to create a perfect balance. Everything is as it should be. I'm pleased that I'm so much more aware of the world around me now.

I lie down on my blanket and open my book, *The Shack*, by William P. Young. I started reading this bestseller a few years before. It tells the story of a man whose daughter was murdered in a shack in the woods. Four years later, a note, seemingly from God, invites him back to the shack. He returns and experiences God in several forms. Though it is a fairly short novel, I never finished reading it. When it began talking a lot about Jesus, I abandoned it. Though I was open to the idea of God at that time, I thought the whole "Jesus thing" was silly and weird. To be honest, I sort of looked sideways at people who bought the Jesus story hook, line, and sinker. A few days ago, I came across the book again and felt urged by God to give it another try. So I began reading it again, from the beginning.

As I read the story of God's reaching out to this despairing man and leading him to love, redemption, and forgiveness, I shed tears of healing and freedom. Like the man in the story, I am changing; I can feel it. I am being led from my sorrow and the shame of my past addictions. I am beginning to connect to myself through the love of my God. In the book, the main character relates more to Jesus, so Jesus works with him on understanding God and the Holy Spirit. I identify with the character's struggle, but in the opposite way. I accept God but have trouble accepting the idea of Jesus.

All my addictions were, in a sense, my protection. When I focused on sex, drugs, cigarettes, food, television, living in my head, music, OCD, PTSD, control issues, gossip, complaining, and so on, I could disconnect from my feelings and not feel heartbroken about the evil I experienced. I spent years and years wrapped up in addictions to prevent myself from breaking. I have a vivid picture of my heart and mind guarded tightly by thorns, broken glass, and vicious dogs. Nothing could reach me.

But the Lord is breaking through! I can feel the change happening, slowly but surely. And I now see my past in a different light. Because I chose to live a life without God, my addictions were the only way to get through the pain. My self-judgment softens. I start to view my addictions less like enemies and more like friends I've grown apart from. The addictions served a purpose at the time, but now that I have God to lean on. They have worn out their welcome and are no longer needed. I grin at the analogy.

Caren, if you could have a conversation with your past addictions and vices, what would you say to them?

Intriguing question. After some deliberation, I respond. "I guess I would thank them for keeping me safe as a little girl, as a teen, and as a woman. But I would tell them I no longer need them. There are no bears chasing me; there are no monsters under the bed. I am ready to face life without them."

A surge of conviction flows through me. I will walk with my sword and shield and become the warrior my God created me to be. I am no longer the little girl that needs to fight for her life. I am the woman who chooses to go into battle for her inheritance!

DATE 9
Live Jazz

I return home from the lake feeling rejuvenated. My mind and heart are buoyant, not only from relaxing outdoors and getting a much-needed break from my uncomfortable work environment, but also from releasing much of the self-judgment and shame about my past addictive behavior.

I putter around the house and scan my emails. An announcement from the Dallas Museum of Art catches my eye. Tonight they are hosting a live jazz and vocal performance. That sounds amazing! I just spent a beautiful afternoon with the Lord, and I don't want to rush things, but I would absolutely love to enjoy the performance with God. "Lord, thank you for our time together this afternoon. Is tonight too soon for another date?"

No, that would be very nice. Let's take your sweet daughter too. I'd like to spend time with both of you together.

I am taken aback at first. My dates with God are personal, and I haven't shared them with my children. Inviting my daughter on one of our dates never occurred to me. Yet, what a wonderful idea! Victoria is my youngest at six years old, and ever since she started attending a Christian preschool, she has loved God as much as I did when I was her age. I decide I will pick her up early from day camp to get ready for the date.

"Thank you for the idea, Lord. This is a nice opportunity to share time with my daughter. Victoria loves to be treated like a princess!"

Yes, she does, and so do you, my beloved. I am proud you are allowing yourself to be treated that way.

How far I have come since my first date with God! At first I turned to Him in broken desperation. Now, instead of focusing on only myself and my brokenness, I look forward to sharing good times with the Lord, and I am even eager to share my special "God time" with my child.

***

Victoria is thrilled at the prospect of dressing up in fancy clothes and going on a date with Mom. As we get ready, I explain in a little more detail what has been happening in my life. She agrees I seem happier than I used to. I no longer cry all the time, and I pay more attention to her and her brothers. I hesitantly describe how God has been using dates to develop a relationship with me. She accepts my explanation with no reservation and is excited to be included in this latest date. I laugh that I had any worries about revealing the truth of my transformation.

As we sit at the art museum enjoying the beautiful music together, I am overwhelmed with feelings of love for Victoria. I have always loved my children the best I was able, but the love I feel right now is deeper and richer than anything I've felt before. I see her in a new light. She is precious and innocent. Her life lies ahead of her, filled with unlimited opportunity. She might have the ability to play any of these instruments or to share her voice as beautifully as these performers. She might have the talent for drawing or painting or sculpting as perfectly as any artist represented in this museum. God offers talent to each one of us; it is our choice whether or not to accept our gifts, our inheritance. Believing Victoria possesses unlimited potential is fairly easy, given her young age. Realizing I have as much potential waiting to be unleashed is a little harder to grasp. But I now believe all I have to do is love myself enough to claim and enjoy my inheritance.

Throughout the evening, I speak to God aloud now and then. "Lord, this food is amazing. Thank you!" and "What beautiful performances, God." Victoria takes my comments to God in stride. In fact, she seems to delight in them.

We share a plate of delicious hors d'oeuvres prepared by an artist of taste. Victoria appreciates the food as much as I do, and I revel in her enjoyment. I love watching how she savors each bite—how her face lights up with a smile when I feed her. When we reach the last mushroom, I immediately give it to her. My only thought is that I can't wait to see her enjoy this last bite. Of course I've sacrificed my desires and given my children plenty of things before because I believe that's what moms are supposed to do, but the emotion behind this act of selflessness feels markedly different. I let Victoria have the last bite because I love her and want to see her happy. I don't secretly feel a little resentful or deprived; my desire to give her pleasure is greater than any desire I have for myself.

As I drive home, I marvel at these new feelings bubbling up inside me. Perhaps less emotionally damaged parents experience this intense love for their children from day one. I wonder if they take it for granted? I haven't been able to open my heart enough to experience fully loving someone without reservation, but my ability to love is growing through this journey. As I allow God to love me and enjoy me, I am finding a deeper, more meaningful way to love and enjoy others. I feel like a newborn first discovering the joys of life.

"Thank you, Father, for a magical evening."

DATE 10
Sunday Service

Driving down the street today, I notice a woman sitting at a bus stop. Her hair is tangled, her clothes are tattered, and she appears hopelessly sad. I am immediately assaulted with memories of my life in poverty like it was yesterday. I remember the desperate feeling of being almost out of food—down to white bread, generic margarine, and Ramen noodles—anxiously waiting for our monthly allowance of food stamps to arrive. Taking the bus to the store, buying our groceries, and then having to "borrow" the grocery cart to transport the food home. It was supremely difficult and demoralizing, but I am certainly thankful that at least I had food stamps. And seeing the woman at the bus stop makes me appreciate more fully what I have today. I say a quick prayer of thanks. The air conditioning in my van doesn't work very well, and the windows don't go down, but at least I have running transportation!

Caren, I am proud of you for remembering where you have been and where you are, and for showing appreciation for it all. You are making great progress.

I flood with pleasure hearing my Lord is pleased with me. I am glad I don't have to hide from Him anymore. "Lord, I know I didn't actually *have* to hide from you. But I used to feel that way."

I understand. Will you go somewhere with me this morning?

"Sure! We haven't had a date in a few weeks. Where would you like to go?"

Church.

Church? This stops me cold. The Lord knows how I feel about church. Ambivalent . . . nervous . . . like I don't fit in since I'm not a "Jesus freak" like everyone else there. Besides, I'm not wearing church clothes, and it is 10:58!

Really, you are worried about clothes? If you do not want to go with me, that is fine. Simply say no. Do not make excuses.

I sigh. I really don't want to go, but I do want to obey God. "Okay, Father, I will go. But where will I find a church open at 10:58?"

I am glad you asked. Look around. See the church to your right? It has an 11:00 service.

Unbelievable. I didn't even notice the church earlier. Suddenly I am frightened. What if there is no 11:00 service? If not, that would prove that God does not really speak to me, that this voice and presence I hear and sense with such clarity is only my imagination. I quickly push aside the thought, gather my courage, drive to the church, park, and enter.

The 11:00 service has just begun.

I am awed once again. I *am* hearing the Lord's voice. God is truly loving me, guiding me, and leading me.

***

The moment I walk into the sanctuary, I feel the spirit of God surround me. I am filled with confusion. I love being in a church, but Christian churches are focused on accepting a relationship with Jesus Christ, and I have not done that. I don't know what I believe. I feel like a hypocrite being here. I resist believing in the reason behind the Church, yet I fear damnation for not believing. I want to be obedient and to be fully connected to God, but I struggle with the Jesus aspect of faith. Why would Jesus have to die for our sins? Why were lambs sacrificed? If God made us, why are we sinful? Why would He call a man His Son and ask Him to sacrifice His life for the rest of mankind's sins, yet never take away our desire to sin? My head spins.

"Father, I am struggling with my beliefs. If Jesus truly was your Son, and if only through Him salvation can be found, please forgive me for doubting and help me understand."

Stop worrying, child. Simply be in this moment. I will reveal to you everything you need at the pace I have designed for you. You have been wounded by man and his word; therefore, I come to you where you are, in a way you can trust and understand. Just enjoy the message you hear today.

Fellowship Church is conducting baptisms today as part of a "Family Sunday" theme. Three women head to the stage, and for reasons I don't understand, I am so moved emotionally that tears begin to pour down my face like a faucet. Before each woman is baptized, she speaks briefly about why she is there. The third woman says, "I want to be cleansed of my sins."

These eight small words affect me so deeply I begin to audibly sob. I hide my face in my hands, embarrassment washing over me. I weep at the thought of being cleansed—not just forgiven, but *cleansed.* Feeling free of all shame and guilt. I have done some horrible, awful things in my life. Imagine if they actually could be washed away forever. If only I could believe in Jesus like I did when I was a little girl, if it could be that easy again.

"Please, Father, show me the way. I want to experience cleansing. Erase it all, everything! Please! I have too much regret trapped inside me. Please remove this heavy garment of shame I wear."

Darling, I have forgiven you, and you can be washed clean. Maybe it is time you forgive yourself as well. Be patient. All will become clear when the time is right. For now, I will reveal one thing to you. All your sins and past experiences brought you to this point in your life. If you let me, I will use you, your life, and your story to help further my kingdom.

My crying subsides and I feel hopeful again. When the service ends, I make my way to the church exit. God stops me.

Before you leave, make a quick stop at the church book store. A book I want you to purchase is on sale.

I obediently detour to the book store. I spot *Fifty Reasons Why Jesus Came to Die* by John Piper on the clearance table. This must be the book God refers to.

Yes, that is the one.

How funny. God asked me for fifty dates, and this book refers to fifty reasons. What is His fixation with the number fifty? I chuckle and buy the book. I don't feel ready to read it yet, but I know God won't mind. He will wait patiently until the time is right for me.

DATE 11
The Harbor

I continue to see changes in myself. I am not as gloomy anymore. I am finding a more peaceful presence. I am starting to
notice others, not just myself. I am more involved and connected with my children. In one way I believe in God's voice more
than ever. Yet . . . something has been worrying me.

I am flat broke. I hate my job now, and since I decline lewd
clients, I have very little income. I try not to fret, to trust that
everything will be okay, but as my money dwindles, I begin to
question my sanity. How in the world can I pay my bills and
care for my children if I'm not earning more? Was I an idiot to
quit the lucrative part of my massage business? Building that
business again would not take long. Should I go back to it? But
the thought of degrading myself again turns my stomach. I am
a different person now. I think going back to that line of work
would break me.

Today I am down to my last twenty-five dollars and feeling
more desperate than ever. I pray, "Lord, if you are really there,
please help me. How can my family survive the rest of the week

with only twenty-five dollars? I can't see why you would want this for me."

Trust me, Caren.

Easier said than done. As I stew a little more, I straighten up the house and get the mail from my mailbox. I am sorting through junk mail when two envelopes catch my eye. One is from TRS, the Teacher Retirement System of Texas. I used to work at an elementary school but quit four years ago. I open the envelope and stare in disbelief at a check from a retirement account that I apparently never emptied. The other envelope is from the Texas Attorney General. I open it and am stunned a second time. I gaze dumbly at a child support check from my ex-husband . . . the man I have not heard from him since he left two years ago and who has never sent child support before.

Moments before I had twenty-five dollars to my name. I am now holding $1,100 in my trembling hands.

My heart fills with renewed wonder and appreciation. "Lord, thank you so much. I am sorry for doubting you. I want to spend more time with you."

Would you like to go to The Harbor in Rockwall tomorrow morning?

I love the idea. The Harbor is a retail development on the shores of Lake Ray Hubbard, a large manmade lake near Dallas. Because of the pretty sunset views, water fountains, and walking paths, it is a popular place to go with a date.

"I'm in!"

***

Today I walk around the lake enjoying nature—the water, trees, clouds, wind, birds. I rest on a large rock and, as on all our other dates, feel the strong presence of God.

"Wow, Lord, I am in awe of your creation! This lake is breathtaking. We needed a lake, so you provided everything we needed to make a lake. Speaking of providing, thanks again for providing for me financially yesterday."

I'm still in shock at the two hefty checks that arrived unexpectedly, exactly when I needed money most. I was doubting myself and God, and He pulled through for me anyway.

Thank you for trusting me and having faith that I would provide, despite your misgivings.

Appreciation fills my heart to bursting. This feeling of gratitude is a relatively new feeling for me. I never thought I had anything to be grateful for, but my eyes are opening. Not only am I grateful for the way the Lord has improved my life in the last month-and-a-half, but I am also grateful for my life in retrospect. I am beginning to see that even in my darkest moments, there were things to be thankful for.

I think about the $1,100 windfall, and I have a strong desire to give part of it back to God. When I was married, I attended church regularly, tithed 10 percent of my income, helped other people, and did all the other things I thought a Christian was supposed to do. While I believed in God as much as I was able to at the time, I did these "good" things mostly because of a sense of duty. After my husband left, I dropped church and all that went with it. Today I have a new feeling. I am so happy that God provided for me that I truly *want* to give back to Him.

"Lord, it has been many years since I've trusted to give back to you in any way, let alone 10 percent of my money. I'd like to do that today. Where should I bring the $110? To the church I used to attend? To a charity?"

The decision is yours, dear. Use your present and past life experiences as guidance. I trust you will do the right thing.

As I gaze at the beauty around me, I reflect on how amazing my life truly is. My entire family is healthy, our stomachs no longer know hunger, we have a roof over our heads and clothes on our backs. My present life is nothing like the poverty of my past. We aren't in a homeless shelter or living from couch to couch. Our clothing is not tattered. I remember a time when my sweet boy's feet smelled awful because we didn't own socks. I remember begging strangers for change to buy my son food when we ran out of food stamps. Yet, even during that season of poverty, we never went without. We might have been sleeping in a shelter or on a friend's couch, but nonetheless, we had shelter. We always had clothes, tattered or not, and we always managed to find something to eat, one way or another.

"Hmmm, that's it, Lord! I want to use the money for people in the same situation I was in. With your help, I will use this $110 to put together gift bags for women and children at a homeless shelter!"

That sounds like a terrific idea.

DATE 12
Shopping

I left The Harbor yesterday energized and motivated to go shopping for the gift bags I've decided to make. I browse the Internet, looking for shelters in Dallas, and find a good recipient for the gift bags: New Beginning Center, an organization that provides many services for victims of domestic abuse, including a Crisis Intervention Shelter. The shelter is a safe haven for abused women and children who have fled their homes and need time, resources, and nurturing as they figure out how to rebuild their lives. After calling the shelter and asking a few questions, I learn they currently house eighteen women, one seven-year-old boy, eight boys four and under, and five girls four and under. I wonder what I can buy that many people for $110.

"Father, I'm extremely excited to shop for these gift bags! Can we go together, as our next date?"

Of course.

***

I walk through the Dollar Tree, open my mind to the Lord, and let my past and present experiences speak to me. What can I purchase that would possibly touch the lives of these women and children? What would have helped me or my little boy when we were in that situation? As I wander the aisles, I filter through ideas.

First, I consider the women. They don't need snacks or perfume or makeup. While fun, that type of gift is just "stuff" that doesn't last. What these women need is *hope*. What might have a real impact on these mothers? Something we could afford with the little bit we have to spend?

I think back to my experience sunbathing on the dock at White Rock Lake while reading *The Shack*. It is a powerful book. Even though I had a hard time understanding and accepting the Jesus piece, it spoke to me in many ways. I envision it as the perfect tool to bring hope to a discouraged woman. Then I think about how writing about my experiences with God has been therapeutic. I could also give each woman a journal in which to write her feelings and thoughts! I can even make them by hand to save money, and making them is much more personal than buying them. As I put my time and love into creating the journals, I can pray for the women who will receive them. Perfect!

Now I think about the little girls. What would have helped me when I was a little girl in this situation? I was never allowed to express myself as a child. How about I give the girls little sketch books and crayons, so they can express themselves with art? And I could give them princess dress-up clothes. After all, they are daughters of the King. What a fun way for them to use their imaginations!

"Lord, what do you think?"

You are doing an excellent job. I am proud of you!

Finally, I turn my attention to the boys. I think about my own sons. They seem to enjoy imagining themselves in powerful roles, where they can be assertive and feel important. I could get plastic policeman and fireman badges so they can pretend to "save the day." Perhaps I can find some toy figurines of strong and mighty creatures, like dinosaurs, lions, and tigers. And I bet they would enjoy sketch journals just as much as the girls.

Satisfied with my ideas, I eagerly scour the store until I find everything I need. The total is seventy dollars. Uh oh. That leaves only forty dollars for eighteen copies of *The Shack*. I might have to change my plan. I don't think I can find eighteen books for that price.

Don't give up so easily, my dear.

Of course, God is right. It won't hurt to at least *try* to find a fantastic deal on the books. There is a huge Half Price Books store in town. I wonder if they have any copies of *The Shack*, and if so, how much they cost.

***

I approach the check-out registers at Half Price Books and request to speak to the manager. I ask him if he has eighteen copies of *The Shack*. He does! But they are priced at $7.95 apiece. I request a discount for buying all eighteen. He is willing to take twenty percent off my price, but even with the discount they would cost more than $100, so the books are still too expensive for my forty-dollar budget. At my disappointed look, he explains that the movie version of *The Shack* is being released soon, at which time the books will fly off the shelves. He will be able to sell them at full price easily. He assures me a 20 percent discount is more than fair.

Before discouragement takes over, I say a silent prayer to the Lord. "Please give me the words to say to this man."

Be assertive and transparent.

I take a deep breath, hold my head up high, and explain to the gentleman why I want the books. Despite a pang of embarrassment, I share that I was once in a shelter like the women I am buying the books for, and that it was the good deeds of others that helped me along my way. I tell him in earnest that if he finds a way to make this happen, he too will anonymously touch lives.

Amazingly, I watch this man's heart soften before my eyes. He looks toward his cashier and says, "Ring them up for two dollars each." With tax, my total is a few cents shy of forty dollars. I sincerely thank the manager for his generous act of kindness and stumble from the store in astonishment.

"Lord, you are so amazing! I got everything I envisioned for almost exactly $110! This is incredible! You *are* real. The voice I hear *must* be your voice. This *has* to be your hand I see at work. I couldn't do these things on my own. I love you, Father. I feel happier than I have felt in a long, long time."

Darling, it is I . . . and we have only just begun.

That night I text Stewart, as I have often have since beginning my journey with the Lord. I tell him when I pray about something, and I follow up with a description of how the Lord provided for me. I do so as a way of documenting the miracles I'm experiencing in a slightly more public way than my book notes—as proof of some sorts that all of this is really happening. But I also do so because I want to share this experience with him. I believe something truly miraculous might be happening, and I want to give Stewart the gift of witnessing it firsthand.

DATE 13
Assembly Line - Part One

When I wake up this morning, I gaze at the table on which I spread out all the gifts I bought yesterday. I am so proud! I take a picture and send it to Stewart. It is hard to believe $110 bought this much stuff. Amazing!

Good morning, Caren. Would you like to start preparing the gift bags today? I would like you to bring them to the shelter on Monday. These bags will have an impact on several special women and children. I am very proud of your idea. You are creative, and your gifts will be effective in more ways than you know.

Today is Saturday. If I want to have them ready for a Monday delivery, I had better start assembling them today. "Yes, Lord. I would love to assemble the bags with you today. Let's do it! And thanks for the compliment, but it was you who gave me the idea for the bags, wasn't it?"

No, dear. The idea was all yours. I simply placed my hand where it was needed to help make your plan a reality. You are very creative. I especially like that you are making the journals and sketch books by hand. Not only are you being a wise steward of your finances, but handmade gifts are more personal and loving than store-bought gifts.

I grab a cup of coffee and sit at the table. I will put together the little girls' bags first. I look at all the construction paper, crayons, and ribbon. Making sketch books for the five girls will take a while. I don't mind, though, because that means a lot of quiet time with God, healing and growing.

As I fold the sheets of paper in half and decide how many pages to include in each sketchbook, I think about the girls who will receive these books. They are exposed to abusive situations beyond their control. Memories of living with my mother as she married and divorced eight husbands, most of them abusive, crash down on me. I vividly remember one of her ex-husbands using me as a shield as my mother hurled a lamp at him, hitting me instead. He and my mother often used my brother and me as a defense against attacks. In the middle of their fights, we watched as they did horrible things to each other. My mother stabbed her ex with a barbecue fork. He burned her with cigarettes. Once he even commanded an aggressive Rottweiler to attack her.

Another memory breaks through. My mom and one of her ex-husbands were fighting violently in the living room. My brother and I cowered in the bedroom, shaking and crying. We eventually opened the window and shouted for help. The neighbors came over, but to our dismay, they didn't try to stop the fighting. Instead they came into the bedroom, moved us away from the window, and told us to calm down. They kept telling us everything would be okay, even as my mother's screams of pain echoed from the living room, worsening the fear in our hearts.

While reliving these painful memories, I am struck by how sweet and loving I was as a little girl, despite being surrounded by a life of sadness and disparity. The girls who will receive these gifts are just as innocent as I was. I experience a strong sense of empathy and sympathy for them. My words come tumbling out.

"Lord, please protect these little girls. Protect their hearts from becoming jaded, their minds from becoming skewed, and their bodies from being harmed. I know firsthand the missteps they might be tempted to take as a result of improper programming. Lord, I ask that their parents' dysfunction not be passed on to them, but that instead you reach your hand into their lives and end the cycle of dysfunction now. Please pursue these little girls like you consistently pursued me. Thank you, Father. In your holy name I pray. Amen."

Though it has been happening more and more, I am still surprised and awed at my newfound ability to step outside myself and care deeply for others. I am becoming a new woman. My concern for the girls in the shelter overrides the sadness I feel about my past. In fact, having endured abusive relationships myself helps me relate more fully to the girls and gives me a more fervent desire to help them.

I think about my own daughter and how receptive she was to my explanation of this journey I am on, dating God. I am thankful I am finally breaking the cycle of poverty, abuse, and self-hate, with God's help. "Lord, I want to ask my daughter to join us in making the girls' gift bags. I love spending time with her, and I bet she will learn a lot from this project."

I think that is a wonderful idea!

I invite Victoria to help, and she jumps right in. We spend hours folding the paper into booklets, punching holes on the edges, and weaving ribbons through the holes, starting from the edges and meeting in the centers in pretty bows. Victoria decorates the covers of the sketchbooks with colorful designs in crayon and inspiring messages like "God loves you!" and "You are loved!" They are beautiful.

My heart soars as I watch my daughter's excitement. As we assemble the sketchbooks and make bundles of crayons tied with ribbon to go with them, we laugh and talk to each other and to God. I think we are both amazed at how much pleasure we derive from helping people in need. We bond as we work, and I find myself discussing deep subjects with her, teaching her life lessons. I share that great pain can lie behind a smile, as mine did for years. I explain that outward appearances don't tell you where people are from, what their struggles are, or what they have been through. We talk about how thankful we are for what we have, and though others have more, there are always people who have less. We celebrate the gift of being in the position to do good for others.

By the time the sketch books are complete, and the girls' bags are filled, I feel closer to my daughter, to myself, and especially to the Lord. I think about all He has seen me through, all He plans to see my children through, and all He plans to see the families at the shelters through. Feeling compassion for the difficult lives the little girls have, and remembering my similarly tragic childhood, has sparked compassion for the little girl I used to be. I was immersed in a toxic way of life from the day I was born—it's no wonder I made mistakes and chose a harmful lifestyle.

Also, the positive experience I had with my daughter today is in stark contrast to the experience of the little girls at the shelter (and my past experiences with my mother). I feel the stirrings of pride for breaking my family's cycle of physical and emotional abuse. My daughter is witnessing a life far great than I witnessed as a child.

"Thank you for this date, Lord. I am finally able to begin forgiving myself. Today we made gifts for others, but I am giving myself a gift as well: the gift of grace."

DATE 14
Assembly Line - Part Two

This morning I wake up in a good mood. My mood gets even better when I walk in the kitchen and see the gift bags Victoria and I put together lined up on the table, ready to be delivered. We accomplished a lot yesterday, but I need to finish the nine sketchbooks for the boys and eighteen journals for the women today. An idea comes to me.

"Good morning, Father. May we have another date today? If so, I would like to work on the gift bags with you and the boys this time! After the incredible experience of Victoria helping, I'm eager to let the boys in on the fun."

I think that is a wonderful idea.

I already told Da'Shon, my seventeen-year-old, and Reggie, my thirteen-year-old, about my journey with the Lord, shortly after the night Victoria and I went to the jazz performance. Both were receptive to my story in their own ways. Reggie was the most accepting; he surprised me by telling me he believes in Jesus and talks to God too. Dae (my nickname for Da'Shon) was less amenable. He is mad at God and doesn't believe in Him anymore, so he thinks dating and talking to God is weird. Yet, he goes with the flow and seems supportive of my experience anyway. I believe he doesn't reject the idea outright because of the tremendous positive change he has seen in me the last month or so.

But I am still a little nervous to invite the boys to join me. Though they know about my dates with God, and they know Victoria has participated in a couple, they have not been directly involved before. As the boys eat breakfast, I take a deep breath and explain that I am going to finish making the gift bags with the Lord today, and I would love for them to join me, like Victoria did yesterday. I am pleased when they both agree right away.

***

We tackle the project with enthusiasm. The boys enjoy decorating the journals and sketchbooks as much as Victoria did. They carefully consider what to draw and write on the covers, trying to imagine what would make a little boy smile. They methodically sort the toys, debating which are best for the older boy and which are best for the younger boys. As we work, I talk about my experience in a homeless shelter with Dae when he was eleven months old. Of course he doesn't remember, but he listens intently to my description of our time there. He is reflective as he absorbs that he used to be in the same situation as the little boys we are making gift bags for. Being empowered to help them in some small way touches him deeply.

Talking about the shelter dredges up a lot of old memories. I describe feeling alone, with no help from Dae's father, family, or friends. At one point, a mother and her two adult daughters at the shelter befriended me. Though they were currently homeless, they were in a better position than I was. The mother's grandmother owned a business and promised them a job and a place to stay in a few weeks. I recall sitting in the rec room one day, feeling broken and lost, when they approached me with an offer to help. They laid out their plan. I could give them temporary custody of Dae, allowing me to get back on my feet financially more easily. He would live with them at the grandmother's house, and they would return him to me when I was better able to care for him. I'll admit that I entertained the idea briefly, only because I thought my baby might be better off with them. But I didn't want to imagine a moment of life without him. Even though things were hard, and I had no direction, I loved him with every bit of my being. I decided that no matter what, I would make things work. I thanked the women for their offer and declined.

Today I am extremely glad Dae and I took that journey together. It was hard at the time, but we got through it. Our lives are much better now, and our past experience feels almost like a gift—because of it, we are able to relate to these women and children with true empathy and love. What God told me before is true. He will use my past for good, if I will let Him. I pray aloud:

"Lord, I wish I could give these mothers hope. I want them to understand they are on a journey, and their current situation is simply a tough spot in that journey. They will get through it, especially with your help."

As is often the case when the boys hear me talk to God, they tease me good-naturedly. "Did the *Lord* tell you how much longer this will take?" Wink, wink. I laugh and roll my eyes.

As the morning wears on, we continue making the books and

chatting, and my youngest son, Reggie, begins to open up. He says that he somehow relates to the boys in the shelter because his dad regularly put him down and rarely showed up for his games and performances. Then, the day his dad left for good, things took a turn for the worse. His father violently pinned Reggie to the wall as he threatened me and the kids, screaming "I hate you all!" He slapped Reggie to the ground, calling him a bitch in the most degrading, hostile tone of voice I had ever heard him use toward his son. His father left that night, and I got a restraining order against him the following day. Reggie was devastated. He carried the hurt for years. So today, Reggie explains, he is happy that he is able to help, in at least this small way, boys who have gone through the same things he did.

By the end of the day, with a few breaks along the way, all thirty-two gift bags are ready. What a feeling of accomplishment! I am giddy at the thought of delivering the bags to the shelter tomorrow. I pray over the gifts, asking God to protect the women and children who will receive them.

Caren, I am proud of your diligence. The gifts turned out beautifully. I especially love how you included your children in the dates with us. Instead of keeping your past a secret, you were open with them, showing them how painful past experiences brought you to the happy place you are today. That is an amazing way to parent.

"Thank you, Lord. I do feel like a great parent right now. Most of the bonding time I have had with my children involves a meal, a movie, or other entertainment. While those are fun activities, spending quality time together making a difference in the world is even more amazing!"

I think about the day and beam with pride remembering how eager my sons were to help. They were able to empathize with people they don't even know, largely because of our past experiences. We became closer to each other as we reflected on life and how it changes—how every experience ties to the next, how God weaves our experiences into a tapestry of perfection, full of beauty and color, if we let Him.

I speak to God again. "Thank you for my children being receptive to the changes I'm going through. You must have prepared their hearts in some way. If my mother had told me she was dating the Lord, I would have thought she'd lost her mind!"

Caren, your children have been there every moment of your journey, watching you. You have made many decisions, some good, some short of good, some with me, some without. You found your way back to me, and together we are working toward incredible victories. You are teaching your children more about perseverance and redemption than you realize. They trust you because you have done your best to do right by them.

The Lord gives me too much credit! I've made most of my decisions without Him, and the majority of those decisions temporarily turned my life into a train wreck. "The only way I was able to fix the mess I made of my life, Lord, was by turning back to you, crying on my knees, begging for help."

Yes, and together we are cleaning up the mess. Every bad situation you have been in can be used to teach a lesson for my glory later. I teach through parables, and the story of your life is a perfect modern-day parable, my beloved. Some of your most imperfect, painful moments provide the most perfect teachings. Today is a good example. You used your past pain for a divine cause.

Joy overflows from my heart, and I pray even more fervently. "God, I pray at least one of these women will read *The Shack* and begin to see you for the loving Father you are. I pray that through these gift bags you provided, that my children and I put together and prayed over, a child discovers the gift of art within, a little girl begins to see herself as your little princess and lets you treat her accordingly, a young boy strives to carry the confidence that wearing a badge for your honor provides, or a woman begins to journal her beautiful journey as she takes the steps to discovering who you created her to be. We send forth these gifts, Lord, and trust you will make your magic happen! Thank you for providing all that you do. I love you."

DATE 15
AutoZone

Life has been rocking along fairly smoothly since I delivered the gift bags to the shelter last week. With the extra money God provided, I am making a bit of progress toward paying off my bills. I am driving around town running errands and chatting with the Lord like I often do these days when the weak air conditioning in my van goes out completely. *Are you kidding me?* It's August in Dallas, Texas, and my windows don't roll down. The high is 105 today!

I call the Ford dealership at once. My heart drops as they tell me that I probably need a new air compressor, which costs about $1,200 to install. I am extra frustrated because I have just learned my best friend Charla is in town from Ohio for a Mary Kay convention. I need a working vehicle! I take the van to the dealership, and they give me a rental car to use as I wait for them to determine exactly what the problem is.

Charla and I have a great time visiting. We haven't seen each other in years, and being with someone who knows me is really nice. On the second day of my van being in the shop, I receive a call confirming the air compressor is the problem, so the $1,200 estimate is correct. I can't afford that much. I return the rental car and pick up my van.

Charla is a good sport about driving in the hot van on the last day of her visit. Not only does she not judge me or get upset, but she also lightens the mood by joking that her thighs are drowning in sweat, and her makeup is melting off her face. She even comes up with a temporary solution to our near-death-by-heat-and-suffocation situation. She holds her door open a crack as we drive, and we both throw our doors open wide at each stoplight. We are able to belly laugh at the situation later. Having a dear friend to talk to and pal around with does wonders for my spirit. Charla loves that I am dating the Lord, and she notices how I have changed. She is proud of the woman I am becoming, and I am proud of her as well. I hope we will contact each other more frequently and consistently going forward.

After I take her to the airport to say my final goodbyes, I drive home and thank the Lord for the wonderful visit with Charla. I then plead with Him about the van. "Lord, please help me! I don't have the money to fix the air conditioning, and I can't continue to drive around like this. Without a vehicle, I'll never get caught up on my bills!"

Darling, things happen in life that you cannot control. How you choose to view and handle those things makes all the difference. Let's go to Auto-Zone together and look for help there. We will make it a date.

AutoZone is a good idea. They sell car replacement parts, so many "backyard mechanics" frequent the store. Maybe I can find someone there who will repair my van for less money than the dealership. But . . . a date? I don't want to seem ungrateful that the Lord wants to spend time with me, but a date to AutoZone doesn't seem too exciting. Then again, time with Him seems to come with great reward, so . . .

"Okay, Lord, let's go."

***

I walk into AutoZone feeling anxious. I scan the store rapidly, listening to conversations around me, searching for someone who appears to be a mechanic I can afford. I immediately spot a man at the counter talking to the cashier. His accent is thick, but I understand him well enough to work out what he is saying. He purchased the wrong part for a car he is fixing, and he wants to return the part. The cashier asks him for a receipt. The man fumbles through his pockets and wallet, searching for it. He cannot find it, so he has to settle for store credit instead of a refund.

Clearly the man is unorganized and doesn't seem too professional, but that probably means he is affordable. He says he fixes cars, and I'm desperate. I decide to ask him to look at my van.

Caren, do you think he is the best man for the job? ━━

"I don't think that matters right now. My van needs to be repaired as soon as possible, the man says he fixes cars, and he looks like he will be cheap."

Almost frantically I ask the man if he can take a look at my van. He eagerly agrees as he follows me out of the store. Using a Freon can I have in my van, he confirms the air compressor is not working. He offers to repair my windows as a quicker and less expensive option than replacing the compressor. Cheaper is better, so I agree.

The man opens his trunk, revealing a mess of tools, hoses, and belts jumbled together. He rummages through the piles to find a wrench that will fit my doors' lug nuts. As he searches, he dumps out bins of tiny nuts and bolts, wrenches, screw drivers, and other tools. I nervously wonder how he will treat my van given he treats his own property so carelessly. He finally finds what he is looking for and begins to unscrew the lug nuts. He manages to lower the driver's side window a couple of inches. Before I realize what is happening, he is ripping off my door! He could remove the door easily by simply loosening another screw or two. Why in the world is he trying to rip the door off prematurely?

I panic. I really need help, but clearly this man is not right for the job.

"Lord, what should I do? This man could cause even more damage to my van!"

I am glad you decided to acknowledge me on our date.

"I'm so sorry! Please help me."

Be assertive. Thank him for his time and tell him you have decided to go another route. Then I suggest you return to AutoZone, with me by your side this time, to look for a mechanic who seems professional.

I thank the man for his time and ask him to kindly put my door back together. I tell him I will take it to a shop to get it fixed. He is kind and does as I ask. At least now I have a couple of inches for a breeze to get through!

The second time I enter AutoZone, I focus on the Lord's presence. I immediately feel calmer and more confident. I scan the store again and soon zero in on a gentleman talking to a couple of men as he stands in line at the counter. I eavesdrop and realize he is giving the men suggestions about air compressors! He wears typical mechanic coveralls and speaks clearly. When he gets to the front of the line, he removes a folded piece of paper from his wallet and reads the year, make, and model of the part he needs.

What do you notice about him, Caren?

"He is organized and appears to know his field."

Yes. Does he seem better qualified than the last person you approached?

"Definitely. He projects a more professional image."

After he finishes his purchase, I approach the man with confidence. I calmly describe my circumstance, and he suggests I bring my van to his shop tomorrow. He says he will evaluate the problem, and then I can decide how I want him to proceed. I thank him, get his business card, and agree to bring him my van the next morning.

I drive home in the stifling van feeling oppressed by the heat but content. I mentally review the date and laugh at myself. The Lord asked me to go to the store with Him, but once I arrived, I abandoned all thoughts of Him and tried to solve my problem on my own! I walked into AutoZone desperate and unorganized and was drawn immediately to someone equally desperate and unorganized. When I finally snapped out of it and asked for the Lord's help, everything changed.

"Thank you, God, for showing me that if I turn to you, I need not operate from a place of impulsive desperation. With you by my side, I was relaxed and confident because I knew I didn't need to sweat the details; you would oversee the situation. I was able to better discern the character of others, and my confidence and professionalism attracted a mechanic with the same qualities."

I feel much better about my air conditioner breaking. The situation is unfortunate and inconvenient, but I will take my van to the mechanic in the morning and handle the problem with God by my side.

DATE 16
The Mechanic

I wake up bright and early to take my van to the mechanic, Michael, I met at AutoZone yesterday. I send up a word of prayer. "Lord, I don't know how you will do it, but please provide a way to get my van fixed within my budget. The weather is simply too hot to drive the children around without air conditioning when the windows won't roll down."

I begin to get ready. I put on a flirty sundress that shows the perfect amount of skin to get a man's attention. I slick my hair back into a neat, sexy bun and begin to apply makeup. I hear God speak to me.

Caren, what are you doing?

"What do you mean? I'm getting ready to meet the mechanic."

Why are you showing cleavage and putting on makeup?

I chuckle. "Wow, Lord—just put it out there, why don't you?" I feel an uncomfortable silence.

"You know how this works, Lord. He is a male mechanic, and I am a single woman! He will try to hustle me because I don't know anything about cars, and I have no man with me.

But if I look sexy and flirt a little, he'll almost certainly give me a better price."

Caren, I am sad you think you need to use your femininity to bargain for a better price on car repairs. Your sensuality is a gift I have given you for the purpose of experiencing intimacy and connecting deeply with the man I have chosen for you. This beautiful part of you is designed to connect you to your helpmate on a deeper level than you connect to the rest of the world. Why don't you take me with you to the mechanic's shop? I want you to experience freedom in being yourself, my dear, without exploiting yourself.

I am taken aback by God's words. I've never looked at seduction in that way. Flirting to get what I want from men is second nature to me. I have always viewed it as fairly innocent behavior—something all women do. I suppose that behavior is ingrained in me because throughout my entire childhood I watched my mother use her beauty and sexuality as a tool to make her life a little easier.

Then again, my mother's life wasn't exactly admirable or easy.

Exactly, Caren. Using any part of yourself for less than I intended is not the easy solution. Doing so negatively affects your self-worth. A low self-esteem keeps you from being all I have created you to be. Now let's go to the shop, with me at your side, and see how well we do.

I am slightly abashed. I should know by now that most of what I was taught about being a woman is off-base and not at all what the Lord wants for me. This is simply one more of the many subconscious behaviors I need to recognize and try to stop.

"Okay, God. I will put away the makeup and change into something more appropriate. Then we'll go together!"

***

I walk into the shop with my head held high. Knowing I am not trying to "trick" or seduce the mechanic gives me a feeling of integrity. I approach him with confidence, give him my keys, and take a seat in the waiting room, feeling like a dignified woman instead of a needy temptress. As I wait, I pray for the strength to handle myself appropriately.

After a few minutes, Michael calls me to the service dock to discuss his assessment of my van. I offer him a genuine smile and thank him for taking a look at my vehicle. I say with a laugh, "Michael, before we begin this discussion, I want to let you know that I walked in here with the Lord by my side. With that in mind . . . give me the damage!"

Michael laughs in return. "Well, ma'am, the bad news is that your air compressor is shot. Given your van is an older model vehicle with high mileage, I don't recommend paying an arm and a leg for new parts. I think your best bet is ordering a used compressor from a junkyard. It will run you about $100, and I'll install it for you for $100."

I am thrilled. The dealership would have charged me $1200! I can't believe this man, who seems so competent and professional and whom I trust at a gut level, can do the job so inexpensively.

"Thank you, Michael, for your honesty and fair pricing. I will buy a used compressor, and I'd be honored if you would do the job."

He orders the part for me, and we make an appointment for the installation. I drive home absolutely delighted. This may be the first time I've felt such a strong sense of dignity and integrity, and it feels amazing. I have been selling myself short all these years!

"Thank you, Father. You are awesome. Life is a lot easier

with you in the driver's seat. I don't know if the outcome of that visit would have been the same without you, but I know I loved leaving it up to you. Being myself instead of playing the seductress was a huge relief. Thank you for that valuable lesson in respecting myself."

I drive the rest of the way home contemplating this new way of looking at sexuality—designed by God to connect me to my mate on a deep, spiritual level. When put in that context, sex no longer feels naughty or forbidden, but like a miraculous, sacred gift instead.

DATE 17
White Shag Rug

As I wait in my van at the traffic light this morning, I see a man walking from car to car, knocking on windows, asking people for a cigarette. I am fascinated this man feels comfortable bumming cigarettes off strangers! The world is full of interesting people and events, small and large, if you look for them.

I think about Stewart. I wonder what interesting things he might encounter today in California. On a whim, I text him, asking him to pay extra attention to the people surrounding him today. I ask him to describe the most interesting person he encounters and why. I anticipate his response with excitement. I am lonely, and he is my only friend. I want some insight into his life—to get to know him better and learn what kinds of things interest him.

A few minutes later, I hear the text ringtone I set up for incoming messages from Stewart. That was fast! I can't wait to get home so I can read his response. But when I finally pull into my driveway and read his text, my good mood evaporates, and a dark cloud settles over me.

My challenge was not well received. Stewart chastises me for trying too hard. He views my fun idea as an attempt to force mechanical conversation instead of letting our friendship develop organically. He tells me I don't have to be "deep" all the time and recommends I relax and simply be myself. I am crushed by his words.

I wasn't trying to force conversation. I was genuinely trying to get to know him better. Other than Audrey, my therapist, Stewart is the only adult I talk to. But I guess he is right. I am not a light-hearted person. I *do* tend to be introspective and ruminate on the deeper meaning of things, which is why I keep a distance from others. But I have a desire for human connection like anyone else, and I have always liked the idea of Stewart filling that need. Clearly he wants to be my acquaintance, not my close friend.

I feel sad and alone. I want to date someone—to be with someone who thinks I'm beautiful and is curious about what interests me. I want someone who thinks I'm worth getting to know and love.

I turn to God. "Lord, will you spend time with me? Can we go to dinner this evening? Will you date me, please?"

Yes, we can go to dinner tonight. But I would like to have a date right now too. Caren, I am happy you turned to me in your time of need. I can never get too much of you. Turn on your mock fireplace for lighting, lie down on your white shag rug, and talk to me.

Still feeling dejected, I walk into my house and get comfortable on the rug. I sit with my thoughts for a while, fighting back tears, before speaking to the Lord again.

"Why did you make me this way? I think too much. I'm too pensive and serious. Stewart says to 'just be myself.' Well, being myself means pondering deep thoughts. My brain just works that way. I desire relationships with others, but my personality scares people away. You designed me, Lord, yet people don't love me the way I am. As soon as I get comfortable with someone, confident enough to step out of my shell, something scares me back in, like Stewart's response today."

Expressing my sadness and frustration to God makes me feel a little better already. I close my eyes and listen to His response.

Caren, you are perfectly made as I designed you. Your tendency to mull over the meaning behind life experiences is a beautiful thing, and, in fact, important to the role I designed you to fill. With more work, that deep-thinking brain of yours will work with me to change the world.

I have big plans for you, dear! Your works will be great; however, great works require great battles. Many people who hear your story will condemn you for the roads you have traveled and choices you have made. Some will call you ugly names. To rise above such negativity, you must be secure, strong, and confident in who you are: the woman I created you to be. You do not need to change your personality to fit anyone else's ideals. Can you accept yourself as you are?

Hmmm. I seriously consider His question. *Can* I accept myself, even if it means scaring off people I want to get to know better, like Stewart? When I envision God's designing me, specifically, in a unique way to fulfill a special role He has in mind for my life, criticizing His work seems wrong. If I trust God, I have to believe that the way He made me is perfect, whether I or anyone else thinks otherwise.

I take a deep breath, dry my eyes, and respond. "Yes, Lord. I will try."

DATE 18
Dinner and Live Blues

As I rise from the rug to get on with my day, feeling much better after my discussion with God, I hear His voice again.

Caren, I want to take you to dinner tonight, as you requested earlier. Would you like to call Terilli's and make a 7:30 reservation?

Would I?! Terilli's is a nice, family-run Italian restaurant that gets rave reviews. The live music playing most nights gives it a romantic atmosphere.

"I'd love to, Lord! How exciting. There is something beautiful about dining in the presence of live music."

Get dressed as lovely as you like, dear. I'd like you to thoroughly enjoy feeling feminine tonight.

Immersing myself in femininity . . . I like that idea!

***

When I walk into the restaurant, I see a beautiful young woman sitting at the piano. She can't be much older than twenty-four. She looks graceful, with perfect posture and an inviting smile.

Immediately after I am seated, she turns around and asks sweetly, "Do you have a song request?"

I thank her and request Etta James.

In a feminine but powerful voice, she says, "Your request is granted." Her hands look elegant on the keys of the baby grand piano as she plays. She begins to belt the words of *At Last*.

Her voice is amazing! It literally gives me goose bumps. I stare at her—admiring her talent, her beauty, her gracefulness—and say, "What a masterpiece you have made in her, Lord! She is beautiful in countless ways."

I glance at the table across from me and see that the other diners are in awe of her as well. The woman at the table closes her eyes and sways slightly to the music. She looks like she is inhaling the art the young singer shares with the room.

During intermission the young singer comes to my table. She introduces herself as Lindsay. I compliment her on her talent. She is sweet and boisterous as she eagerly points out her parents and brother sitting at the table across from me. They are the ones I have been observing! Her father's birthday is tonight, and her brother leaves for his first year at college the next day. I love that she felt the desire to tell me about her family.

As the evening carries on, I am taken aback by how her family looks at her—how they feel her music as deeply as if her voice were a brand new discovery. I can almost see love for Lindsay embedded into every fiber of her mother's being. That kind of love is powerful.

Caren, the amount of love those parents feel for their daughter is only a fraction of the love I feel for you.

I am compelled to visit their table. I introduce myself and compliment the family on having such a gifted daughter and sister. I relay how Lindsay told me about the father's birthday and the brother going to college, the pride in her voice unmistakable. Her parents are thrilled and hang on my words. Before I excuse myself, I ask her mother, "What does it feel like to watch your baby girl?"

Her mother replies, "Words cannot explain how amazing it is to listen to and watch her. I am in love."

I return to my table with many emotions. I hope I am making my heavenly Father proud of me, as Lindsay makes her family proud. I hope my love for my children glows as brightly as the love Lindsay's parents have for Lindsay. I then think about how completely different my parents treated me—and amazingly, instead of the usual bitterness, I feel sad for them, actually *sad* for them! Instead of being angry that they didn't love me enough, I see that they cheated themselves out of an amazing gift: loving a beautiful, unique daughter and watching her flourish from that love.

"Lord, if my parents had given me a fraction of the love, encouragement, and time you've given me, the sky would have been my limit. I believe I could have been talented. If they had only loved themselves enough, they would have been able to love and nurture me. Not only would I have benefitted, but their lives also would have been greatly enriched as well."

I am glad you have empathy for your mother and father. Words cannot explain how amazing it is to watch you become the woman I created you to be. You are making me very proud, and I have always been in love with you!

I finally believe in my heart that I am not unlovable and never have been. God has always loved me, even though my parents couldn't. Now I have the power to love myself, and therefore, to love and nurture my children.

"Thank you for loving me so much, God. Thank you for making me *me* and for giving me the gift of my amazing children."

DATE 19
Candy-Coated Picnic

Today I am in a bit of a funk, but something Victoria says lifts my spirits. God must have been listening . . .

Caren, thank you for encouraging Victoria to spend time with me last night. She is a special little girl, and we had a wonderful time together. I love her so. She reminds me a lot of you at her age.

Last night Victoria was bored. When she complained that she doesn't have anyone to play with, I remembered how lonely I was when I was her age. I used to talk to the Lord a lot back then. He was my best friend and a big comfort to me when I was lonely or hurting. I remembered listening to cassette tapes of Bible stories from the Old Testament over and over, entranced. I thought about how, after so many years, God is once again my friend and comfort. Victoria has been on a couple of my dates with the Lord, so on a whim, I suggested she have her own date with Him.

"Victoria, why don't you spend some time with the Lord before going to bed? Maybe you can have a daddy-daughter tea party together."

She perked up, smiled, and skipped off to have her tea party. Then this morning: "Mommy, last night I asked God why you are so nice. He said because He made you that way."

I respond to God, "You're welcome, Lord. I love Victoria so much. I want her to know you, to share what we have—to give her the opportunity to know she is perfectly made. I want her to understand that her earthly father's abandonment has nothing to do with her. You are her true Daddy, and you take delight in her. Thank you for her and all my babies. They are each special and amazing!"

Speaking of your children . . . let's enjoy a day at the lake together. We will stop at Central Market first. I have a special surprise for you there."

I love the idea of having a date with the whole family for the first time. Central Market is an upscale grocery store targeted to "foodies." They have an extensive selection of breads, cheeses, beverages, produce, desserts, and more, and they carry many unique brands not found in other grocery stores. We don't usually shop there because of the higher prices, so it will be a treat to visit today. I eagerly gather the troops for our adventure.

***

As we enter Central Market, I tell the children that the Lord has a surprise for us, but that we are on God's time, and we can enjoy all the store has to offer first. We browse for a little while. Because it is Saturday, many vendors are distributing free samples. The kids enjoy tasting new foods.

I feel God urging me to go to the bulk candy bins by myself. I tell my children to take their time exploring and tasting, but to meet me at the candy bins when they are done. They are happy to oblige.

Unfinished

God's making Masterpiece

My mind races as I take a shortcut through the store to get to the candy section. What does God want to show me or teach me? I am as excited as . . . well, a kid in a candy store!

I reach my destination and look around. There must be close to a hundred varieties of candy to choose from!

"Lord, why did you call me over here without the children?"

Caren, when you look at these many bins, what do you see?

I chuckle. "Umm . . . tons of candy?"

Look deeper, Caren. I want to address something important.

A flicker of mild panic rears its head. This sounds more serious than a fun time at Central Market. I wonder if God is going to dredge up the ugly secret buried deep within me that, lately, has been harder and harder to keep suppressed. I haven't talked about it since it happened—not with my therapist, not with Stewart, not with God. The shame is so great that I can't even think about it. Surely God doesn't want me to address my secret in the middle of a store on a date with the children!

Relax, dear. This is a simple, light-hearted question. Look around with joy in your heart and tell me what you see.

Whew! Relief floods through me. I look at all the candy bins again.

"I see rows and rows of bins. Each bin contains a different kind of candy. There are so many to choose from! Colorful, sour balls, chewy gummy bears, sweet milk chocolate, wax soda bottles, bitter cocoa, caramel, red Swedish fish. Some I really like, such as the dark chocolate-covered espresso beans over there, some I don't enjoy at all, like those sour tear jerkers, and some I'd have to taste to know whether I like them."

Very good, dear. If you and the children pick out a variety of candy and have a "candy picnic" at the lake, will the picnic be ruined if some of the candy you try does not taste good?

"No, Lord, of course not. A candy picnic would be fun no matter what!"

Exactly. Think of life as a shopping trip through a candy aisle, culminating in a candy picnic. Life is full of choices. Every decision you make is simply one of those choices. Some of your choices are "sweet," and some are "bitter," but as a whole, they are a collection of life choices that, with my help, can be used for a wonderful "picnic." Do not let disappointment and regret about the bitter choices ruin the picnic. Caren, keep walking with me, and you will understand. I have a great plan for us.

I have a fuzzy vision of what He might mean. Despite how far I've come in the last two months and how much happier I have been since dating the Lord, I still cry sometimes and have guilt-ridden feelings about the poor choices I've made since my ex-husband left. Before turning to God, I wasn't doing a very good job mothering my children. I often worked late, and on my free nights, I went on dates with men instead of staying home with my children. When I was home, I cried much of the time, worrying the kids. I didn't teach them about God or take them to church. I was not emotionally available to guide them toward making good choices themselves, and as a result, my sons in particular struggled and made mistakes I wasn't even aware of at the time. I am glad they have started to confide in me, as I've become more open and present with them, but I regret I wasn't there for them earlier.

Looking around at the candy thinking about God's analogy, I understand that guilt over my choices prevents me from fully moving forward toward the "picnic" God has planned for me, whatever that may be. Yes, many of my choices caused pain. But some of my choices helped others. And some caused joy. And the choice to reach out to God instead of killing myself changed the tide of my life. Though I can't envision what my future might hold, I find myself believing that God can use *all* of my choices, good and bad, together for something meaningful.

"Father, thank you, I get it. Using the candy aisle was a fun way to demonstrate your point! I feel like a little girl again, and I feel as if you are loving me like a perfect father would."

I am happy you are starting to find the sweetness in your life. I can turn each experience in the past and each experience in your future into a blessing, if you let me.

I am smiling broadly when the children arrive. I tell them excitedly, "Kids, God's surprise is a candy-coated picnic! Pick the candy you want, be thankful, and let's get out of here to enjoy it at the lake today!"

Their eyes widen in pleasure. Moments later, all four of us go wild, choosing all sorts of candy, having the time of our lives.

***

With our dog and ridiculous amounts of candy in tow, we scope out a place to picnic on Lake Ray Hubbard near The Harbor in Rockwall again. The lake bottom is muddy, but we don't care. We have a blast swimming in it, teasing each other, splashing, getting filthy. When we've had our fill, we sit on a blanket drying out, laughing, and talking.

As we select from our candy smorgasbord, I explain to the kids what God taught me in the candy aisle. I tell them the Lord doesn't want us to beat ourselves up for the mistakes we make, but instead to learn from those mistakes and try to do the right thing next time. Even though I am teaching them a lesson, the mood is happy and light. We begin joking about how our different "choices" taste. Some are delicious, and some are rather disgusting. But hey, it's all candy!

When the ants finally drive us to leave, we are a happier, closer family than when we woke up this morning.

Amen.

DATE 20
Sunrise

My massage clientele has dwindled to almost nothing. I do have a few respectful clients, but I struggle with massaging even them any longer. I am almost completely broke, however, so I've scheduled an appointment for later this evening.

I am an emotional mess. I've been dwelling on my deepest secret more and more, the shameful thing I feared God wanted to address at Central Market a couple of days ago. I am back to crying often, feeling guilty and ashamed. I know why, but I don't want to deal with the memories. Bringing this issue to the surface terrifies me—it will be like opening Pandora's Box, and I will fall apart. I'd rather ignore the issue so I can enjoy the happiness I've found the last few months as I've slowly been changing inside. Yet, it is precisely because of these changes, because of my newfound self-awareness, that repressing the memories is more difficult. My secret has been simmering a long time and is now in danger of boiling over. I am determined to stay busy so I don't have to think about it.

***

My client arrives at 8:30. I *really* don't want to deal with anyone right now. I fight back tears as I've done most of the day. As soon as my client lies down on the table, I dim the lights and push play on my iPad. Norah Jones sings "After the Fall." The song reminds me of Wallace and our time together. I really liked him . . . and I thought he liked me too. He said he was single, but that was a lie. Why it is that all the men I pick lie to me? Had he not lied, maybe I wouldn't have had to do what I did. I hate him for that.

In the middle of my ruminating, I feel God's presence. He interrupts my thought process, gently asking me to focus on the part I played in the situation, rather than on Wallace's part.

My heart races. I have always been too afraid, filled with too much shame and regret, to think about that. But in this moment, the Lord gives me the strength to face it. I begin to revisit the events of the past in my mind while massaging on autopilot.

I remember first meeting Wallace. He was a respectful, handsome, charming client. We spent a lot of time talking at his appointments. He said he was ready to retire from professional sports in the next couple of years and wanted to settle down. I imagined he was hinting at settling down with me. We started seeing each other out of the office. In the six months prior to meeting Wallace, I had intentionally put dating on hold. Though Stewart made it clear we were just friends, my running fantasy was that one day we would be together, so I would wait for him until then. Even so, I developed a crush on Wallace. He was kind to me, and he said he was single. Eventually, I gave into my physical desire for him.

Shortly after we became romantically involved, I discovered he was engaged to be married. I was devastated. I had believed he would fall in love with me. The hurt and self-loathing I felt was unbearable. In a desperate move to feel better about myself, I called one of my male friends, Danny. Though I viewed Danny in a strictly platonic way, I knew he had adored me for a long time. I preyed on those feelings to ease my loneliness. We went out that evening for cocktails. I drank too much, one thing led to another, and I found myself at his apartment the next morning. Full of regret, I dressed while he was sleeping and called Uber for a ride home. I acted like that night never happened and blocked Danny's number from calling me.

A few weeks later, I realized I was pregnant.

I told Wallace I was pregnant, and he insisted I have an abortion. He said he really liked me, and if he weren't engaged, maybe things would be different, but as it was, we couldn't have a child together. This broke my heart a second time. My fantasy of possibly sharing a life with him was shattered for good.

And now I was alone and pregnant. I couldn't have a child with no father in the picture! My sons were old enough to understand the situation. They would lose respect for me and probably always view me differently. Plus, how could I put them through the embarrassment of our community knowing I was pregnant? After my ex left and I returned to a wild lifestyle, some of their friends' parents had already begun distancing themselves from us. My sons were no longer included in all the activities they used to be. They were having trouble in school too, in large part because I wasn't there for them emotionally at home. I couldn't bear watching them suffer from yet another one of my mistakes. And I didn't want to endure that kind of humiliation either.

I made an appointment to get the abortion in Fort Worth. A few days prior, I went to a mandatory pre-appointment to determine how far along I was, get a sonogram, and go over my options. Everyone at the clinic did their best to make me feel good about my decision. After hearing my circumstances, they assured me that an abortion sounded like the best thing for my family. Before holding up the sonogram, they apologized and explained they are required by law to show it to me. They encouraged me to glance at it for only a brief moment. They determined I was four weeks pregnant to the date and told me that all I was seeing was a mass of cells this early in the pregnancy. They explained why a vacuum abortion was the best choice for me, and I agreed. I chose medication that would lessen the pain and make me feel drugged, but not put me under. When I left the clinic, I felt that my decision to abort confirmed.

On February 26, 2013, Wallace drove me to the appointment and stood by my side during the process. I signed a release stating that once the medication was administered, there was no turning back. The nurse inserted an IV into my arm and started the medication. I immediately felt a haze come over me, as if I were standing outside myself watching what was happening. I heard the vacuum that would remove my child switch on. Everything suddenly became real. The baby I was carrying was not "just a mass of cells." What I was about to do was against everything I once stood for. I was scared and ashamed, and I hated the woman I had become. I felt tears running down my cheeks and heard myself screaming as the doctor sucked the baby from my womb. "Please, God! I'm sorry! No, no, no . . . I'm killing my baby."

And then it was over. I couldn't undo what I'd done. I couldn't place my baby safely back inside my womb. The finality of it overcame me, and I sobbed uncontrollably. Everyone was ordered to leave the room, even Wallace. As the doctor left, he told me sternly that I needed to be quiet because my crying would scare the other patients. Then I was left completely alone for a half hour while the medication wore off.

As we left the clinic, pro-lifers lined the driveway and shouted at us. These were not peaceful demonstrators. These were vicious extremists. They held up pictures of mangled full-term babies; they spewed hateful words. They waved signs that read "Jesus hates murderers" and "You are a murderer." I remember thinking, "I don't blame your Jesus for hating me. I hate me too."

The ride home was a long and silent one. Wallace and I didn't speak a word. After he dropped me off at home, I texted him that I hated him for what he made me do. He responded with an apology, but I didn't want to hear it. We had a few more short communications after that, but the relationship was soon completely over.

For three days, I alternated between my bed and the bathtub, sobbing almost constantly. I almost took my life during that time, but concern for my children stopped me. I eventually reached out to my DBT (dialectical behavioral therapist), who advised me to take an ice cold shower. She explained that the human brain can't think about anything else while it handles the sudden frigid temperature, and the shock of the cold water can help with depression.

She was right. After the shower I was able to stop sobbing and pull myself together long enough to make a decision. I could survive the immediate future by sweeping the last few months under the rug. Wallace. Danny. The abortion. One day I would be able to address it, but I simply could not handle it then. I told my therapist I did not want to discuss it until I felt ready. She understood and never raised the subject again.

***

I snap out of my painful reverie only to realize tears are running down my face, and I've been massaging five minutes longer than scheduled. I wipe my face and tell my client his time is up. After he leaves, I continue with the Lord where we left off. His voice is gentle but assertive.

Caren, your first step to healing is to be truthful with everyone involved.

I know exactly what He means. But I open the calendar on my phone anyway to be sure. With a sinking heart, I confirm that the date I learned Wallace was engaged was exactly four weeks before my pre-abortion appointment. And I remember it had been a week before that since I'd seen him. In that moment, I know Wallace was not the father of my child. It was Danny.

How could I have ignored this fact before?

No sooner did I ask the question than the Lord answered me. His words are matter-of-fact but compassionate.

Wallace being the father fit into your fantasy. If Danny were the father, you would have to admit to yourself what you did with Danny that night.

"Lord, I can never undo the horrible act I committed. I know that. But how can I begin to make amends for something like this?"

You tell me, Caren. How do you think you can make restitution?

I pause for a moment to consider His question. As I think, a vision passes through my mind: Wallace with his wife as she gives birth to their first child. I fear that if I don't confess the truth to Wallace, one of the most joyful moments of his life might be clouded by the shameful secret he shares with me and God. A secret he will bear forever. What if the birth of his first child reminds him of the abortion clinic? I have been assuming that because he is a man, the abortion didn't affect him. But he might feel as much shame and regret as I do.

The answer is clear. I have to tell Wallace. I don't know what he will do with the information or how he will react, and I don't need to know. My only responsibility is making sure he knows the truth.

I text Wallace immediately. I explain that because our last sexual encounter was five weeks prior to the pre-abortion appointment, at which time the doctor told me the fetus was four weeks along, I am almost certain Wallace is not the father of the child. I also tell him that nobody could have "made" me have an abortion. I take full responsibility for my part in the decision, and I admit to him (and myself) that I could have made a different choice had I truly wanted to.

That done, I wince as my conscience prods me to do another difficult thing. Before I lose my nerve, I text Danny. I apologize for using him that night and cutting him out of my life afterward. I tell him that I discovered I was pregnant after our encounter, and I chose to abort the baby. I confess there is a strong possibility that the child was his, and I regret what I did.

Having confessed to the two men feels right. I know I am one step closer to forgiveness and healing. Then I realize I have even more confessions to make. I remember that I told my therapist and Stewart about the abortion, naming Wallace as the father and playing the victim. As embarrassing as it is, I must tell them the truth and clear Wallace's name. I text Stewart right away and vow to tell my therapist at our next session.

I drive home, feeling some relief from taking action toward restitution. But coming clean and apologizing didn't take away this suffocating weight of shame and sadness. In fact, I am even more ashamed. This is the first time I've let myself feel the truth of what I have done. The pain is so great that all I can do is crawl under my covers and cry myself to sleep.

***

Good morning, dear. Rise and shine! I would like to watch the sun rise together.

I awake, groggy, peering at the clock through squinted eyes. "Good morning, Lord? It is 5:24 in the morning. I'm sleeping!"

You cannot watch a sunrise after the sun rises. Come, dear.

"I had a hard night last night. Please just let me sleep."

That was yesterday. Today is today.

I throw off my covers and groan. "Alright, alright . . . whatever happened to *free will?*"

You are more than welcome to choose, dear. Sleep or sunrise?

"I'm up, I'm up. Let's go watch the sun rise. Where do you even go in Dallas to watch a sunrise?"

Our dock at the lake will do just fine.

I'm not so sure about that. I grab my iPad and type "best place to watch the sun rise in Dallas" in the search engine. The answer pops up: White Rock Lake. Well . . . our dock *is* at White Rock Lake, but the sun rises in the east, and I don't know if our dock has a good view of the east.

Our dock is perfect.

I download a compass on my iPad just to be safe. After studying it for a few moments, I determine that our dock faces south, giving me a view of the east to the left and the west to the right. I sigh.

"Lord, no I-told-you-so's please."

Never, love. You will learn to trust me one of these days.

***

I sit on the dock, get comfortable, take a deep breath in, and prepare to reflect. I know why we are here. Yesterday I chose to address a shameful sin I committed. I hid my wrongdoing under a rug for eight months, but the rug wasn't big enough to keep it hidden any longer. I am ready to face it.

I start a conversation with the Lord, telling him how hard yesterday was for me.

Yes, I know it was difficult. But you did it. You confessed and are now ready to face your biggest regret. You allowed your secret to surface so we can address it and move forward, dear. The good thing is that yesterday is yesterday. With this sunrise, I gift you a new day.

A surge of guilt sears me. "Lord, how can you gift me anything? How can you look at me after what I did? I committed a horrendous, unforgivable act to avoid public shame. Then I didn't even have the courage to face what I had done! How dare I blame others and bury the truth so I wouldn't have to feel bad about it? But the pain never goes away. Look at me, Father. I don't deserve life! I don't deserve happiness! I *killed* my innocent child!"

Darling, in a life without me, there is no absolute truth, no genuine freedom, no true happiness. I am proud of you for living these new days with me. I want you to truly examine what life without me leads to.

The truth is that I took it upon myself to end an innocent life. I took it upon myself to stop possible generations. I can't change the fact that I aborted my baby. My reckless sexual addiction led me to a darker place in sin. I went from adulterer to murderer.

"Father, I've made so many horrible mistakes. *So many mistakes.* Can you please forgive me?" I sink forward, my head on my chest, weeping.

Lift your head, sweet child. I forgive you. The question is, do you choose to accept my forgiveness? Do you choose to forgive yourself? Will you embrace your decision to abort your child as a mistake—a mistake that is part of your past, which has led you to this very sunrise?

"There are so many mistakes to forgive. How can you forgive them all? Some were horrible. Just terrible!"

How? Because I love you. Forgiveness provides freedom. Living free from shame allows you to love yourself and others. Caren, you can become the woman I created you to be only if you allow yourself to live a life pleasing to me, without toxic shame. I ask of you, daughter: will you learn from your mistake, walk with me, and forgive yourself?

At His words a peaceful feeling washes over me. Nothing has changed, yet everything has changed. The burning feeling of self-loathing and hopelessness I've been carrying deep in my soul lessens, and my heart feels lighter. "Yes, Lord. I love you so much. Thank you for forgiving me, and thank you for loving me."

Then I think of the one other person I want to ask forgiveness from: my child. I close my eyes and think of my unborn baby. I whisper, "Dear, sweet child, I am so sorry for what I did to you. I embrace you with my arms and give you a name. Your name is Divinity, and you will always be with me. You led me to redemption. You will forever be a reminder of why I now choose to live a life guided by my heavenly Father. Your short life was not in vain. Because of you, I am choosing to become the woman God created me to be. I am sorry, sweet child, and I love you."

Good work, Caren. Now I want you to sit back and appreciate the sunrise. It is a reminder of the new beginning I offer to you.

As the sun rises over the horizon, I am stunned by its beauty. I've never watched a sunrise before. I can't imagine anything more perfect.

DATE 21
Sushi

After watching the sun rise, I head back home. How emotionally exhausting the last twenty-four hours have been! The day passes in a bit of a blur as I try to get some things done around the house while I mentally sort through new thoughts and feelings. I sit down to collect myself when the Lord speaks to me again.

Caren, I am proud of you for beginning the process of forgiving yourself this morning. I know there are a few questions you would like to ask me, and I want to spend more time together today. Would you like to go to dinner?

That sounds like exactly what I need right now. I feel such freedom from our sunrise experience this morning, and yet the wound feels so fresh. I thank the Lord for thinking of me and try to put my thoughts of today into words. I explain that because I didn't allow myself to dwell on the abortion beyond the first few days, I haven't yet processed all the pain it caused. I haven't truly grieved for the loss of my baby. Make no mistake, I have experienced plenty of pain since that day, both consciously and subconsciously. For months afterward I'd catch myself holding my stomach in longing. Seeing pregnant women filled me with despair. I still can't bear the thought of holding a baby; guilt and sadness overwhelms me imagining it. And not a day has gone by since the abortion that I haven't felt a deep sense of loss and regret. But every time I felt despair, I chastised myself and tried to think of something else. I didn't believe I had the "luxury" of grieving about something I brought upon myself.

"You are right, Father, I do have a question for you. If I hadn't gotten an abortion, I would be eight months pregnant right now. My child would almost be born."

I trail off, pausing, imagining my stomach big with a child. The Lord prompts me.

Yes? I am ready for your question, dear.

"If you are an all-knowing God, like the Bible says, then you knew I was going to have an abortion before I did it. And if you knew, and knew how much pain I'd be in, why didn't you stop me?"

I would have liked to stop you, but my love is based on free will. I did show you other possibilities, though. I spoke to the heart of your friend Lindsay. Remember when she visited you to talk about other options? I spoke to the heart of your DBT therapist. She had a stern conversation with you two days before your abortion. I even spoke to your heart. Do you remember when you considered calling a pregnancy resource center? I encouraged you to make a different decision, but I allowed you to make your own choice.

"Father, I wish you had stopped me!"

I know you do, dear, but that is not how our relationship works. There is no need to waste time and energy on wishing things were different. Instead, remember where you have been, learn from your missteps, and go forward with your eyes on me. Caren, if you let me, I can turn all your past sins, no matter how big or small, into good. And you can allow me to use your decision to have an abortion as a way to help others.

The thought of the Lord using my experience to help others makes me feel slightly better, but mostly I can't imagine anything good coming from the abortion. I can't imagine it as anything other than a shameful and horrific act. But if the Lord can use my experience to prevent another woman from having an abortion, or to help another woman find freedom from the painful aftermath of abortion, then I humbly accept that. I would do anything to make amends.

So, my love, would you like to have sushi for dinner?

"Yes, Lord!"

***

I sit in my favorite sushi restaurant and peruse the menu. The spicy tuna roll looks delicious, but I decide to order the vegetable roll instead. Since losing over a hundred pounds a couple of years ago, I've been a vegan, and fish is not part of a vegan diet.

The Lord questions my decision to resist ordering what I like.

Why are you vegan, Caren?

"Because I'm terrified of becoming fat again."

Do you truly believe you will let yourself become obese again, and that eating animal protein was the reason you were overweight?

"I'm not sure. But I don't want to take any chances."

Is that living free? Or is it living according to fear-based restrictions?

His question takes me aback. I've never equated my decision to eat a vegan diet with fear. But He is right. I am not a vegan because of personal beliefs about the morality of eating animal protein, or for health reasons, or because of my taste preference. The sole reason I became a vegan is fear stemming from my past weight issues.

Darling, to truly live free from bondage, you must learn from the past, but you must live in the present with love as your guide, not fear. Try to

love yourself and others the way I love you. Though I mourn when you make a choice that causes yourself or others pain, I do not control you nor frighten you into obeying me. I simply love you and offer you redemption if you choose to accept it. Despite the consequences of your past choices, try to make present choices from a place of love, not fear. Allow yourself to choose the things you want.

At His words I feel a surge of disbelief. I shouldn't allow myself to make a *bad* choice if I can help it, should I?

There are no "good" or "bad" choices. There are only choices made with me and choices made without me. When you walk through life with me by your side, you often see possibilities that you would not have seen as a choice otherwise.

I certainly wasn't walking with the Lord at the time of my pregnancy. It never crossed my mind to ask Him to guide me as I struggled with what to do. In the context of my life at that time, it seemed as if having an abortion was a choice I had to make for the good of Wallace, my family, and myself, albeit a painful choice. But now that I am walking with God in my life, I can rely on Him for wisdom and guidance. I must forgive myself for my past choices. God doesn't want fear or guilt about the past to prevent me from making wise choices today, with Him by my side.

Exactly. Good job, Caren.

The waiter arrives to take my order. "I'll have a spicy tuna roll and a vegetable roll, please!"

DATE 22
Hiking

Lately I have had a strong desire to be around people. I enjoy
my dates with the Lord, like eating sushi with Him a few weeks
ago. I enjoy being around my children, and I appreciate being
able to lean on Audrey and Stewart, but I crave true friendship. I know I'm not ready for a close relationship, but I feel
under-socialized to the point of being anti-social. Meanwhile,
I feel like God is asking me to get a part-time job. I suspect the
two things are connected. He knows how lonely I am, so He is
probably suggesting an extra job as a way for me to be around
more people.

I remember an old friend who owns a casual fine dining
restaurant downtown. Though I don't have much work experience other than massage, child care, elderly care, cooking, and
cleaning, I am nice, accommodating, and, despite my depression, I really do love to smile. Perhaps he is hiring hostesses. I
decide I might as well ask him. Being around people other than
my massage clients would be a nice break and might even help
me build my social skills.

I call my old friend and ask if he is hiring. I tell him I'm looking for something part-time, just to get out more. He tells me to come in for an interview with his restaurant manager this evening.

***

The interview goes well. I am hired on the spot as a hostess and scheduled to begin training tomorrow! The position pays only ten dollars an hour, but I'll only work part-time on my slow massage nights so I'll be able to keep my regular massage clients.

On my second night of training, one of the servers shares with me how much she made in gratuities that evening. I can't believe it—$400 in five hours! I'd have to work forty hours as a hostess or give four massages for that kind of money. I wish I had serving experience.

On my third day working as a hostess, the general manager approaches me. He says I have an incredible personality, and he thinks I'd be an amazing server. He offers to train me, saying we'll take it slowly. I'm flattered, and of course I want to earn more money, so I take him up on his offer. I think it will be fun.

***

I've been working part-time at the restaurant for a couple weeks now while maintaining my massage practice. The money has been great, but more and more, I'm feeling uncomfortable about the massages. Today when one of my regular clients, Josh, came in, that feeling intensified. Like all my other clients, he found me through my ad on the adult website. Sure, my massages are strictly therapeutic now, but he and my other clients were attracted to the sexy picture in my ad. Whether overtly or subconsciously, they probably think a sexual "bonus" is a *possibility*, and even if they don't, having their naked bodies rubbed by an attractive, flirty woman in sexy clothing likely feeds their fantasies. I don't ask, but I suspect many are married, and their wives don't know they are here. I am tired of being a secret, closed behind these disreputable doors. I decide to confirm my suspicions.

"Josh, does your wife know you schedule weekly massages with me?"

He admits she does not.

"Would she be upset if she knew?"

"I don't think she'd be upset," he answers. "Disappointed is a better word."

"Can you explain?" I probe.

"Well, I guess coming here is equivalent to me going to a strip club with the fellas. She wouldn't fight with me about it, but she would prefer I didn't do it."

His response infuriates me. The thought that my work is comparable to a woman dancing naked for money makes me sad. I begin to assess who I've become.

"Then why do you come here?" I ask him.

He sighs. "My wife doesn't give me a lot of attention, especially touch. She's busy with the children, and by the time I get home from work, she is exhausted and doesn't have any energy for me. We're more like roommates than a married couple. I would never cheat on her because I love her and want to honor our marriage, so seeing you once a week for massage helps me to stay faithful."

After Josh leaves, the weight on my heart is even heavier, and I want to talk to God about it.

"Lord, I feel troubled. Can we talk?"

Of course, Caren. What is on your mind?

"Well, I am tired of feeling like other people's dirty secret. I feel ashamed and hidden from the world."

I know, dear. Would you like to explain?

"As far back as I can remember, people have been ashamed of me. When my mom dated a new boyfriend, she'd tell them I was her sister, not her daughter. In high school boys dated me secretly, asking me not to tell anyone. My husband never took me out to show me off. He would go out with his friends and leave me home. And of course Wallace was seeing me on the side, and even Stewart has rules about how I can contact him. I've never liked feeling like someone's dirty secret, but it is especially bothersome now. I mean, if I had a husband, I wouldn't want *him* seeing a sexy massage therapist because he thinks doing so is the only way he can stay faithful to me. After all, if Josh is sneaking to see me, is he really being faithful?"

All of a sudden I see a bigger picture, beyond how my massage practice makes *me* feel. What if weekly visits with me prevent Josh from working harder in his marriage to receive the affection he wants from his wife? What if my massages make it easier for him to accept the status quo at home and less likely that he'll address the real issues in his marriage? He could be helping with the children, preparing dinner, doing laundry, and otherwise easing his wife's exhaustion, which would increase her loving feelings toward him, but instead he is avoiding home and seeking physical pleasure from me.

And what is his lack of involvement doing to their family? Maybe getting massages from me reduces his motivation to pay special attention to his wife, to say sweet things to her and make her feel beautiful. If so, their children aren't witnessing a healthy family unit. They are not exposed to fun, romantic, playful parents. I've had enough therapy to know that children learn from their parents' example, and most adults pursue relationships that mirror their parents' relationship. I certainly don't want to contribute to generational family dysfunction.

As I imagine the possible consequences of Josh's massages with growing alarm, I realize that a couple of months ago, I would have never even thought about this couple. I wouldn't have considered that my actions might have an impact on their relationship, nor would I have cared. But the Lord is changing me drastically. Now, as I think about the potential effect I'm having on other relationships, I feel a sense of urgency to get out of the massage business. But I don't know how.

Caren, I am happy you are starting to see things on a deeper level with conviction.

"Yes, but where does this leave me? I feel like I have no way out. If I quit massaging, we will be poor again."

I will provide what you need. Do you trust me?

"Yes, but…" I don't share that I sometimes still question whether my relationship with Him is even real. I quickly change my thoughts, lest He hear what I am thinking, and finish answering His question. "What are you asking me to do?"

Start by closing your office doors. Leave the massage life behind. Walk out on faith with me and believe that I will provide for you and the children.

The thought of quitting my massage practice entirely both terrifies and comforts me. I would have to cancel nonessentials like cable, Internet, and Netflix. I would need to cut back on food and utilities. Adjusting to a lower income would be tough. But in this moment, quitting seems like the right thing to do. I don't hesitate any longer; I cancel the rest of my appointments for the day and start packing up my office.

***

Seven days have passed since I closed my office doors, and the reality of my situation becomes more apparent every day. I changed my entire lifestyle with no planning. I quit a job that brought in good money when my only other income is what I earn working a couple of days a week in the restaurant. Now I am worried about keeping a roof over my children's heads. Most people would view my actions as crazy and impulsive. How can I be sure I am really hearing the voice of God? I know God and I have addressed my doubts before, but I still fear that what I am really hearing are my own ideas and thoughts.

And yet . . . things are happening that I can't explain. A couple of days ago my friend Julie brought us tons of leftovers from a party. She felt led to check on us and bring us the extra food. She is a pastor's wife, so I felt safe sharing some of what has happened and my fears, and she supported my decision to quit my business. Then yesterday, when walking home from my son's football game (because I had no money for gas), I found a fifty-dollar grocery store gift card on the sidewalk. I felt conflicted—I desperately needed the money but felt guilty about taking it from whoever lost it. I called Julie's husband, Pastor Steve, for advice, since he now knew of my financial situation, and he recommended I accept it as a gift from God. He suggested that since they had just brought me food, why not use the card to fill my tank at the grocery store's gas station? So I did.

Still, quitting my practice on the spur-of-the-moment is foolish and irresponsible! I need to talk to God and share my fears.

"God, please make it clear that I'm doing the right thing. I am trying to convince myself to have faith and follow your lead, but I'm beginning to doubt. Am I truly supposed to believe that you will provide all we need if I listen to you? I have been leading my own life since my youth. Giving up control to follow your path doesn't feel normal or sensible."

Caren, your life with me is not intended to feel "normal." Normal for you is living your life on your own with no guidance from me. It is taking the paths you choose and letting them take you where they may. Living a life in faith instead, relying solely on me to provide, is intended to give you freedom, if you let it. Caren, dear, would you like to go hiking in the morning?

"Yes, I would love to. Thank you for asking. I would love to get out of this house and into nature. I've never been hiking before!"

I know. This will be a fun experience for us both!

How exciting! I've heard others talk about hiking. I've seen people hike in movies, and I've read about people hiking. It sounds fun. Yet allowing myself to experience hiking never dawned on me, even though putting on tennis shoes and packing a backpack is a simple thing to do.

I prepare for the hike with enthusiasm. I search online for places to hike in Dallas. I am drawn to a natural park in Richardson, a suburb of Dallas less than fifteen minutes from my house. I feel the Lord telling me that He will meet me there.

***

The next morning, I arrive at the park in anticipation. Signs lead me to the start of three hiking trails. The first path is new and freshly paved. It appears clean and smooth as the sunlight shines on it through the trees. The second path is unpaved, old, worn, and somewhat overgrown. The third path looks worn as well, and its sign cautions hikers to stay on the trail to avoid snakes.

Which trail should I take? The first path seems too easy. I suppose walking on a paved path could be considered hiking, but when the Lord suggested hiking with Him, surely He envisioned my breaking a sweat. I rule out the third path because I don't want to encounter any snakes.

I start down the second path, confident I've made the wisest choice. But in less than a minute, the path dead-ends into a clearing with a bench. It is a peaceful place to sit and relax and take in the pretty surroundings, but the Lord asked me to hike, not sit. I guess He meant for me to meet Him on the first path.

When I reach the first path, I hear the Lord's voice.

Hello, dear. Thank you for meeting me here.

"Hello! I wasn't sure which path to meet you on, Lord, but I'm glad I found you. I am *so* excited that we are really about to go hiking! I brought a backpack, organic mosquito spray, a big bottle of water, and, of course, trail mix. I was just thinking I should have brought a big stick, but—oh, look! A trail to the woods! And I thought this path was going to be too easy. Let's go!"

As I start down the trail, the woods quickly become overgrown. I can still make out the trail hidden underneath some brush, so I keep going. The further I go into the woods, the narrower and steeper the trail becomes. I start to wonder if I should turn around, but I persevere. After all, hiking isn't supposed to be easy! I stumble over a rock and begin to slide down the hill. As I start to fall, I struggle to hold onto a tree. When I look backward, worried about touching poison oak or poison ivy, I realize the trail has disappeared. In its place are vines and thorny pricker bushes. Meanwhile, my organic bug spray is not effective; mosquitoes are attacking me. I swat at one buzzing by my ear and then freeze when I hear a stick crack in front of me. I look down to see a huge snake slithering past my feet. I am scared, and I do not feel the Lord's presence. I don't like it here anymore. When the snake disappears from my sight, I climb back up the hill and return to the path.

As soon as I reach the path, I feel God's presence again. I tell Him with relief, "Wow, that was close, Lord. I could have easily been bitten by that snake. Where were you?"

Yes, it was close. I was near, waiting for you to come back up the hill. You could not see me because you were too busy getting lost.

"Well, why did you ask me to go hiking if—"

The Lord interrupts me. *Darling, I never led you down that trail. You went there without me.*

I think about it and chuckle. "I guess you're right. I was so excited that I didn't let you get a word in edgewise, did I?"

No, dear, you did not.

"Instead of asking you to lead, I led myself, and ended up heading further and further away from the path you chose for our hike today. Had I been patient and followed your lead, we could have been enjoying a nice hike together. Instead I led myself deeper down that scary, dangerous path."

Ohhh! As the parable dawns on me, I laugh again. "Now I get it, Lord. Basically you are showing me that I need to have faith in you and take the path you have chosen for me. Not only will I get to my destination sooner, but I'll also get there more safely."

Great job! Now, are you ready to go on our hike?

"Yes!" And this time, I let Him lead the way.

***

The Lord and I have an amazing time today. As we hike I thank Him for what He is doing in my life, for how He is changing me into a better person who has convictions and acts on them.

I also share how much I appreciate His spending time with me. We work on some of my childhood issues and painful memories from my mother as well. What a gift it is to be fixed by God! My heart is bursting with joy. I fervently hope this is truly the voice of God I hear.

DATE 23
Five-Mile Run

Working as a waitress has been surprisingly fun. I'm realizing more and more that people actually *like* me. I served a group of people last weekend who gave me a lot of compliments, like "Your smile is infectious!" and "You have the best personality!" and "You should hang out with us sometime!"

I like the idea of having friends. I watch these people having fun together, being close to one another, laughing, and playing, and I yearn to have what they have. I can't help but wonder what's wrong with me. I appear to be likeable, yet I spend all my time without friends. I put on a great show in front of strangers, acting like the person I want to be, but when I'm around people who know me, I am scared and feel insecure.

A surge of determination washes over me. I'm going to take a step in the right direction. I will gather my courage and invite someone over for dinner. I decide to invite Kate, an old friend I haven't spoken to in a year or more.

***

I am so glad that Kate accepted my dinner invitation yesterday! I bought everything to prepare a perfect southern dinner: chicken fried steak, homemade mashed potatoes and gravy, green beans, and a salad. Though we are on a strict budget, I splurged because I really want to make a good impression. She will be here at 6:00 tonight, so the children and I begin to cook. We have a great time. I think they are as excited as I am that I have a friend coming for dinner.

At 6:00 the text notification on my phone rings. I hurry to read it, thinking it's probably Kate having trouble finding my house. My enthusiasm disappears, and my face drops as I read, "Caren, are we having dinner tonight? I completely forgot I have somewhere to be."

I send a response. "Don't worry about it. Go where you need to be. Maybe we can do this some other time." But as I type the words, disappointment and negativity overwhelm me. I put a lot of effort and money into this dinner. I never should have invited someone over. People don't want to be around me.

I call the kids to the table for dinner and explain that my friend had a change of plans. As we eat I try to act like nothing is wrong. First I act silly, and then I make small talk. However, within minutes I can't pretend anymore, and my tears begin to flow. I am heartbroken that nobody who knows me likes me. Only strangers find me fun.

I quickly recognize that what I am doing is not healthy for the children. I apologize for crying at the table. I explain how excited I was to have a friend over, and I share how disappointed I am that she canceled. They are so sympathetic and understanding that I make a conscious decision to change my behavior. Instead of dwelling on my hurt, I focus on how wonderful my children are and proceed to enjoy their company.

They deserve to be enjoyed!

***

I wake up the next morning and kick off the covers, glancing down at my thighs. My first thought is, "I am getting so fat!" The thought quickly turns into a feeling of disgust. The Lord encouraged me to quit taking ADHD medication several weeks ago, and I am rapidly gaining weight. I go to the mirror to get a better look. Ugh! I hate my body! I quickly turn from the hideous sight. Even though I feel repulsed, I also feel ashamed for thinking such horrible things about myself. I hate feeling this way!

"Lord, please help me. I feel so fat! I've gained twenty pounds since I've gotten off my medication. I despise being fat! I can barely look at myself in the mirror."

Darling, that is an awfully intense statement, is it not?

"I'm just telling you how I feel. I don't like feeling this way, but I absolutely *hate* myself when I'm fat."

You hate yourself when you are fat. There is a LOT of judgment in that statement. Does the size of your body determine who you are?

I shake my head.

Would you hate someone you loved if he or she got fat?

"No," I sigh. "I understand what you're getting at. I know I shouldn't feel this way, but I can't help it. Sometimes I am disgusted with myself."

Did you feel this way about yourself yesterday?

I shake my head again.

I see. Caren, I would like to go for a run together and talk about what is really bothering you. We will make it a date.

I groan. I *really* do not like running, but I agree anyway.

"Where do you want to run to?"

How about from here to Northwest Highway and back?

"Are you kidding me? That's over five miles! I can't run that far! Besides, I have bad knees."

You do not have to run the whole way. You can run, jog, and walk.

Disgruntled and hopeful at the same time, I get dressed in athletic clothes, lace up my tennis shoes, and take the kids to school.

***

As I start running toward Northwest Highway, I pour out my heart to the Lord. I explain how sad I am that Kate canceled at the last minute. I overcame my fear of getting close to other people, reached out to her, and prepared a beautiful dinner, and then she didn't show! I tell God that if I am supposed to lead a life of solitude without adult relationships, I want Him to remove the desire for friendship from my heart. All my life I have wanted to love others and be loved in return, yet having friends is scary and uncomfortable. I worry that they won't truly like me . . . that they will talk about me when I'm not there. Given my fears, I don't even know why Kate's canceling dinner bothers me so much.

I slow down to a walk, exhausted and out of breath. I pant, "You see how sad this pattern of wanting to be loved but not being lovable makes me, Lord. Why won't you fix it, one way or another?"

I am sorry Kate did not show, dear. I know you were looking forward to spending time with a friend. I want to talk about how and why you interpreted her canceling as meaning you are faulty, fat, and unlikable.

I think for a while before answering. God's question makes

me consider for the first time that Kate might have canceled for reasons that have nothing to do with me personally. "I guess I'm reacting this way because of my insecurities. And out of habit. This kind of thing happened to me a lot when I was young. I always assumed the reason must be that I wasn't good enough . . . too boring, too fat, too weird, and so on."

The Lord assures me that to Him I am beautiful and lovable. He reminds me that He made me exactly the way He wanted, so I am in no way faulty. I speed up to a slow jog.

We have more work to do together, Caren. Your feelings about yourself are easily distorted. A simple thing like a friend canceling plans caused you to tailspin into self-doubt and insecurity. If you continue to spend time with me, you will soon see yourself through my eyes. Once you know your true worth, you will not define yourself by what others do, think, or say. You will eventually be strong enough in me that only my *opinion of you will matter. Be patient; this will take time. Your "self-worth muscle" is already stronger than it was before you reached out to me, but you must continue to walk with me in order to strengthen your self-image.*

I slow down again. Now I understand why God asked me to go for a five-mile run/jog/walk. Building my legs and lungs is like building my self-image. Today I can't imagine running the whole distance, but if I continue running this route, I will eventually be able to run without stopping.

"Thank you, Father. I will continue to walk this path with you. But please understand how deeply I am affected by not having friends and feeling unlovable. Please plan your teachings accordingly."

I speed up to a run, adding, "Please forgive me if I seemed ungrateful yesterday. Preparing that meal wasn't in vain. My children and I spent precious time together preparing it, all the while talking and building a closer relationship."

Caren, when you chose to enjoy your children's company instead of sulking, I was very happy.

"That was a good moment, wasn't it? My relationship with my children is priceless. I am so thankful for them! Having children who love me unconditionally, and I them, is an amazing gift."

I slow my pace again and walk the rest of the way. When I reach home, I feel empowered. The run was hard work, but like all other areas in my life, if I push past the pain, I will become a better, stronger version of me. I whisper another, "Thank you."

You are doing great, Caren. Keep following this path with me, and I will lead you to an abundant and fulfilling life. You watch and see!

DATE 24
Chocolate, Candles, and Canvas

This evening I am feeling especially feminine and I long for "him"—that is, the man God has picked out specifically for me. I envision that man being Stewart. I want to sit together and enjoy each other's company. I long for him to appreciate my beauty and be interested in what I have to say. I desire to feel mutual admiration, to be in a safe place with each other because our love revolves around the Lord. I think I am ready. I think I now love myself enough to embrace a man's love for me and to love him beautifully in return.

"Lord, please send my true love to me. I yearn for his companionship."

Be patient, darling. I am still preparing you to accept him. Rest assured, the man I have picked for you is a mighty man who is loving, selfless, strong, and powerful. He has sacrificed much to be with you, and he longs for you even more deeply than you long for him. I will rejoice the day you are ready to be united. The two of you will be a powerful pair who will do many works for my kingdom. He will lift you up as his queen, and you will honor him as your king. He will admire your beauty and nurture your femininity.

You will treasure his wisdom and embrace his love. Keep working, dear. If you stay on the path I have paved for you, you will not have to wait much longer.

Wow, this man sounds incredible and definitely worth waiting for. Knowing he is coming helps, but I still feel a sense of discontentment. I switch gears and ask God for something different.

"Lord, help me to be the joyful and amazing woman you've created me to be. Help me to find contentment being in my own skin, to feel whole and healed. Please teach me how to love myself completely."

The Lord assures me that we are doing just that and asks for my patience again. He tells me He is proud of my continued growth.

What can we do together this evening that will help fill the void you feel? How can you show Caren *love and appreciation?*

I try to imagine what would make me feel pampered and content. I associate candlelight with a cozy, romantic evening. And flowers certainly make me feel feminine. Ooh, a few of those dark chocolate espresso beans I love would be a nice treat . . . and painting! Painting makes me feel artistic and creative. I imagine experiencing all of that wrapped snugly in my white robe. What a beautiful way to treat myself! But is this too much to ask for?

The Lord assures me that it sounds like a perfect date. He tells me I should enjoy this type of evening more often.

You do not need to wait for someone else to provide you the quality time you desire, Caren. You have the power to enjoy your life now. You simply have to decide to treat yourself the way you would like to be treated by others.

Of course He is right. Enjoying my own company and doing things I love are simple choices. With a buoyant heart, I send the children to bed, slip on my favorite white robe, grab a few chocolates, light some candles, and prepare an area for painting. At first I have no idea what to paint. I start by picking colors that suit my mood. Then I turn off all judgment and conscious thought, pick up my brush, and let myself create. Before I know it, it is one o'clock in the morning, and I have painted a beautiful flower. As I painted, I pondered a little about the man the Lord described to me. I have a sneaking suspicion he is referring to Jesus.

DATE 25
Olive Garden

I have been a more present parent lately, emotionally and phys-ically. The more time I spend with my children, the more I face their personalities! I love my amazing children, but shifting the dynamics of our household by taking reign of our home has proved to be challenging, especially with my middle child, Reggie. We used to get along quite well. Now we argue often, and the arguments usually end with me yelling something like, "Because I said so! Now be quiet and go to your room!" I know that's not a kind or effective way to talk to him. But the older he gets, the more stubborn and mouthy he becomes, and I don't know how else to assert my authority. As the parent, I want the final say in our arguments. After all, I am the mother, and he is the child. I think he needs to respect me and listen to me. But my approach is not giving me the results I want. I ask the Lord for help, and He responds right away.

Caren, parenting is difficult, especially with teenagers. You think Reg-gie is stubborn and strong-willed. Well . . . many times I have wanted to end my conversations with you by saying, "Because I am God! Now be quiet and go to your room!" However, saying that, dear, does not leave you room to express yourself or develop into the woman I created you to be. I set standards and rules for you to live by, but I do not force you to follow them. If you choose to do things your way instead of my way, you must deal with the natural consequences of your sins. Because if I do not allow you free will, you are simply the woman I forced you to be. There is no freedom in that. I want you to be the woman I created you to be because you desire and choose that path.

God's allowing His people free will makes sense to me. However, I'm not sure how I can apply that to the parent-child relationship. Letting Reggie do and say whatever he wants does not seem appropriate.

I agree. You are his parent, and you need to establish rules that will help him grow into a responsible young man. When he does not follow those rules, let him experience natural consequences. He will learn much better from consequences than from your yelling at him. And let him have a voice as long as he is respectful. He needs to express his opinions and feelings, but he will only do so if he feels safe with you.

When put this way, God's advice sounds more reasonable, though I know putting it into practice will be difficult. As I imagine different scenarios and possible rules, God asks me if I would like to go out to dinner tonight with Reggie and Him.

"I'd love to! Where should we go?"

Reggie feels loved when you feed him, and the more, the better, right?

"Yes, that is true! You know, I think Olive Garden has an all-you-can-eat pasta and salad deal for $9.99."

I find Reggie and ask him if he'd like to go on a dinner date with the Lord and me tonight. I am pleased when he agrees, and I smile when he suggests the all-you-can-eat buffet at Cici's Pizza. The Lord and I were right about his liking large quantities of food! I explain the Olive Garden special, and he is eager to go.

***

The aroma of fresh bread and pasta is deliciously intoxicating, and we are hungry. The restaurant isn't very busy, but we've been seated for fifteen minutes with no service. I notice with frustration that the people who just arrived at a nearby booth have already been served salad. As I'm wondering where our server is, their server returns with drinks and begins to take their orders.

My hunger makes me bold. I turn to their server and say, "Excuse me, ma'am. I'm sorry to bother you, but I am wondering why we have been sitting here for fifteen minutes with no service when these people just arrived and are already eating salad and placing dinner orders."

Before the server can respond, a woman at the table lashes out at me. "Lady, you're so rude! Maybe you should worry about yourself instead of us."

I am shocked and taken aback. "Excuse me? I didn't say anything against you, and I wasn't talking to you. I was talking to the server."

"Well, you were being rude by speaking."

Now I am angry. In a steely voice I respond. "Like I said, I wasn't talking to *you*." I look pointedly at the server again and ask, "Ma'am, can we please have some service?"

I look back at my son, who is watching me throughout this interaction. He jokes, "Hey, Ma. Do we need to switch seats so you're not facing her?"

When the woman continues to gripe loudly, using profanity, he says, "Ugh! No she *didn't* just call you the B word. She must not know you're on a date with the Lord and me!"

Clearly Reggie is trying to diffuse the situation with humor.

He is such a funny young man! And his tactic works. I immediately realize that I am not setting a good example. I'm not using a tame tongue or self-control. And his "joking" words speak to me. Yes, he was talking about the other woman's behavior, but his words are also a clever and respectful way to call me out on my own behavior.

I make a conscious decision to adjust my attitude. I let go of my irritation and become present for my son. I thoroughly enjoy the rest of the dinner as I listen to him—what's important to him, how he views life at this moment, his sense of humor. I appreciate his intelligence and insight into how life works. As we are wrapping up our dinner, I feel a pull in my spirit to apologize to the people at the neighboring booth. But my pride whispers to me that the conflict wasn't my fault.

At that very moment, Reggie says, "Hey, Mom. You know you should probably apologize to them, right?"

I sigh. "Yes, dear, you're right. You must have read my mind. I was thinking the same thing, but I'm still dealing with my pride."

"Yah, Ma, but you'll feel better about the situation if you apologize anyway. Try to see it through her eyes. Maybe that will help."

I only have a few seconds to decide because the woman and her party are about to leave. My mind races. What if she rejects my apology? What if she causes a scene? I take a deep breath and catch the woman's eye. My son is right. Apologizing is the correct thing to do.

"Ma'am, I want to apologize. Can you forgive me for my behavior? My delivery could have been much better, and I should have waited until your waitress was finished taking your orders."

The woman walks over to me, pauses, and replies, "Yes, I do

accept your apology. I have to say, I admire you for apologizing to me. I'm sorry too. I was very rude to you, and I'm sorry for that."

She shakes my hand, and she and her friends walk away.

"See, Ma! Doesn't that feel better?" Reggie asks.

"It sure does, son!" I beam.

I feel a great sense of peace steal over me. My son and I learned a valuable lesson this evening about humility. It's a lesson I'd definitely like to apply to our relationship.

***

Later that night, I thank the Lord for our date. I learned a great deal in one evening. I realized how often I see things through pride's eyes and that an argument takes two people, regardless of who is "more right" or "more wrong." I learned that with humility in mind, I can end an argument as easily as start one. I was also reminded of how sweet and intelligent my son is. I saw firsthand that letting him speak gives him room to grow into his own person. I better understand that loving others is giving them a chance to express themselves, not silencing them when they express opinions or views different than mine. I smile as I remember one more thing.

"Lord, one of the best parts of that date was that my son remembered you were in the room with us!"

DATE 26
Sunset #13,966

I have been working at the restaurant now for a couple of months, and I don't do massage anymore. I've completely stopped all inappropriate relationships with men. I still love Stewart and long for a romantic relationship with him, but he has made it clear that he and I are just friends. Other than my relationships with the Lord, Stewart, my children, my therapist, and coworkers, I am alone. The Lord and I don't spend as much time dating as we did at the beginning of this journey, and I feel restless. I still have a dark, empty place in my heart.

I want to have friends and feel connected to my extended family, yet the thought of a relationship with anyone else scares me. I'm caught in a horrible back-and-forth dance of emotions. I want love, but I fear love. I want close friends, but I'm terrified of getting close to anyone. I feel especially vulnerable now that I am trying to live on faith, to rely on someone other than myself. I'm not used to living my life like this. And I can't explain why, but I sense that God (if, in fact, God is who I have really been talking to) is about to change something else in my life, and I'm apprehensive that the change involves other people.

"Lord, I don't know why I have this suspicion, but you are preparing me to leave my solitude, aren't you?"

Yes, Caren. You are correct. I have great plans for you, and they involve your being in a full relationship with me and, soon enough, with others.

"But I don't want others! I want only you! I know that sounds odd, given all the tears I've shed longing for personal relationships, but I am accustomed to living a fairly solitary life. And the thought of your asking me to build intimate friendships makes me want to hunker down in my nest with only you, my children, Stewart, and Audrey."

Yet I know this is my fear talking. God designed us to be relational. Staying in solitude would stunt my growth and not allow me to shine as brightly as He desires. The Lord confirms this. He tells me He enjoyed our time alone while we worked at reprogramming my thought processes, but keeping me all to Himself would be selfish. He explains why it's time for me to branch out.

You have much to offer with your sweet personality and innocent take on life. You are strong enough in me now that you are ready to have healthy relationships with others. I am excited for you, sweet daughter. You are about to have a lot of fun in the next phase of our journey . . . if you let yourself.

His words take the edge off my anxiety. I miss our time alone together.

"Lord, between working and taking care of the children, I haven't had time for a date with you in at least a week. I am craving some time with you."

I miss you as well, Caren. Would you like to watch the sun set Friday evening?

"Yes, please!" I am excited. It sounds wonderful. I've never watched a sunset before. But of course God knew that already.

I feel special as I get ready for my date with the Lord. I want to dress up for the occasion, so I choose a lovely formal dress and heels. While applying makeup, I muse about not having seen a sunset before—I'm thirty-eight years old and then some. I do the calculations . . . there have been 13,965 sunsets in my life, and I've never taken the time to witness a single one of them! I could feel depressed about that, but instead I take joy in knowing that tonight I will finally witness the 13,966th sunset of my life with the sun's Maker Himself!

***

As I sit on our dock on White Rock Lake, I am breathless. I thoroughly appreciate this gift from the Lord. The view to my right is absolutely beautiful. The sky is clear, allowing an unblocked view of the sun above the horizon. I hear an orchestra of sounds—crashing waves, singing cicadas. My Father is amazing!

A few moments into my experience, a woman approaches the dock. The Lord and I have always been alone on our dock dates, so her presence feels like an intrusion at first. But then, inexplicably, I feel led to speak to her. I invite her to share my blanket and watch the sun set with me. She eagerly accepts my invitation.

As we watch the beautiful oranges, pinks, reds, and even purples of the sunset, I tell her that I am on a date with God and that this is my first sunset. I immediately feel silly for sharing something so personal with a stranger, but she loves my story and is excited to be a part of it. We begin chatting, and before I know it, an hour has passed. Here we are, two complete strangers, choosing to engage in meaningful conversation as if we have known each other for years.

On the drive home, I thank God once again. "Father, I ac-

tually enjoyed our company this evening. We are officially out
of solitude, aren't we?"

Yes, we are. You have grown a great deal over the last three months and
twenty-six dates. You have chosen to let me into your heart, allowing us to
heal many wounds together. You are ready to trust and love people in a much
healthier way.

I beam at His words, feeling much more optimistic after
my positive experience with the woman on the dock. Then He
drops a bombshell:

It is also time to take our relationship to another level. Your separation
from me caused darkness in your heart. You are ready to meet a different part
of me, the part who will remove that darkness. Darling, it is time for you
to know me as Jesus.

DATE 27
Blind Date with Jesus

All week I have been wrestling with what the Lord told me on our last date. I know it's silly, but I feel like God is leaving me. He told me I'm healed enough to be with other people, and He told me it's almost time to accept Jesus. To me, this equates to "God is tired of me." Intellectually I know that's not true, but I feel it all the same. Also, I don't *want* to accept Jesus. Why do I need Jesus when God is enough for me? I decide to go for a walk. The fresh air might do me some good.

As soon as I open the door to walk outside, I see an envelope marked "Dear Neighbor" on my door step. I open it with nervous curiosity. Who would leave me a letter? I hope it's not a complaint about the noise level of my children. Please, God, I can't handle anything negative right now! But instead of a complaint, the envelope contains two tickets for a Christmas Cantata performed by the Gracias Choir and a note that says "With Love." Hmm . . . that's intriguing. I have no idea who would give me these tickets.

As I start my walk, I hear the Lord's voice. *I arranged for the tickets to be placed on your doorstep. I would like this to be our next date so you can begin getting to know Jesus.*

"Why, Lord? I am obedient, so I will listen to you, but I can't help but feel like you are abandoning me! You have taken a lot of time to get close to me, only to leave me to another man."

God assures me He will never leave me and explains He simply wants me to be whole. He says the only way I will feel peaceful and content is to connect with this other piece of Him.

My son will fill that aching spot in your heart. He will complete and fulfill our relationship. He is what you deeply long for, what you have been longing for since your youth. You are ready to let yourself experience him now.

My mind rebels. "You know I don't understand the whole Jesus thing, Lord! I certainly don't consider sacrificing your Son a loving act. If I believed you did that, I would never trust you as a loving and faithful God! I used to believe in Jesus when I was very young. But when I was ten years old, I walked away from that belief, in large part because I didn't like the idea of your asking Jesus to die on the cross. And I still don't like it!"

Instead of answering right away, God leaves me to my thoughts. I think back to my young self, and I remember that when I believed in Jesus, I experienced happiness despite my sad, difficult life. The peace and joy I used to feel disappeared after I rejected the idea of Jesus. In fact, my first suicide attempt was at age ten. I've lived all the years since then discontented, fighting thoughts of wanting to die and searching for something to make me happy again. Now God is telling me that the only way I can find true happiness is to embrace Jesus again.

I could turn back home but decide to walk a little farther as I wrestle with my thoughts. The problem is that I loathe believing God has a wrathful side. Why would He require his own Son to be sacrificed to "even the score" of our sins? That makes no sense to me. And am I to believe that if we do not accept the Jesus story, then we cannot fully connect with God? And that if we do not accept Jesus we will . . . what, *go to hell?* A God like that is too much like the people who abused me throughout my life. "Do what I say and act like I want you to, or you will suffer my wrath." I don't want to believe that my loving God, the only one other than my children who has truly loved me, could be vindictive.

"Lord, I feel like you are coercing me into believing in Jesus by threatening that we won't get any closer if I don't, and I'll never feel whole unless I do. I feel like you are abandoning me, like so many other people in my life have abandoned me."

Sweet daughter, you have so many questions. I love this about you. You have a precious child-like innocence. I am thrilled that you know I am Love, and I appreciate that you refuse to see me any other way. You are right. I do love you, and everything I have done is out of love; I promise. Caren, your perception of my sacrifice is skewed. I can reveal the truth to you. Will you let me?

I turn around and head toward home while I consider it. Everything the Lord has said so far has turned out to be true. I do trust Him, even if I'm frustrated. I acquiesce.

"Yes, Lord. I guess our next date is October 9 at 7:00. Who should use the second ticket?"

Please bring our sweet Victoria.

***

As I sit with Victoria waiting for the show to start, I am conflicted. I want to obey God, but this situation feels, for lack of better words, "not fair." It's the same way I would feel if the man I loved were to set me up on a blind date with another man.

But God has come through for me over and over the last four months, so I know if He says He will reveal the truth, He will. I put aside my reservations and become present for the Lord, for my daughter, and for myself.

The show begins. The musical performance depicts the world before and after the birth of Christ. In the first act, all is dark and dreary. People are searching for hope and peace but are full of emptiness. The scenery, the lighting, and the way the cast portrays themselves evoke the exact feelings I have in my heart.

The second act takes place after Jesus is born. The stage transforms into a beautiful place full of light and joy. The people are thrilled the King is born, and their hearts fill with hope, even though their circumstances have not changed. They live in the same place, make the same amount of money, work at the same jobs, and have the same families, and yet their spirits are drastically changed. I am moved as I watch. The production now looks and feels like what I have been searching for: the joy I had as a girl.

After the show, I am full of emotion and yearning.

"Father, please bring me that kind of peace. I want to know that kind of contentment for myself, but also teach my children what I am missing. I want them to have internal happiness, no matter what is happening in their lives. I won't watch them go through life the way I have. I love them and can't bear the thought of their experiencing the emptiness I feel."

I love you, Caren. The joyfulness you witnessed in the performance, the same kind of joyfulness you remember as a young child, is possible for your children—and for you, as well. Follow me to where I am leading you, Caren. We are almost there.

Even though I still don't accept Jesus or understand how doing so will change anything, I respond, "Yes, Lord. I will follow."

DATE 28
Jesus Study Date

My feelings from seeing the performance last night—a cocktail of hope, confusion, nostalgia for Jesus, and resistance to the idea—linger. I start my day with a prayer.

"Father, thank you for last night. It was a nice treat. Although the show didn't make me any less ambivalent about Jesus, it did make me want the type of joy I saw in Act Two. I know you promise that kind of joy with Jesus. Please make everything clear to me. I want to trust and love all of you, and if Jesus is the essential piece of you, then I want to understand Him so I can accept Him."

Caren, I am proud of you. Even though you struggle to understand, keep your mind open to what I will reveal. Your faith will set you free. Would you like to have a Jesus study date today?

I agree readily. I yearn to fill the empty part of my heart. I will do anything God asks if it will bring me closer to clarity. I have let go of all the harmful behaviors He has asked me to. I have forgiven myself. I have learned to lean on Him when I am hurting or confused instead of turning to my vices. Yet I still feel sad and hurt a lot of the time. I still have this aching desire for something "more." I want what the Lord promises He has for me.

He tells me to get the book I bought at the church bookstore back in August, on our tenth date.

"Oh! I was going to grab a book that someone gave me several years ago named *Jesus* by Beth Moore. Seems like an appropriate title! I don't remember where I put the book you're talking about."

Caren, dear, will you please get the book I suggested? It is on the bottom shelf of your cabinet in the dining room.

Whoa, that is specific. I head to the cabinet and begin looking for the book. I don't see it. I lift a few papers and books with no luck. I move the last pile of junk, and there it is: *Fifty Reasons Why Jesus Came to Die.* I am awe-struck. In the back of my mind, there's a constant, niggling doubt about whose voice I hear. There's a part of me that always wonders if "God's voice" is actually a figment of my imagination. Yet, other times that voice has told me things I simply didn't know . . . like that Stewart would be in that sports bar, that across the street from me that day was a church with a service starting moments after I entered, and now, the location of this book. And the title of the book, which I had forgotten, is too fitting for the questions that have plagued me the last twenty-four hours. I can't believe all of these incidents are simply coincidence. These are the times that help me believe I am truly speaking to God.

I take a deep breath, sit on my couch, and begin to read.

As I read the introduction, I take to the author's unique writing style immediately. His voice is gentle, yet clear. By the time I get through the first page of Chapter One, my tears are flowing. It's uncanny how appropriate the book is for me at this point in time. On the first page of the first chapter is the answer to the question I have been wrestling with all these years, written in a way I truly understand! It all makes sense to me now. God is the creator of everything. Sin continually destroys and hurts His children, creatures, and world through its actions. God's Word clearly explains that our sin brings death and brokenness. Therefore, God has a righteous wrath against sin. He wants nothing to do with our sin, an evil not created by Him. Because of our sin, He must be separated from us, but His love for us is so great that He cannot rest being apart from us. So He sent a part of Himself, in the form of His Son, to absorb His wrath and bear the punishment for our sin so He could be near us once again. God's sacrifice explained this way makes sense to me. I call out to Him.

"Lord, this book is written as if the author were literally answering my questions on a personal level. My sweet and loving Father, you truly love me, don't you?"

As I weep, I see my past flashing before my eyes so clearly it is breathtaking. I see all the events and mistakes and good and bad choices that led me to this point, as if I'm watching the pages of a book being flipped. All my doubt vanishes. My human need to submit to the Lord overwhelms me, and I drop to my knees, bowing my head to my sovereign and loving God.

"Father, please forgive me for doubting. You didn't sacrifice your Son because you are hateful. You love us so much that you couldn't stand to see us suffering the consequences of our sin. Sin separates us from you, so you put laws into place to guide us away from sin. But because we are human, following your laws perfectly isn't possible, so you put yourself into human form as your only Son. You let Him bear the punishment for our sin, and He was the ultimate pure Lamb of God sacrificed for all of our sins."

I no longer see God as mean and wrathful. I see Him as the perfect parent—one who sets down the law as warranted when His children do wrong, but who can't bear to watch His children suffer, separated from Him, without giving them a way to make amends and come back to Him.

My desire to sin is unavoidable because I am a child of Adam and Eve, who fell in sin. When I live a life of sin, I am in pain and feel like death . . . because sin *is* death. When Jesus walked this earth, He felt the pain of our sin, yet He did not sin Himself because He needed to be a perfect sacrifice. He showed us that we can overcome sin through Him. God sent Jesus to teach us how to live, to show us how He wants us to give and experience love. He did so not to control us, but because He loves us and wants us to have the opportunity to live a joyful life. Sin takes away our happiness, our peace and joy. It separates us from our Creator. God wants a relationship with us, so He sent Jesus to be our way back to Him, our way to overcome sin, our way to a life with Him.

I walked away from Jesus at age ten, when my youth pastor described the crucifixion. Hearing how the soldiers tortured, beat, and killed Jesus turned me off. I decided if God allowed that, then He was no better than the people who abused and tortured me. I began to drift away from Jesus and hang out at my friend's house, where R-rated Showtime movies, Playboy magazines, and junk food was easily accessible. I chose sin over my relationship with God and Christ, and I was separated from my one and only love. That was the year I started thinking about dying and tried to kill myself for the first time. As I grew older, I used men and other vices to fill the void. Ironically, even though I had a horrible environment as a young child and experienced unspeakable things, I was happier and peaceful at that time. I knew Jesus and talked about Him to everyone I knew. I invited friends to church with me. I skipped up and down the street singing "Jesus Loves Me." I loved Jesus because He loved me and brought me pure joy amidst pain. And He never left me—I left Him! I turned to worldly things in an attempt to ease my painful life instead of continuing to turn to Jesus for contentment.

I marvel that had I not listened to God's prompting to go to church that day, the day of our tenth date, I would not have bought this book, this very, very important book.

I knew this book would speak to you when the time was right. I am very happy you have allowed yourself to accept the truth about Jesus. You can now receive all the freedom that truth offers, if you choose.

I see a picture unfold that portrays what God is saying. I understand that the next step is completely up to me. God healed me in the areas that were stopping me from accepting Christ. He led me to read a book that explained Jesus in the exact style and language I needed to understand. I now know the truth, and I have no further questions. God led me to His Son, and whether or not I engage with Him is my choice. The ABCs from my childhood church come to mind: **A**ccept Jesus, **B**elieve in Him, and **C**onfess. Today I can choose to love Jesus again, I can let Him teach me how to live my life in order to truly "live," and I can choose to bear witness to life with Him and death without Him.

But I am simply not ready.

DATE 29
Book of John

Since reading the first few pages of *Fifty Reasons Why Jesus Came to Die* yesterday, I've been frozen. I sense that God is waiting for me to engage. I want to be open and accepting of a relationship with Jesus and begin the process of connecting with people, but I am stuck. I don't know how healthy relationships *work*, let alone how they *start*.

I developed most of my relationships when I was unhealthy, and I handled them poorly. The Lord says I am ready for healthier relationships now that we have spent a good amount of time correcting my faulty thought processes, but He hasn't taught me how to restore old relationships or start new ones. I don't know where to begin. What am I supposed to do? Call someone out of the blue and say, "Hi, it's Caren. Sorry I dropped off the face of the earth, but I'm a much healthier woman now and would like to be friends. Wanna chat?" I can't imagine making that kind of call, especially after my unsuccessful dinner invitation to Kate last month.

Even if I *were* willing to make that kind of phone call, I

don't have anyone to call! I interacted with tons of people in the past, but I can't think of a single person I'd feel comfortable initiating a conversation with right now. I blame myself. Many people tried to reach out to me, but I ran from them every time they got too close to my heart. The only relationships I put effort into were those with people who mistreated me, who didn't want a relationship with me, or who could not commit to a deeper relationship with me, like my therapist and Stewart. This realization makes me sad.

But the Lord is calling me out of solitude, and He is kind and loving. Surely He will teach me how to develop healthy relationships if I ask for help.

I am proud of you for seeing these truths, dear. You have indeed run from constructive relationships. You have sought unhealthy relationships because they fit your version of normal. You have embraced relationships that cannot evolve into deeper relationships because they make you feel safe. This is where a relationship with Christ comes into play. Through learning about and developing a relationship with Christ, you can learn how to love the way I intended you to love and be loved. I am excited for you! Let's start today by reading the Book of John.

I dig out my Bible and flip to the New Testament. The Book of John talks about how the true light who gives light to everyone is coming to the world and that through Him we can all be one with the Father. I immediately think of the performance we went to last week. It depicted Jesus' coming in exactly the same way that John describes it: *The world was dark and then Jesus brought light* (John 1:9-13).

I continue reading. When Jesus called the disciples to follow Him, they left everything in their lives behind and followed. They made a huge commitment! I think John is saying that to become a disciple of Jesus, I can't "kind of" follow Him; I have to leave my current life behind. Then I read something that outright frightens me: *Whoever believes in the Son has eternal life. Whomever does not obey the Son shall not see life but the wrath of God remains.* I am conflicted. The commitment seems too large, yet the payoff is the light that Jesus offers, which sounds beautiful.

John Chapter 4 talks about the Woman of Samaria. She reminds me of myself. She is obviously searching for love through men. Jesus knows her, her sins, and her brokenness. He tells her that if she drinks from the water He offers, she will never thirst again. A well of eternal life will spring within her. This sounds wonderful to me.

The more I read, the more I discover about Jesus' character. I recognize a lot of it from my childhood and from past church sermons, but I understand it much differently now. What Jesus says and how He acts is the key to helping me develop relationships, with Him and with others, so now I listen with an invested ear. For example, Jesus doesn't judge people. This simple fact takes on new meaning for me. I think about the kind of woman I have been. I imagine sharing something shameful from my past like my abortion with a friend, and that friend not viewing me negatively. I try to imagine that not even a tiny part of her would view me as "less than" because of what I did. That's hard to imagine.

Yet the Bible says Jesus would not judge me at *all*. He would simply forgive me and ask me to follow Him. If I truly follow Him as the disciples did, I come as I am. He would change me from the inside out through His love and teachings. God has been telling me the same thing, but picturing Jesus as my savior and teacher, rather than God, gives me a much different feeling.

I finish reading all of John, and then I reflect about his teachings and contemplate my relationship with God. When I think of God and pray to God, I envision Him in the sky and do long for this indwelling deep closeness the Bible describes with Jesus. All these months God has helped and guided me, and now it is clear that He has been slowly but surely guiding me toward His Son so that I can experience this deeper and closer walk with Him.

I think about what the relationship the book of John describes with Jesus and I want it—I desperately want it!—but the enormous commitment scares me.

I feel God nudging me more strongly than ever. He tells me it is time to make my commitment to Christ. I shake my head. I can't do it. I am just not ready. I am not ready to drop everything and commit my whole life to following Jesus.

I close my Bible and set it aside.

DATE 30
Break-Up and an Altar Call

Something is wrong with me. About a week ago my severe depression returned, worse than ever. I'm sitting on my couch, listless, wanting to die for the first time in months. The familiar whisper from within tells me, "There is no God. This pain is too big. You can't handle feeling this way anymore."

I think the whisper is right. I should have known the last several months were too good to be true. I can never escape this immense emotional pain for good. This whole "God" thing was a figment of my imagination. I must be mentally ill, and the "voice of God" I've been hearing must be part of my illness. I'm humiliated that I believed I was talking to God all this time. I am sick, sick, sick. There is no "personal relationship" with God, and no Jesus. I am damaged goods. I ruin everything I touch. No one is going to magically save me. I'm too broken to fix. The only way out is to end my existence.

But if I take my own life, what will my children do? I can't leave them behind. I love them. A selfish act like that would ruin them. They would suffer immensely. But I can't stand to

I don't believe this—but many do

live anymore!

I separate myself from my thinking and wonder where these thoughts are coming from? They are so loud in my brain, telling me I should take the bottle of pain pills under my bathroom cabinet. What is wrong with me? Why am I thinking this way? I cry out, "Shut up! Shut up!" I need to get medical help. I'm obviously not thinking rationally. I have an appointment with my therapist in a few hours. I decide to just get out of the house until then, tell her what is happening, and ask for her advice.

***

I arrive at Audrey's office in tears. I choke out between sobs, "I was so much happier for so long, and now I am back to feeling hopelessly sad and desolate, more than ever before! Maybe I'm bipolar or something!"

"Caren, you've never exhibited any signs of bipolar disorder."

"Well, something is happening to me! I feel like a flip was switched in my brain, turning on a horrible depression. It feels bigger than this room. Negative thoughts have surrounded me for a week now. I am overwhelmed with the conviction that I shouldn't be alive."

Audrey says, "As your therapist, I must take what you're telling me very seriously. You need to see a psychiatrist."

I cry even harder. "But I don't have any money! Because I was 'listening to God,' I shut down my massage practice! I barely make enough money as a waitress to pay my bills!"

Audrey sooths me and calms me down enough to help me find a free mental health clinic. She makes an emergency appointment for me to see an after-hours psychiatrist that evening. I promise to call Audrey's answering service when I arrive so she knows I am safe.

***

I stare at the psychiatrist, quietly crying. She asks me to explain what has upset me. Through my tears I try to describe all that has happened.

"I don't know exactly. I was depressed and suicidal, so I called out to God about four months ago and . . . well, I think He answered me."

She looks surprised. "He answered you?"

"Yes. I heard Him say that if I went on fifty dates with Him, He would heal me and lead me to the one who would complete me."

She wants to know what has happened since then. She asks whether I've made any drastic life changes.

"Yes. I closed my business, for one thing."

"Explain that to me," she prompts.

"Well, the Lord has been working with me. He helped me realize that massaging men for a living isn't what He has planned for me."

"So you abruptly closed your business because the voice of God told you to. Were there other reasons? Perhaps you weren't making enough money?"

"No, I made a lot of money . . . " I trail off.

"Okay, Caren. I want you to hear what you have told me. You are suicidal. You hear a voice you think is God, and He is asking you to date Him. And you impulsively shut down a lucrative business to become a part-time waitress. What you are experiencing are textbook symptoms of bipolar disorder. You are delusional right now. Believing you have a personal connection to God, that he is *dating* you, is classic grandiosity."

I shake my head. Even though I'm not fully convinced I am hearing God's voice, when I hear her interpretation, I have the urge to defend Him and myself. "It's not the way you're making it sound. It seemed real. I wanted to die, so I called out to God, and He came to my rescue. He really was helping me change my life. I was starting to learn how to be happy!"

The psychiatrist looks at me with genuine sympathy and compassion. "We humans are very interesting. We have a strong biological need to survive. I believe your brain created this experience. You desperately needed something to save you from your suicidal depression, so your subconscious created a 'voice of God' scenario. And it was successful for a while! But tell me, Caren. If you are truly dating God, and He is truly healing you, why do you want to die again?"

"I don't know!" I snap. "I mean, maybe because He hasn't finished healing me yet. We only made it to date twenty-nine of fifty. On our last date, He told me it was time to accept Christ, but I ignored Him."

I pause, dumbstruck that I hadn't thought of this sooner. "That's it! I was reading the Book of John last week. It said that the Father will lead me to the Son, and if I accept His Son and His sacrifice, He will give me eternal life. But it also said that if I refuse to accept Him, I have no life within me. That must be why I feel like this! God led me to his Son, but I refused to accept Him, which is a sin. And the Bible says God can't be present in the midst of sin!"

For the first time today, I feel the tiniest sliver of hope. But then the psychiatrist's voice brings me back to reality.

"Ms. Bright, I have heard all I need to hear. The way you are speaking tells me you are clearly manic. From the ups and downs you've described and because of the severity of your depression, I believe you have Rapid Cycle Bipolar 2 Disorder. One of the wonderful things about science is medication. I'd like you to get on an antidepressant and an antipsychotic and see what happens. Without medication your condition might progress, which could lead to you being committed to a psychiatric facility. Do you understand the severity of your situation?"

"So you're saying this has all been a fantasy? I haven't been talking to God? Which means His promise of complete healing and a purpose-filled life is false too? I like having the Lord and His guidance! I feel safer! I feel loved, and—"

"Caren," she cuts me off. "There is no cure for bipolar disorder, but you can learn to manage it with medication and therapy. Many people live successfully with BP. The best approach is to take medication and, as tempting as it may be, resist falling into your fantasies. I'm writing you a prescription for 300 mg of an antidepressant named Wellbutrin. That's a high dosage, but I believe you need it. I'm also giving you Ambien to help you sleep and Risperidone, an antipsychotic that will inhibit your delusions. I want you to follow up with a psychiatrist in a month. Okay?"

I finally give up and face the truth. I am mentally unsound.

"Okay."

***

I've picked up my prescriptions, and now I sit with the pills in my hand, weeping. Even though I sometimes doubted I was truly talking to God, facing the truth, that the whole thing really was a fantasy I created, is devastating. It seemed so real . . . but I guess all crazy people who hear voices think that. I believed I

was special. I believed that God loved me so much that He actually spoke to me and promised to heal me. I thought God had
forgiven me for my horrible mistakes in the past and was bringing me to a beautiful place of purpose and meaning. The worst
part is that, for the first time in my life, I believed I was lovable.
That too was just another horrible trick my mind played on me.

Shortly after taking the antipsychotic I feel like my brain
is breaking. What is wrong with me? I thought this was supposed to help, but I feel much worse. The urge to take my life
is all-consuming. The suicidal ideation is strong and insisting I
take my life, I am scared and don't know what to do. Stewart
is out of the country, so I can't reach him. I talk to myself in
desperation.

"Logic, Caren. Use logic! What you're feeling is just a horrible side effect of the medicine. There is no one to turn to but
yourself. If you reach out to a professional, they will force you
to take this medication if not, you will be committed. So think,
Caren, think of your sweet children. What can you do?"

Finally, I remember the sleeping pills. I decide to take a few
of them so I can sleep. When I wake up, the antipsychotic will
have worn off, hopefully, and I can put all of this behind me. I
have to overcome all crazy behavior—Bipolar Disorder and my
God delusion. I believe in God, but I must stop the fantasy that
I am dating Him, that He talks to me. I have to get out of my
head, or I will be committed. My children need me, and I am
all they have.

***

When I awake, I feel normal again but so very, very sad. It
dawns on me how much I will miss my time and talks with God.

But what if the doctor is wrong? I'm so confused! I decide to reach out to God one more time to explain myself, just in case He is actually there.

"Lord, if our conversations were real, then I am truly sorry for turning my back on you. I don't want to believe it was all a fantasy, but for the sake of my children and my sanity, I can't risk believing it was real. I can't risk being committed. I am closing the chapter on us. I am breaking up with you *and* with the idea of being bipolar. I will begin taking my antidepressants, figure out how to start my massage business again, and move on with my life like a normal person. I will ignore this emotional pain and simply exist in logic. If our time together was real, Lord, please find another way to reach me."

Caren, you do not need to leave me. I have—

I block out God's voice, or whoever's voice I am hearing, before it can finish. Walking away from what I thought was my one true love, the only glimmer of hope I've experienced since I was a child, hurts badly. But I fear the doctor is right, and I am completely delusional. I can't take the risk of that being true. Even though my heart hurts, I will try to forget about the last four months and move on.

***

The last couple of months being "normal" have been fairly successful but difficult. I've been using a dog training clicker to retrain my brain. I click it every time I notice that I'm living in my head or starting to talk to "God." Doing this increases awareness of my thought processes. It has helped me focus on reality instead of dwelling on my thoughts and emotions. The down side is that I feel numb and empty, as if I've lost my best friend.

I now work out two hours a day, six days a week, so my body looks great. I began a sexual affair with my male workout partner in an effort to feel connected to someone other than my kids, but I don't feel connected at all. I actually miss being sexually pure. I regret breaking my almost year-long abstinence for an unsatisfying fling. I started a new waitressing job at an upscale restaurant in Highland Park Village, and they are grooming me to be a cocktail waitress. I will make a *lot* more money than waiting tables. All I'll have to do is wear sexy dresses while I bring drinks to high profile customers who give huge tips. I have also gone back to massaging part-time to earn more money. I am no longer suicidal, and I am firmly planted in reality, but I feel like the living dead. I've accepted the harsh reality that I am broken beyond repair and that this is just what my life looks like.

***

Victoria dances up to me and says, "Mommy, can we go to church tonight? Please? They are having a candlelight service for Christmas Eve! Please, Mommy?"

What can I say? I'm not going to tell her there is no such thing as Jesus. I want her to believe in a savior because the antithesis would leave her empty. I never want her to feel the way I do. I have to take her. I'll pretend I believe, just as I pretend to believe in Santa and the Tooth Fairy.

"Yes, dear. Pick out a nice dress, and we'll go."

As I watch Victoria singing praise and worship songs during the service, I feel happy for her. I am glad she believes in something. I wish it was safe for me to believe. Thinking I would be completely healed one day was exciting. I miss that. I also miss believing in Jesus like I did when I was little. What is wrong with believing, after all? Wasn't I becoming a better person when I thought I was dating God? Yes, I closed my office doors . . . but that was a good thing! I hate massaging men. The way most of them look at me and act around me makes me feel dirty and impure. Shutting down my business so quickly may have been impulsive, but it was also a reasonable decision! I no longer felt like a prisoner to the business, fearing I couldn't survive without it. I found freedom in letting the Lord take care of us. Somehow I was able to still pay the bills and put food on the table.

The pastor Pamela announces that the altar is open, and several people go up to pray. I feel a pull to join them. I quickly shake it off. I think to myself, "Be present, Caren. This type of thinking is dangerous. Those people are simple-minded. They believe that a man named Jesus came to save them."

I don't believe that . . . do I? I *want* to believe in Jesus. Just look at the contentment in all the people around me. They are happy loving Jesus. What if He is real? When I was listening to God, my life was changing for the better. He promised me that my life would change fully when I accepted Christ. Maybe if I had accepted Christ that day, I would have begun the next part of my journey instead of spiraling into out-of-control depression.

Caren, dear. Meet me at the altar.

I know this voice. It brings me an incredible amount of comfort, the same kind of comfort I knew as a child. I do not want to block it out. I want to invite Jesus into my life.

Yes, my beloved. I am here. Meet me at the altar.

I no longer want to fight this. I don't care if I'm simple-minded! I felt hope believing in God. I run to Him!

I kneel at the altar and pray, "Oh, Lord. I want this to be real. Please. I miss you. I need you."

I am suddenly sobbing, and at the same time, my mind is filled with peace. The Lord then speaks to me in a different way than He has before. Images of hope and love flash through my mind, as clearly as a movie. I see myself as a writer, a speaker, and a missionary. I am being used to help lead others out of oppression. My children are happy and content. I see myself as a woman of integrity, and all that once soiled me is washed clean. I am strong and confident yet humble before my Maker. I am connected to others. I have friends, and the Lord is pleased with me and I have purpose.

Caren, I have plans for you, plans for a hope-filled future. Come back to me, and we will continue where we were interrupted.

"But the doctor sincerely believes I am mentally unbalanced. If she is right, returning to you now will eventually take me down a dark path. If she is wrong, and my experiences with you are real, then I've betrayed you! I'm not pure anymore either, Lord. I've slipped back into some of my old behaviors."

Caren, accept me into your heart, repent, and follow me. I will forgive you. I will wash you clean. I came to give you salvation. Let me be your comforter. Let me finish what we began. I will not only heal you, but I will also save future generations from brokenness.

With that, I capitulate completely. I no longer have the energy or desire to resist the love and comfort I feel from the Lord. I crave what He offers me. I want Christ in my heart. I will believe. I accept Him right there, on my knees, still weeping tears of joy.

"Oh, Jesus. I have missed you so much. I am so, so sorry."

I missed you too, dear.

PART TWO

"I am the light of the world. Whoever follows me will not walk in darkness, but will have the light of life.."

-John 8:12

DATE 31
Aquarium

A month has passed since I accepted Christ at the altar on Christmas Eve. I am finished denying Christ. I have chosen to accept Him as my savior who brings me more peace. I feel safe near Him, so I spend time thanking Him and letting myself feel His love for me. I know He is waiting for me to be ready to do more together, but I am still a bit hesitant to engage. He is so loving and patient. I hear Him all around me professing His love. I feel a comfort inside my soul that I haven't felt in many, many years. My thoughts of suicide are completely gone. I have a new perspective on life; I am honored to exist and look forward to what lies ahead. As nice as this month has been reveling in Christ's love, I know I need to move forward with Him. I just don't know how. I decide to ask Him for help, like I do with God.

"Good morning, Jesus."

Good morning, my dear.

"Jesus, I am happy to be together, but I am scared to commit to following you. However, my love for you is greater than my fears, and I recognize that I can't, nor do I want, to live without you by my side. I want to choose you as my savior, and I want to start connecting with others. Will you please teach me how?"

I understand your fears and where they come from. I want to give you a gift of true happiness and freedom. Walk with me, and I will teach you how to embrace this gift. Will you come with me to the aquarium today? I have something beautiful for you to experience.

I agree with anticipation.

***

As I walk through the aquarium, I feel Jesus' presence as if He is walking beside me. It's a more intimate feeling than how I felt on my dates with God before I accepted Christ. Now, I feel an intimate relationship with Jesus that is so deep it has filled that void and connects me completely with all of God. I also feel oddly connected to my environment. Life seems to slow down, allowing me to better observe the creatures that surround me. I notice how the animals and fish are bonded in relationship with one another. They work beautifully together in a close, intimate community, almost completing each other. Some lead, some follow, others drift . . . but none go far before heading back to be together.

I reflect on my own life and how I spend most of my time alone, drifting and wandering. I have much love inside me, my heart is kind, and I am filled with wisdom. But what good is a wise woman who doesn't share her wisdom? What good is a loving and kind heart if it isn't shared with others? And I am also missing out on the love and goodness of others.

Jesus tells me that the animals I'm observing at the aquarium exemplify how God designed humans to interact. He wants me to "do life" with others. He wants me to share myself with people and let others share themselves with me.

"Jesus, thank you for taking me here today! Thanks for walking with me and lovingly showing me what you offer through relationship with you and others."

You are welcome, but we are not finished just yet. I would like you to have a bite to eat in the aquarium restaurant.

Lunch sounds wonderful, so I make my way to the restaurant. I am seated next to a family of five: a husband, a wife, and three young girls about five years old and younger. The mother seems tired and overwhelmed. I notice, without judgement, that she would benefit from learning more effective parenting skills. The girls start talking to me and showing off for me. One even gets out of her chair and hugs me, a complete stranger! The mother says to me, "Wow, my girls are really drawn to you."

"I seem to have a way with children and animals. I love them. In fact, I was a nanny for a number of years," I share.

"Being a nanny must require a lot of patience."

"Yep, I do possess plenty of patience!"

She exclaims, "You're lucky! I don't have any patience at all."

The woman, who I learn is Julie, sits down at my table. As her husband takes care of the girls, Julie and I begin a deeper conversation. She shares that she was abused as a child. Her husband wanted her to have the children, but she doesn't know how to be a mother. With tears in her eyes, Julie confesses that she is afraid her inability to bond with her girls is ruining them. My heart goes out to her. I tell her that I too was an abused child, and there was a time not so long ago that I cried for the same reasons she is crying. I assure her that we have a loving God who can heal her past wounds and show her how to connect with others through Jesus. All she has to do is seek Him with prayer, humility, and obedience. Just as He did with me, the Lord can restore what was taken from her and fill her with tremendous amounts of patience and love, a beautiful godly love that will pour from her into her sweet girls.

Julie confides in me that she gave her life to Jesus at church last week. She is ready to get to know Him. This feels like a perfect moment to tell her why I am at the aquarium today.

"I am writing a book called *Fifty Dates with the Lord*, and this outing is our first date since accepting Jesus into my life. You and I are in an amazing moment right now. I believe the Lord specifically placed you and me together today."

Julie and I end our chat with a hug. She tells me she is excited to be a part of my date with Jesus. "Caren, I believe God brought us together to give me hope and to show me that He is real. I know your book will be amazing. I look forward to seeing it on store shelves someday."

As I float out of the aquarium, I talk to Jesus, my words tumbling over each other in excitement. "That was so amazing! What a beautiful gift! You first showed me what being in community with others looks like, and then you gave me the opportunity to put what I learned into action! I was able to share my wisdom, love, and kindness with another woman, and in return I received her love and openness. It was so easy and rewarding! The way you work is amazing, Lord. You put people together so they have the opportunity to touch one another, and through those connections, their lives change. I want to learn more."

Darling, we have only just begun. Keep seeking, and I will show you a life greater than you ever imagined!

DATE 32
Blankets, Pizza, and Hot Cocoa

Brrrrr. The weather is freezing this morning. I lie in bed, burrowing deeper into my covers, delaying the moment when I have to get up and wake the children for school. I want a few more warm and cozy minutes. Suddenly I hear Jesus' voice.

Yes, today is very cold. Imagine how those less fortunate than you must feel not having a warm, cozy bed and blankets to snuggle up in.

"Gosh, Lord. You are right. I am so thankful for the luxuries I have right now!"

Would you like to be my feet today?

"Um . . . sure, tell me how."

Jesus explains he wants to take blankets, pizza, and hot cocoa downtown to the homeless. I can't wait to start after I take the children to school.

Instead of waiting, will you leave your cozy bed right now and ask the children to help you? Their hearts are like yours. I am sure they would love to donate some of their things.

I kick off the covers with enthusiasm, no longer bothered by the chill in the house, and call for the kids to get ready for school. When they come downstairs I say my good mornings and tell them about the date Jesus and I are going on today. I ask them to say a quick prayer about it and, if they feel led to contribute something of theirs toward our date, bring it to me. They are more than eager. My daughter runs upstairs and comes down a few moments later with her warm, fuzzy, pink comforter and one of her favorite stuffed animals, a brown puppy from Build-A-Bear Workshop named Cocoa. My sons each grab a pair of shoes from their closets. Reggie donates a pair of his size ten-and-a-half basketball shoes, and Dae donates a brand new pair of size fourteen basketball shoes he was planning to sell on eBay. I thank each of them for their generosity.

"Thank you so much! If these are the items you felt led to give, then these are the exact items we need!"

Before we head to school Victoria tells me, "Mommy, I want to pray over my puppy before I give it away." She then says a sweet prayer out loud. "Dear God, please watch over whoever gets my puppy and blanket and help keep them safe and warm. Amen."

I have tears in my eyes. A feeling of gratitude blankets me. I am very blessed to have these exact children. They are amazing human beings.

I drive the children to school happily. The temperature is in the twenties, which is much colder than usual in Texas, but instead of feeling disgruntled and complaining, I feel thankful for my life, and I eagerly anticipate bringing warmth and comfort to others with Jesus by my side.

"Wow, Jesus. I am so excited right now! These are new feelings for me. I've been happy and even felt real gratitude for the first time in the last few months, but not on this level. My gratitude feels more genuine—not just a thought, but a feeling of thankfulness from deep in my soul. And man, my children are pretty great!"

Yes, they are wonderful children. There was splendor in watching them gather their things. Seeing you happy on a deeper level, filled with internal peace and joy with me in the center, brings me great pleasure. Are you ready to be my feet?

"Yes, Lord. I'm ready! I'm assuming we need to buy a few things first. Shall we use the fifty dollars I set aside for tithes?"

That is a wonderful idea. Fifty dollars is the perfect amount.

Jesus tells me to stop at Goodwill first. He instructs me to pick up four blankets but to ignore the asking price. He tells me to instead explain to the cashier that the blankets are for homeless men and women. He says the cashier will lower the price.

I drive to the nearest Goodwill and search for blankets. They have exactly four available, and their price tags total $18.44. When I check out, the gentleman at the counter happens to be the manager. I explain why I am buying the blankets, and he offers them to me at two dollars each, a total of $8.62 with tax.

"Well, that happened just as you said! What next?"

Well done. It is time to buy pizza. Go to the CiCi's Pizza at White-hurst and Skillman. Order five large pepperoni pizzas and explain our mission to the cashier like you did at Goodwill.

Once again the scene plays out exactly as Jesus predicts. The total cost of the pizza is normally $37.92. After I talk to the manager, he offers them to me for five dollars each, lowering the total to $27.13.

Now I want you to buy five hot cocoas from the gas station around the corner.

I obey, and the total cost of the cocoas is $8.95.

"Unbelievable, Lord. We bought all these blankets, pizza, and cocoas for only $44.70. You're pretty good on a budget!"

You should see what I can do with some fish and bread . . . read about it in your Bible.

I chuckle as I get back into my car. Jesus then instructs me to head downtown. As I approach the downtown area, He directs me to pass Lamar Street and go under the bridge. I sense He wants me to turn left. As soon as I turn, I see a man walking alone pushing a grocery cart. The Lord wants me to give him one of the pizzas and tell him that Jesus loves him. I feel a little self-conscious as I get out of the car with the pizza.

"Excuse me, sir. This pizza is from Jesus, who loves you."

The man gives me a sweet, almost toothless smile that stretches from ear to ear. "Thank you, little lady. I sure love Jesus too! I am blessed and highly favored, yes indeed! Thank you kindly. Now you be safe out here, little lady."

Before I drive away, I ask him if he needs a new pair of shoes or a blanket. He politely declines both—the blanket because he doesn't want to lug around another item, and the shoes because neither are his size. He explains his shoes might not look the best, but they fit perfectly. Because of the amount of walking he does, having comfortable shoes that do not give him blisters is more important than having shoes that look good.

I say goodbye and contemplate my experience. Saying Jesus' name out loud to the man was a little uncomfortable. Telling him that God loves him would have felt more natural.

I continue driving around downtown, passing out the pizza and cocoas to folks Jesus leads me to. I give and receive a few hugs as well. At each stop, saying Jesus' name becomes more comfortable. To my surprise, all those I talk to already believe in Jesus, trust Him, and know He loves them. This challenges my assumption that people who are down and out do not know the Lord.

Finally, I have passed out all the pizzas and cocoas. Despite offering the shoes, blankets, and stuffed animal to each person we encountered, I still have them. Nobody wants them for the same reasons as the first man. I start to doubt that it was the voice of the Lord who told me to ask the children for items and to buy the blankets. Perhaps those were my own thoughts and ideas. I suddenly feel foolish and discouraged. Obviously homeless people don't need these items. Maybe this whole thing was silly—the dates with the Lord, writing a book . . . everything! After all, if even one of the things the Lord tells me proves to be false, then none of it can be true. As I spiral into negative thinking, I think back to how I found Stewart at that sports bar. And how I was guided to a church moments before the service started. And how I found a book I had forgotten about exactly where God's voice told me it would be. I decide to bring my doubt to Jesus.

"Jesus, why did you tell me to buy these blankets from the thrift store and to get items from the children if nobody wants them or can fit into them?"

Sweet Caren, you still have such little faith. You are so quick to give up, so quick to believe that I am not the voice who is guiding you.

His words sound slightly exasperated but teasing.

"I'm sorry, Lord. I have trust issues, and—"

I know, dear. Continue to come to me with your doubts, and I will help you. I never said we are done with our date. We are finished with that part of the date, but I would like you to stop at the gas station over there and get five more hot cocoas.

"But I have only five dollars and some change left from my tithe money, and perhaps a few quarters at the bottom of my purse."

Do not worry. These cocoas will cost less than they did at the previous store. Tell the woman at the counter they are for the homeless, and ask her to donate one for the cause.

I do as Jesus instructs, and the woman is happy to give me a free cocoa. With the three quarters I find at the bottom of my purse, I have exactly the right amount of money to buy the other four. Truly amazing!

Now get in your car, turn left, and go straight for about half a mile.

I follow His directions and run into a group of six homeless people standing in front of the library. He tells me to bring them the hot cocoas.

"But there are six people and only five cocoas."

Trust me.

I introduce myself to the group and offer them the cocoas. "Sorry, guys. I have only five."

They eagerly grab the cups. One of the men declines and says, "Give the last cup to the lady." I admire his noble gesture. His "others first" mentality is inspiring, especially since he is cold and homeless.

I then offer the blankets. A few need them, and then one of the men takes the rest, explaining that his friend at his homeless camp can use them. I next offer Victoria's stuffed puppy. A woman says she would love to bring it to her seven-year-old daughter, Lily. I sit with the group and tell them about Jesus' love. After a few minutes I feel it's time to go. I say my goodbyes, give a few hugs, and turn to leave when I remember the shoes. I turn around.

"By chance do any of you wear a size fourteen or ten-and-a-half shoe?"

One of the men shouts, "I wear a fourteen!"

I can't believe it. I jokingly ask to see his shoe size. Yep, it's a fourteen! Then the woman tells me her boyfriend wears a ten-and-a-half. As the man puts on his new shoes, the woman's boyfriend walks up and joins the group. They are all extremely thankful, and I am in awe of what has taken place.

I drive back home, again on Cloud Nine. "Jesus, that was perfectly orchestrated! You are amazing. Everything went smoothly as perfectly planned."

Yes, I am a man with a plan. I am pleased with you. Thank you for being my feet on our date today.

Is He kidding? The pleasure is mine! "Doing this with you today made me feel beautiful. You couldn't have planned a better day for me. I adored loving others and meeting their needs with you by my side. Please keep teaching me this love, Jesus. I'm sorry for doubting you, yet again. It's just that—"

No need to explain. I understand you. Just keep following me, Caren. We have only just begun.

DATE 33
Diaper Stand

My last date with Jesus was almost two weeks ago. I am itching to do something with Him again. I really liked helping others. Maybe it is time for another date?

"Good morning, Jesus!"

Good morning. It is nice to hear from you first thing in the morning and with so much joy!

"Well, it's because of you! I feel a new kind of happiness that grows every day. I am excited and thankful. Life is less of a struggle now that I've found joy and comfort being in a relationship with you."

He tells me He is pleased. He reminds me the reason He came was to bring joy, truth, and light. It's funny because that is exactly how I would describe what Jesus is becoming to me: joy, truth, and light. The children notice too. Last week Da'Shon came into my bedroom, gave me a kiss on the forehead, and told me he loves me. His show of affection is a sign that things are improving between us. I thank Jesus and ask Him if we can go on another date helping others.

First, you are welcome. Watching you experience this freedom is my pleasure. Second, I would love to go on a date. How about next Thursday?

"Of course! But why next Thursday?"

We need time to prepare for our next date.

"Okaaaaay. Can you explain?"

Think of a time in your past when you struggled and felt alone—when you needed help, and someone came to your rescue. Tell me the first thing that comes to mind.

I immediately think of when Dae and I lived in a homeless shelter, and he came down with diarrhea. The shelter provided us with only three diapers a day, and I didn't have any money to buy more. I called family members, but they were upset with the way I was living my life and didn't believe they should help me. So I had to make the three diapers last for twenty-four hours, and Dae developed a severe diaper rash.

"Gosh, Lord. Remembering this makes me sad again."

Stay with me, Caren. Do not get lost in the sadness of the memory. You are no longer in that stage of your life. Shift your mind to the part where you were shown love and given a gift.

I wrench my thoughts from that horrible, desperate time and continue remembering. In the early afternoon, after I put my last diaper of the day on Dae, the house manager asked me to come to her office. She presented me with an envelope and a large box of diapers, explaining that a man dropped them off for me. The envelope contained twenty dollars. I didn't know who the man was, but his gift came exactly when I needed it— and what a gift it was!

I am glad that moment is branded in your heart. It was a proud moment for me. I loved watching him show you love when you were in need.

"Wow, you are right. Who was that man anyway?"

That is not important. What is important is that he listened to my voice. I brought your struggle to him in the unique way that I do, and he was loving and obedient enough to let us all reap the reward of being my hands and feet.

"You are amazing! What a beautiful thought to know you have been looking after me all this time. You continue to surprise me with your love for others and me."

Would you like to use your memory as inspiration for next Thursday? I will give you a vision. Use your gifts and abilities to make it a reality.

This sounds odd, but I quiet my mind until I see myself standing at what looks like a lemonade stand. But instead of selling lemonade, I am giving away small gift bags of diapers, wipes, and baby lotion. It is a nice scene, but how would I pay for those items?

Go out and ask my people.

I scoff. "What do you mean? Why would anyone give me money for something as odd as a free diaper stand? People will think I'm crazy!"

It is your choice; you do not have to do it. But I promise you this. If you put aside your fear of what others will think and go for it, everyone involved will be blessed. The gift givers will experience the joy of giving to a worthy cause. The gift receivers will experience the joy of receiving something they need. You will experience the joy of being my feet again, and I will experience joy from watching my love flow among my people. Caren, will you be my feet?

How can I resist? But even as I agree, several questions come to mind. Who will come to my diaper stand? How will I know that the people who take the gift bags really need them? Jesus reassures me that He will provide everyone and everything to make it happen.

You need not question how it will come together, Caren. And do not worry about who comes to receive my love. My love is for everyone. This is about giving and being a gift, no questions asked, and no strings attached. This is how I love, dear.

"The way you love is beautiful. I am honored to have this date with you next Thursday."

***

I begin asking people to help me, in person and via Facebook. Sharing my vision feels awkward, to say the least. My relationship with Jesus has been fairly personal up until now. Only a few others knew about it. Now I have to explain why I am asking for contributions. As the week goes by, I become slightly more comfortable sharing the vision Jesus gave me. I am humbled by the generosity of others. Nobody questions why I am qualified to coordinate a diaper stand. They simply give a few dollars here, twenty dollars there, and the next thing I know it is Tuesday, and I've raised $350.

Now it is time for the fun part: shopping! I feel like a kid at Christmas as I buy diapers, wipes, lotions, and gift bags. Words cannot explain the joy I feel being Jesus' hands and feet. When all is purchased, the children and I fill forty gift bags and make a homemade card for each bag that reads: "Will you be mine? Love, Jesus." Per Jesus' instructions I make several signs that say: "Need diapers? Come to the corner of Whitehurst and Skillman today at 4:00 p.m. Love, Jesus." I load the bags and signs into my van and turn in for the night. My mind races. I feel insecure about what tomorrow will bring, but somehow I fall asleep.

***

Good morning, love. It is Thursday! Rise and shine. We have a busy day ahead.

I am wide awake with anticipation and nervousness. I open up to Jesus about how weird I feel. Even though everyone has been receptive to my plan this week, I feel exposed and vulnerable. The thought of actually posting our signs in neighborhoods scares me. I fear people in this small community will think I am odd. Isn't it strange to set up a table and give bags of diapers away? Who does that?

"And Jesus, what if nobody comes? Then I'll have wasted my time and everyone else's money. Nobody will trust me again!"

Sweet Caren, I invite you to push away your fear and self-doubt so you can enjoy this experience. Even if only one person comes, everyone involved will receive the gift of love. Why let negative emotions rob you and everyone else of the joy that will come from this venture? Today is the reward for your hard work all week.

He is right, of course! If even one person comes for a gift bag, that one person will be blessed. If we have any bags left over, we can donate them to the New Beginnings Homeless Center for women and children. I take a deep breath and let go of my anxiety.

I hang the signs and experience waves of emotion—excitement, nervousness, fear, comfort—throughout the day until 3:00 finally arrives. I then firmly put all doubts aside, pull close to Jesus, and go for it. I pick up my daughter as the Lord encouraged me to do (she loves this stuff as much as I do!), and we stop at a store to buy balloons. Then we go to the corner and set up and decorate a table. People begin to arrive. The joy on their faces is an amazing blessing. One woman explains that she saw our sign as she was literally on her last diaper, wondering what she would do until she got paid tomorrow. She tells us we are the answer to her prayer, and she is thankful. I respond that Jesus came to her aid, not us, but she insists that if we were not obedient to His call, her needs wouldn't have been met. I remember the feelings I struggled with last night and most of today. More than once, I told myself I shouldn't do this. Knowing that the Lord used my daughter and me to answer another woman's prayer for her child has a profound effect on me. It makes me want to keep following Jesus' gentle, loving voice.

Many women take comfort in knowing the diapers are from the Lord. A few of them weep openly as they tell us what a blessing receiving our gift is. One woman even says it is an inspiration to see someone out here on the streets *being the feet of Jesus*. Wow.

By 6:00 the gift bags are gone, so we pack up and head home. What an amazing day. What an amazing week! Everything went beautifully. At least seventy-five people took part in the event, either by giving or receiving. And that's not counting those who simply witnessed it.

"Lord, you are incredible. All the diapers were taken! That is pretty cool. Please keep teaching me about your love and using me to share it with others, even when I resist. I want to be closer to you."

I agree. It was amazing, and you are amazing, Caren. Good job. I am proud of you. Keep following me, and we will do much more together. We have only just begun.

DATE 34
Be My Valentine

Yesterday's successful diaper giveaway should have me feeling elated, but I am instead in a strange place mentally. An old friend contacted me on Facebook this morning, asking how things went yesterday. She asked what prompted me to not only raise money for diapers but also to personally pass them out to people in need. I responded honestly, explaining it was Jesus' idea, and I simply did His footwork. I did not receive a reply. Now I feel exposed and vulnerable. I suspect she thinks I am one of those "Jesus freaks" and is too uncomfortable to respond.

Why does this bother me so much? As close as I felt to the Lord yesterday, I should embrace our plans together and disregard what other people think. Instead I feel self-conscious and embarrassed. When I was dating God, our relationship was mostly private. But getting to know Jesus involves an outward display of our relationship and my affection for Him. I hate feeling exposed this way, but the way I felt when I was doubting and running from the Lord felt even worse. The best thing I can do is turn it over to Him.

"Lord, I am struggling with my feelings today. I'm making a lot of changes in my life, following the voice I hear in my spirit. But do you hear how crazy that sounds? How does one hear a voice in one's spirit? I've been telling people Jesus said to collect money for diapers. They have to think I've gone off the deep end! Imagine what people thought when they read my signs advertising a gift of diapers from Jesus . . . what was I thinking?! This is all too much. I don't know any more. What if that doctor was right, and this is a fantasy I'm creating in my head?"

My sweet and precious love, I am sorry that thought continues to torment you. I understand where it comes from. Could your doubts have anything to do with how much time we have been spending together lately?

"What do you mean?"

I am referring to your commitment issues.

I mull over His question for a minute. "Are you implying that I'm running away from you because we are getting too close? That I am so afraid of a true connection that I'm putting space between us by attributing all that has happened to an overactive imagination?"

He responds with a smile in his voice. *You said it, not me.*

I don't know what to make of that. I am torn. Am I making up a fantasy to feel special, or am I refusing to believe the truth because I subconsciously want to push Jesus away from me?

My dear, if you choose to walk away again, I will be here when you decide to come back.

But I don't want to walk away from Him again. I love Jesus. I love the idea of Him! I want to truly believe and place my life into His hands. But there is something stopping me. Perhaps it's because I've never heard of anyone else having a daily dialogue with Jesus like I do. Here I've been worried about being a Jesus freak, and it appears that I'm the freakiest of them all!

"No one I know says they speak to you and hear you speak back, Jesus—much less go on dates with you! The few people I tell about our relationship kind of look at me sideways. I know if I stick with you, I'm going to have to share our relationship with more and more people. That is an uncomfortable, daunting prospect."

I want to have a date with you today. After all, it is Valentine's Day!

"Ugh, is this a joke to you, Jesus? I don't have time today anyway. I have to do a little Valentine's Day shopping for the children, pick them up from school, and then go straight to work."

I am a simple man. Our date can be Valentine's Day shopping for the children together.

I know Jesus is teasing me, but I'm not in the mood. "Okay! Fine! We'll go to TJ Maxx."

***

As I walk through the discount department store, I look for gift ideas for the kids. I want something fairly inexpensive that will speak to them on a personal level but also be of real use. I decide on school backpacks. As the school year is halfway over, their current backpacks are getting shabby, and I can choose a different fun design for each of them. I browse the available choices and begin feeling remorseful. I know I am supposed to be on a date with Jesus, but I have been purposely ignoring Him. I've given Him the cold shoulder for no real reason other than my fears and second guessing. I feel like a jerk, so I decide to let Him in. As soon as I open my heart to Him, He speaks to me.

Those are nice bags. Good job staying within your budget as well. Let me ask you something. How did you know which backpack to get for each of your children?

"What do you mean? I simply looked at the size, design, pattern, and shape of each bag and thought about what each of my children like. Victoria loves flowers and pretty things, so she'll love this one. Dae's favorite color is red, so he'll like this one, and this one is for Reggie because he likes blue."

So you would not give the floral backpack to one of your sons? Or the blue backpack to Victoria?

"Of course not!" I laugh out loud at the thought and then quickly scan my surroundings to make sure nobody is looking at me.

Why not?

"Because they wouldn't appreciate the gifts if they weren't tailored to what they like as individuals! You know that, Lord. Why are you asking me?"

I stop short, realizing Jesus' questions aren't really about the backpacks. I sense He wants me to explore His analogy. I guess He is saying the backpack gifts I am buying for my children are like the gifts He gives me. The way He deals with me and the nature of our relationship is based on what I need. He knows what I appreciate, and He designs my experience with Him in a way that speaks to me specifically.

Exactly. I love you and know you. How I interact with to you is different than how I relate to someone else. Our journey together is different and unique because you are different and unique, Caren.

How sweet! I can't help but break into a wide smile, regardless of who might be watching.

"I sure do love you, Jesus. I'm sorry for pushing you away today. You are so good and loving to me, yet I continue to run from you. I will work on doing better, okay?"

I understand. I will encourage you to become more aware of when you are running away from me out of fear. I love you too, Caren. Happy Valentine's Day.

I am back to feeling close to the Lord. He continues to pursue me, but not in a forceful manner. When I consider backing away from Him, He gives me the freedom to do so, yet reassures me that He loves me. He prefers that I stay with Him but promises He will be waiting for me to return if I leave. How is that possible? How can He love me so much? I struggle accepting that He loves me so deeply, especially when a voice in the back of my mind still whispers words of disbelief. "You are a broken woman creating a love story because in reality you are unlovable." How dare I entertain that whisper when the Lord has fixed so much in my life? He has proved Himself time and again, and I still have the audacity to doubt Him.

"Jesus, I want to confess something to you."

What is it?

"I still have doubts about our relationship. I need to work through more of my trust issues."

I know. You still have several problem areas that need repair, especially when it comes to trust. That is why I asked you for fifty dates, my dear. Not thirty-four.

I can almost hear Him smirking.

DATE 35
Mirror, Mirror

Ugh. Looking at myself in the mirror is harder than usual today. I know I look the same today as I did yesterday, but today I am repulsed by what I see. I've gained twenty-five pounds since last July, and it feels more like fifty. Even though I was once 100 pounds heavier than I am now, I feel completely and totally FAT. My eating is once again out of control, and I've even made myself throw up a few times after eating this week— something I've done on and off since I was twelve years old. I despise feeling like this and don't want to hurt myself anymore. Why is loving myself so difficult sometimes?

My relationship with food is twisted. Every time I eat a bite of food, I calculate how many calories it contains. I plan what meal I'll skip tomorrow to justify eating something fattening today. I constantly think about what I can or can't eat, what I should or shouldn't eat, what I will or won't eat, and berate myself for what I have already eaten that I shouldn't have. I notice what other people eat and compare their food choices to the food on my plate. I worry about my children eating too much. I believe skinny women are somehow better than I am. When I look in the mirror, I see a fat face and big body, and I don't even have clothes that sufficiently cover my flaws. I want to feel beautiful, but all I see and feel is ugly right now.

I realize this issue is no different than the rest of my issues. I must stop trying to fix it on my own and ask the Lord to help me.

"Jesus, I need you. I have a tremendous need to feel beautiful right now. I don't know what triggers these feelings of self-disgust. All I know is that today is one of those days when I wake up repulsed by my body, and my sole desire is to be skinny."

Jesus suggests going for a drive while we talk more about my struggle. I get in my van and begin driving aimlessly as I continue to talk to Him.

"Can you help me with this issue? I know you don't want me to hate myself. I am doing better at loving myself for who I am, not for what I look like, but there are still plenty of days like today when I feel like a prisoner trapped in an ugly body."

I am glad you came to me about this. I have been waiting to help you with your body image issues for a long time. First, how do you define the word "beautiful"? You say you are ugly, but just three days ago you were handing out diapers to women and children in need. Caren, your beauty radiates from you. I look forward to the day you can see it and believe it yourself. What are you feeling right now?

I obviously feel self-loathing. I make a turn and think about it a little more. I realize I also feel sad and a little lonely. I feel ashamed too because I know the way I feel about food, and my physical appearance is distorted. I know my attitude stems from the way people treated me as an overweight teen, but even so, if I am not the "correct weight," I feel ugly. I have avoided dealing with this issue because it seems too huge to take on.

The Lord tells me He'd like to explore my feelings more

deeply and assures me that if I get too uncomfortable, we can stop talking about it. He wants me to truly understand the root of this problem and its magnitude so I can give myself some grace and understanding. I take a deep breath and start remembering my story.

My mother had an obsession with weight. Her ideal weight was ninety-eight pounds. When her weight rose to 105 pounds, she would refrain from eating for a few days until she was back to ninety-eight pounds. Being fat repulsed my mother. Unfortunately, I was a chubby kid, so she put me on many restrictive diets throughout my childhood. She packed my school lunches, giving me about 150 calories of raw fruit, vegetables, and sliced turkey. If she caught me eating something fattening, she made me spit it out into her hand. She even put me on Phentermine, a prescription weight loss medication, when I was twelve. Can you imagine encouraging a twelve-year-old to take legal speed? But I know she meant well. She struggled with her own demons, and to her, being fat was ugly, so she wanted to save me from being ugly.

Sometimes I lived with my father and stepmother for several months, or even years, at a time. They didn't patrol my eating at all, so I would binge until I couldn't eat any more. Sometimes I'd eat so much that I would make myself throw up. My life fell into a pattern. I'd become obese when I lived with my dad, and when I returned to my mother's house, she'd put me on food restrictions until I was skinny again.

During my obese times, my brother, stepbrother, and classmates made fun of me. They sang insulting songs to me, like "Christmas is coming, and Caren's getting fat. Please put a penny in the old man's hat." I often heard "Fatty, fatty, two by four. Caren couldn't fit through the bathroom door. So she went on the floor, wiped it up, and did it some more." They were immature kids who viewed their actions as harmless teasing, but I cried every time. Even grown-ups said hurtful things. More times than I can count I heard, "You have such a pretty face. You would be beautiful if you lost weight!" When I wore my purple bathing suit, my brothers taunted me by calling me Grimace, referring to the large, purple, blob-like McDonald's character. I was so self-conscious in it that I asked my stepmother to buy me a new bathing suit. She responded jokingly, "Did you already put away the tent from your backyard campout last night? If not, you can wear it for a swim suit!"

Conversely, I received compliments when I was in the process of losing weight or had reached my low weight. People told me I was pretty. My mother often said, "Look, Caren! Your collar bones are showing now! You look beautiful!" It's no wonder I did not feel lovable unless I was skinny like most of the other little girls I knew.

By the time I was an adult, I had gained even more weight. Being obese was difficult. People stared at me with thinly-veiled disgust. I heard them whispering behind my back. It seemed that the only thing people around me cared about was whether I lost a pound or two or gained a pound or ten. My ex-husband lost interest in being intimate with me or touching me.

Tears fall as I drive around reliving these horrible memories. I turn back toward home. "Lord, this is extremely painful for me. The memories cut too deep. I don't want to work on my weight issues right now. I'm afraid I will fall apart. I don't want to unravel again. I just want to be thin and beautiful and not have to think about all of this!"

He compliments me on expressing my feelings and then says, *I am so sorry for how others treated you. People often do not think before speaking. What they said was hurtful, and it pained me watching you go through it at the time. I understand you are not ready to deal with the whole issue, but we can work on a small piece of it now, if you are willing.*

I am open to the suggestion.

Okay. Other than losing weight, what do you think makes you beautiful?

"Taking the time to fix my hair, putting on makeup . . . and wearing stylish clothes."

How do you feel when your hair is not styled, your face is bare of make-up, and you are wearing clothes you do not particularly like?

"Ugly!"

I want you to do an experiment. For the next two weeks, do not wear makeup. Wear your hair in its natural state and wear simple clothing. Focus on who you really are—on your personality and how you treat people. Then we will talk about how you feel. Deal?

"Umm . . . okay, I guess."

I can't believe I'm agreeing to purposely look ugly for two weeks! But I know Jesus is trying to teach me something, so I'll do it. I'll start tomorrow.

I am excited you are willing to try this. When it gets hard, do not give up. Come to me for strength.

***

The first few days of "going natural" has been upsetting. I am so self-conscious that I don't even want to look at myself in the mirror. I notice every blemish on my face, my stubby eyelashes, and my thinning eyebrows. My pale lips fade into my pale skin. Without my blow dryer and hair products, my hair is a mass of frizzy, yet limp, curls. I am a nice looking woman when I make an effort, and sometimes people notice me when I'm out and about, but now I feel invisible as I run my errands throughout the day. I don't like the feeling, but I can handle it because I haven't been anywhere that really matters to me. But that is about to change. I am getting ready to go to work tonight!

I put on my waitress uniform, a white button-down dress shirt, black tie, long black skirt, and knee-length apron. I usually wear heavy makeup, slick back my hair into a tight ponytail, and wear nice earrings. Serving people confidently without feeling pretty will be tough. I remind myself to focus on what people see in me as a person and server instead of focusing on being physically attractive.

I am nervous as I walk in and see the general manager at the door. He likes his girls pretty, so I fear he will be disappointed when he sees me. Not surprisingly, his first comment to me is, "Are you okay? You look sick." I have an overwhelming urge to run to the bathroom and apply makeup. Instead I consider my manager's personality. He is a self-proclaimed "ladies' man" who thinks women should wear a lot of make-up and as little clothing as possible. I remind myself that his opinion is simply that: an opinion. It is not a true reflection of who I am.

I continue through the restaurant, determined to hold my head high. A few other staff members and the maitre d' tell me how fresh and natural I look. I immediately feel better, but just as quickly I realize their opinions are equally irrelevant to who I am as a person. The Lord wants me to find freedom in being myself without factoring in what I look like or what others think of me. The rest of the night I make an effort to be especially personable to my customers and forget about how I look. The maitre d' receives an unusual number of compliments about my service that night. I later share what I am doing with a few co-workers. They are inspired, and our hostess even decides to forego makeup the next time she works as well. Knowing my actions inspired others feels amazing.

***

My two-week experiment is coming to a close. My perception of myself is changing. I am much less focused on my physical appearance, and I don't feel the need to "look good" like I did. I draw strength from compliments about things I do and say rather than my looks. The best part of this experiment is that I've been able to share my experience with Victoria. Unfortunately, my past behavior made it crystal clear how important physical appearance is to me. I often made comments about my weight in front of her, and I wouldn't leave the house without using a flat iron on my hair and "putting my face on." Putting all that aside these last two weeks has allowed me to share the value of being natural with her. We've learned together that who you are on the inside is more important than making yourself up to look like the world's version of pretty. She stopped asking me to straighten her hair and instead embraced her natural curls. What a beautiful outcome! I don't want my little girl to struggle with self-image like I have, so I am thankful I am re-engineering the way I think about self-image while she is still young. This experiment has given me the opportunity to redefine beauty to my sons as well. We have talked about actions and hearts versus good looks.

***

The experiment is over. I thank the Lord for His challenge and tell Him all I learned. It was an amazing two weeks! I felt incredible freedom to be who I am as a person. Makeup, hair, and clothing no longer define me. I can feel beautiful with or without it. I like a little mascara and lip gloss, but I don't *need* them anymore—which feels incredible! I still have a lot to work on concerning my weight issues, but I know we will work on them when the time is right. For now, I can celebrate that I am one step closer to being the woman I was created to be.

DATE 36
Memoir and Barbecue

I have been taking a writing class and a speech class at the community college since mid-January. If the Lord is truly calling me to be a writer and a speaker, I need to improve my writing skills. I dropped out of school after failing ninth grade twice; my reading comprehension was at a sixth grade level. I do not plan to get a degree in writing, but I want to at least learn how to better communicate my thoughts and words.

I enjoy my classes. My instructor is a Christian man who has gone on mission trips. I love this because the Lord tells me I will be a traveling missionary in the future. I hope all the exciting things Jesus predicts for me really do happen—I can't imagine waiting tables the rest of my life. Besides writing, the only other skills I have are cooking, cleaning, childcare, and massage therapy. I'm not sure these are the skills I need to lead the purpose-filled life Jesus showed me at the altar. It's hard to imagine a woman with no formal education or accreditations becoming a speaker and writer. It's no easier imagining that woman, who has never flown on an airplane and lives paycheck to paycheck, traveling around the world doing mission work! I am scared to bank on what Jesus showed me, but He has been truthful so far. I think it's time to start embracing His plans for my future.

Last week's writing assignment was to write a memoir about a childhood memory and end the story in present day. Part of embracing my future is confessing to those around me about how Jesus is working in my life, so I decided the assignment was a good place to start. I wrote about a time when my mother kicked me out of her house. I was thirteen-years-old, and I confided in a friend that the bruise on my face was from my mom hitting me during one of her angry fits. My friend told her teacher, who called Social Services. My mother was afraid she would lose her children because of the incident. She was so angry with me that she packed my bags and dropped me off in my father's driveway. Her parting words were, "Have a nice life."

I was too frightened to go inside my father's house because I knew my stepmom would be upset. She was a nice lady, but my brother and I were troubled children who brought a lot of chaotic drama into her home. The last time I lived with my father, I attempted suicide for the second time. I was kept in the hospital for a month and then sent to the Ohio Veterans' Children's Home in Xenia, Ohio, where I was supposed to stay until I was eighteen years old. After a few months, I ran away and returned to my mother. And then there I was, standing in my father's driveway again, abandoned and unwanted. I wanted to die.

I hid my bags behind a bush and walked up the street to a creek in the woods nearby. As I sat by the creek sobbing, I heard the Lord speak to me, in the same way I hear Him today. I didn't know it was the Lord at the time but, looking back, I am certain it was Him. He soothed me as I wept, telling me everything was going to be okay. He encouraged me to return to my dad's house and assured me he would give me shelter.

I ended my memoir describing where I am today, building a relationship with Jesus. I explain that His voice has once again soothed my broken heart and led me to a place of comfort and safety.

I received an A on my paper, and my instructor gave me a note that said I was an AMAZING (yes, he used all caps!) story-teller. Nobody has ever described me as a storyteller—amazing or otherwise—so his compliment surprised me and made the idea of becoming an author a little more conceivable.

***

I drop off the children at school and notice that some of the plants outside are green. It is early March, the beginning of spring in Dallas. I marvel at the warmer weather and decide to wear a skirt today. I give my legs a rub and determine I want to shave them first!

When I get home, I settle down into a warm bubble bath and chat with the Lord for a bit. Soon He tells me He wants me to do something that requires a complete act of faith because it won't make sense to me.

"Well, Lord, you have been faithful thus far. Everything we've done together either teaches me something or brings me a blessing, so . . . bring it on!"

I like your attitude. Remember the Bible study your friend told you about?

He is referring to a woman I know through my gym. Last week she greeted me as I was leaving and mentioned a small Bible study that meets at Smokey John's barbeque restaurant on Tuesdays. Her comment seemed a little out of the blue, and I had forgotten about it until now.

I would like you to go to the Bible study today and bring the memoir you wrote. Ask Smokey to let you read it to the attendees. Tell him I told you to.

Whoa, He wasn't kidding when He said his request won't make sense to me! I am to walk into a Bible study I've never been to before, tell a man I've never met that Jesus wants me to read my memoir, and then read part of my personal journey in front of complete strangers?

"Jesus, they will think I am absolutely nuts! Why do you want me to do that?"

I have my reasons. Do you trust me?

"Yes, but——"

But nothing.

I sigh. "You want me to walk in faith to——"

Yes, He interrupts.

What can I say? I get out of the tub, get dressed, grab my memoir, look up the restaurant's address, and hop in the car with butterflies flapping in my stomach. Why, oh why, does Jesus want me to do this? I am not prepared. I have never spoken in front of a group of strangers before. What if they don't let me read it? I find myself wondering, yet again, if the Lord really asked me to do this. How do I distinguish between my own thoughts and His voice? I resign myself to going through with it. If the Lord really told me to do this, then it will all work out the way He said it will.

Half of the restaurant is set up for the Bible study. I approach a man sitting to the far left of the room, setting up a keyboard. We exchange hellos, and then he asks me if this is my first visit.

"Yes. Actually . . . the Lord sent me."

He nods his head and drawls, "He calls us all if we listen."

"I'm glad you feel that way. Maybe you'll be open-minded

when I tell you that the Lord called me here today to read a short memoir."

"Oh!" he replies, looking slightly surprised. "Did ya speak to Smokey 'bout it?"

"No, who is Smokey?"

"He's the man in charge of this here meetin.' If the Lord told you, then He'll have to tell Smokey too 'cause he's a little old-school and funny about women speakin.'"

I thank the man and find a seat, feeling panicky. "Lord, what is going on? Why did you ask me to do this? People are already giving me sideways glances!"

I am right here beside you. Thank you for being obedient.

When Smokey arrives, the man points him out to me and introduces us. He tells Smokey what I said about reading my memoir.

Smokey examines me for a few seconds before saying, "Hmmm, the Lord sent ya, huh? Well, He didn't say nuthin' to me 'bout it. 'Til He speaks to me, we'll carry on like we usually do."

Feeling defeated, I sit down again, my inner voice talking a mile a minute. This was stupid. Talking to Jesus silently in my head is one thing, but going around telling complete strangers what I hear Him say is quite another! If I'm supposed to speak here, Smokey would have agreed to it. Then again, the meeting hasn't begun yet. Jesus still has time to tell Smokey to let me read my memoir, in which case I might have to actually get up in front of thirty to forty people and read something I wrote! My hands begin to sweat, and I feel short of breath at the terrifying thought.

The meeting opens with hymns and prayers. Smokey begins speaking and does not acknowledge me. I notice he is talking in circles and not making much sense. He starts and stops a few times, glances at me, and addresses the group. "We're gonna do somethin' a little different today."

This must be it! The Lord must have spoken to him. I get even more nervous, but at least that means that Jesus really did want me to come here.

But Smokey looks at another man in the audience and says, "Hey, Johnny. Why don't you come on up here and give testimony to what the Lord is doin' in the lives of some of the folks in our group?"

I sink into my chair. So the Lord didn't speak to Smokey after all! My own silly imagination put me in this spot!

John gets up with a startled look on his face. "Okay . . . "

He talks for about five minutes, telling us about a few things going on with some of the group members. Like Smokey, he hesitates and stumbles over his words while he speaks, looking puzzled. He looks back at Smokey and says apologetically, "Well, that's all I got today. Cat must've got my tongue."

Smokey glances at me again, a little longer this time. Then he says, "Thanks, John. Brothers and sisters, we have a special visitor here today. She says the Lord asked her to pay us a visit and read a short story. Ma'am, come on up and introduce yourself. But let me tell ya . . . " He glances around the room and chuckles. "If we don't like what ya gotta say, we'll ask ya to leave!"

Though his voice is light-hearted, he shoots me a meaningful look.

I stand up shaky with nerves and self-doubt. "Help me, Lord!"

I am with you. I called you to do this for a reason.

As soon as I begin talking, my nervousness vanishes. I speak with an unfamiliar confidence, and my words flow with ease. "Hello. My name is Caren Bright. I don't know why, but Jesus wants me to share with you a memoir I wrote."

I tell my story about an abandoned and abused little girl who, in the midst of her bleak circumstances, found strength to carry on. She got lost for many years and made many, many poor decisions. Her life choices led her to a dark place filled with brokenness and despair. But God's love was bigger than any of her sins. He pursued her until she was ready to return home. He dusted her off and wiped her clean, and they picked up their friendship where they had left it twenty-eight years earlier.

When I finish reading, I feel as if I am coming out of a trance. I'm not sure exactly what happened or why. A few people approach me, some with tears in their eyes, and tell me how moved they are by my story. They believe God specifically wanted them to hear it. Of course I am happy that the Lord worked through me, but I am ready to leave. I feel overwhelmed and vulnerable. As I head for the door, a man stops me.

"Ma'am, that was an amazing story. You're a talented speaker and writer. I'm not sure what the Lord is doing, but I feel led to give you this phone number. Call this woman and tell her that Randy wants you two to get together. I'll be interested in hearing what comes out of this."

I thank him and take the phone number, wondering what it has to do with my story. Perhaps the woman is a publisher or author or something? I get into my car, my emotions high. "What are you doing, Lord? What are you up to?"

So many questions! I am proud of you for going on this date with me. Enjoy this moment and know that each step we take together is part of my plan for you. I want you to go home, relax, and reflect for a moment, and then I want you to call the number Randy gave you. We will be going on another date later today, so be prepared.

DATE 37
Meeting with a Stranger

I am stunned as I think about what happened this morning. I watched Smokey try to avoid letting me read my memoir, but he couldn't. He tried to give a sermon but couldn't think clearly enough. He literally grasped at words until he gave up and asked another man to take over. Then *that* man was inexplicably tongue-tied! Smokey finally allowed me to speak, albeit begrudgingly. I shake my head in amazement.

I look at the name and phone number a man gave me at the meeting. *Amity*. What am I supposed to do with this? I mean, of course I know I'm supposed to call the woman named Amity, but I don't even know her! What can I say without sounding insane? I would say I must be crazy to go through with it, but I just witnessed something equally crazy and unbelievable unfold that tells me I am not.

"Lord? Things are getting strange. I want to trust that today's events are part of your plan. Things like this cannot be explained logically in the real world. I feel safe with you in our own little world, but now you are asking me to be radical—to confess our relationship to others. Not that I want to hide it, but people today are quick to judge. Saying that Jesus 'told me to do something' is almost considered taboo."

Caren, dear, calm down. It is not as if we raised someone from the dead! I hear genuine amusement in His voice. *You read your memoir as I asked you to. That took courage, and I am proud of you. Some of the people in that room needed to hear what you read. Know that your story inspired and encouraged others. You are correct that many people dismiss those who speak about me because my name is often misused. So you must use discernment about when and with whom you discuss our relationship. However, if you live your life according to my plan, your actions will do most of the talking for you.*

That makes sense. However, I am still freaked out about calling the number.

"Who is this Amity person, and why am I calling her? Is she a publisher for the book? What is her role in my story? Where are you headed with this?"

I feel as if Jesus is smiling at me. *So many questions, sweet girl! Put one foot in front of the other—one step at a time. You will find freedom from worry and anxiety by simply focusing on the present moment without worrying about the end result. Right now, you have a phone number. You can do one of two things: call it, or do not call it.*

I ignore the whisper in my mind that mocks me for believing and deliberately switch gears. Laughingly I tell Jesus, "This is a bit like a treasure hunt! Turn here, go there, take four steps to the left, and dig a hole to find the treasure!"

Great analogy. I promise treasure at the end of this hunt, as well as throughout the rest of your journey. The beauty of faith is that it leads you to treasures unknown, treasures I am delighted to bestow upon you.

Finally, I call Amity. The conversation is not nearly as awkward as anticipated. She acknowledges knowing Randy and is eager to meet me. We make plans to meet at her house at 5:00 this afternoon. I hang up with the strangest sensation that I am a character in a movie. I am headed to meet a woman I do not know, for an unknown reason, to discuss an unknown subject!

***

I pull up to Amity's home in Highland Park, an affluent town in the middle of Dallas. Her house is so beautiful it's almost breathtaking. Amity greets me with enthusiasm, saying she is excited to see what the Lord is doing with us today. We say a quick prayer and then chat for a bit, getting to know each other. I share some of my story with her, both the good and the bad. I tell her about the book and about my relationship with the Lord. She is very receptive and shares her story with me as well. I am surprised to learn that she too has a constant dialogue with Jesus. She tells me that if I continue to listen, He will lead me to great places.

Amity suddenly takes my hand and looks me in the eye. She says in a serious tone of voice, "Caren, I believe the Lord sent you here for a few reasons. Number one: I think He wants me to tell you to let go of any remaining shame you carry. A few times as you spoke about your story, you hesitated and even hung your head. There is *no* reason to hold on to shame. Your story is incredible. Clearly the Lord is preparing to use you for an amazing purpose, and shame will only slow you down or even *prevent* you from being used in the colossal way He desires.

"Number two: I think the Lord wants me to encourage you to get connected to the Bible and to other believers. Following Christ and resisting worldly temptations is a battle—a good battle, but one that is difficult to fight alone. You need to know

God's Word and have His people beside you—mentors, pastors, friends, community, Bible studies. God is preparing you for something huge. It is time to build an army with Him.

"Number three: I firmly believe the Lord is indeed calling you to be a speaker and a writer, so hold on to that. You need direction and information about what is required to get a book published. I have a successful author friend who can help you.

"And most importantly, number four: I believe Jesus wants me to help you get His Word! You need a few scriptures close at hand for your journey. I will give you colorful construction paper, index cards, markers, and a glue stick. Go home right now and find at least seven Bible scriptures that speak to you. Write each one on an index card, paste the cards onto the paper, and decorate them the way you like. Keep these scriptures with you in your purse, around the house, and next to your bedside. When Jesus has a great call for His people, the enemy doesn't like it and will try to use your weaknesses to get to you. You can pull strength from scripture when you feel weak.

"Caren, I am glad the Lord sent you here today, and I am honored that He used me as a piece in your puzzle."

I leave Amity's home feeling simultaneously excited, spiritually exhausted, and overwhelmed. I have the same "is this real?" feeling that I did after the barbecue Bible study. This entire day feels like a *Choose Your Own Adventure* book. I don't know which option I want to choose nor what ending my choice will lead me to. Is the Lord truly going to use me for great things? I don't want to get my hopes up in case I am crazy, but if I am crazy, then everyone I met today is crazy as well!

All of this would be much easier if I could rid myself of doubt and simply trust and believe completely.

DATE 38
Walk to Emmaus Weekend

What peeth for me Lord?

For the last two weeks, I have been embracing Jesus' plan for me more and more. I am trying to mentally claim my new position: speaker and book writer for Christ. I follow up with Amity's author friend. She recommends I put together a book proposal to send to agents. She warns me that getting a literary agent interested in your work is very challenging. A proposal is vital. I think writing a proposal is important for another reason: confirming to myself that I am truly pursuing this path.

She sends me a link to a website that lists step-by-step instructions for writing a book proposal. When I look at the list of ten or so steps, I feel overwhelmed. I don't know how to do this! But the Lord tells me to tackle one thing at a time. He assures me that each step is doable on its own, and He will even send a friend to help me.

I got this

This morning I kick this "writer thing" up a notch. I sort all the notes I've taken, all the texts I've sent to Stewart, and all the photos I've snapped into chapters, and I begin transforming them into actual sentences and paragraphs. I work on the first chapter.

Caren, I absolutely love that you started turning your notes into chapters today! You are walking in faith a lot more lately. Beginning the book is another big step of faith. I would like to go on a weekend getaway with you. Are you interested?

"Am I ever! I'm sure you know that I've never been swept away for a weekend before. Where do you want to go?"

On a Walk to Emmaus Weekend.

That sounds familiar, but I don't know exactly what it is. I ask, "How do we make it happen?"

I want you to text three women from your old church, all of whom loved you very much: Mrs. Pam, D'Lane, and Libby. Tell them I have asked you to go.

Yikes! I haven't talked to them in a while. Getting a text out of the blue from me will seem strange to them.

Do not worry. Just text them.

I agree but want to know what the retreat is before I text.

You will see when you get there, dear. For now, know that the Walk of Emmaus is a seventy-two-hour spiritual retreat where you learn more about yourself, me, the body of believers, and interpersonal relationships.

It sounds nice. I want to develop relationships with people, but I've been in solitude so long I don't know where to begin. I long for a connection with others so deeply sometimes that I feel an almost-physical ache. Talking to the woman at the aquarium was wonderful, but I haven't reached out to anyone since then. I guess I am afraid of being hurt. How would I act? What would I say? Who should I be? Will others judge me? Will they think I'm weird? Being alone with Jesus feels safer than trying to make other friends.

I know your heart, Caren, which is exactly why I am suggesting this getaway. The body of believers is a beautiful thing that you are ready to experience.

I text the ladies as the Lord instructed. Their responses shock me. They simply agree without asking any questions! Libby agrees to sponsor me, D'Lane agrees to co-sponsor, and Pam signs off as my pastor. I am scheduled to attend the March 27 weekend.

I am unbelievably excited! A weekend with Jesus sounds wonderful, even though I don't know what the weekend entails. I feel completely loved by Him. I want to tell Him something important.

"Hey, Jesus. Guess what? I no longer doubt you are speaking to me! The day after I read my memoir and met with Amity was a turning point. I decided I had to make a choice: either believe I am delusional, meaning your voice and all the love I've felt from you has been a figment of my imagination, or believe you are truly speaking to me and act accordingly. When I thought about how many times you've proved your love and authenticity to me over these last thirty-seven dates, and how much more emotionally healthy I am since we began this journey, the choice was simple. I'd have to be insane NOT to believe in you! I have tried to overcome my emotional wounds by myself all of my adult life with no success . . . until I allowed you into my life. The amount of progress I've made in less than a year can only be attributed to you."

I am very happy to hear that. Now that you fully believe and trust in me, we are almost ready to move mountains. The one missing piece is the body.

"I am ready, as long as you stay beside me and teach me like you have thus far."

Deal!

***

Two weeks before our weekend getaway I get a disappointing text from Libby. She can no longer sponsor me because the dates of the retreat conflict with the date of a previously-scheduled surgery. Initially I feel gloomy. The Lord said I should go on the retreat. If it doesn't happen, what does that mean? But I am able to stop worrying fairly quickly and instead rely on my newfound faith. If Jesus said we're going on a Walk to Emmaus weekend, then we are!

I ask, "Jesus, I need a sponsor to attend the retreat. If Libby can't do it anymore, how can I go?"

Trust in me, love. Have faith the retreat will happen.

Okay. I can do that. I determinedly ignore the faint whisper of doubt.

***

Two days later, I receive a text from an old friend named Virginia. She tells me she would like to sponsor me since Libby can't. She also informs me that my old friends Trey and Amy have offered to watch my children while I am away.

I can't contain my excitement. I shout, "Jesus, you are a miracle worker!"

I've talked to these friends only a few times in the last several years. How can they be willing to take on extra work for me? Virginia and D'Lane are already sponsoring the entire event; now they are paying my fees, making all arrangements, and driving me to and from the retreat too. Trey and Amy are watching my children for seventy-two hours. D'Lane is taking care of our dog. Why? I have been flighty around them and completely abandoned our friendship for three years. Not only do they appear to have forgiven me for walking away, but they are also embracing me as if nothing ever happened!

My love is shining through them, dear. This is a beautiful example of the body as I intend it to be.

I remember back to my third date with God, when He led me to get a massage. I was lonely and angry that He wanted me to remain in solitude, and He assured me that when I was ready, we would work on restoring friendships. I must finally be ready.

"Thank you, Lord, for bringing my friends back to me. Please teach me how to be a true friend to them in return. They deserve my love, and I desire to give it to them. But I need to learn how to do so."

You will learn, my love, when the timing is perfect for you.

***

March 27 has finally arrived! I feel giddy with anticipation; Jesus wants to spend the entire weekend together! I am excited when He wants to spend time with me. I feel content and safe in His presence. When He asks me to do something, I trust it is in my and everyone else's best interest, even when I don't understand it. I have never trusted anyone this much. I look forward to spending more time with Him this weekend.

I have a wonderful time on the retreat. I learn about living a life of piety through God's grace in the body of Christ. I learn that each of us are to use our unique spiritual gifts in unity to fulfill the Lord's divine plan together. The weekend is filled with an astounding amount of love from the Lord and from others. I receive handmade gifts every day, made specifically for those of us on this retreat, Emmaus Walk #252, from people all around the world. I read dozens of cards and letters from people at home telling me how much I am loved, what I mean to them, and how proud they are that I have chosen to take this walk with Jesus. All of the attendees are surprised with a lovely candlelight vigil, in which at least 150 people from near and far come to sing songs of love to us. Hundreds of God's people have come together, each fulfilling a different role, to make our Walk to Emmaus weekend a success. And it is a success indeed!

When I return home, I am profoundly changed. The Lord's plan for me feels much more real. Truly understanding that I was perfectly created to fulfill a role only I can fill and to work with others as they fulfill their roles makes me feel special. I now understand that only togetherness can bring forth God's ultimate goal for mankind. We are like the human body, comprised of many parts to make a whole. An eye is an essential part of the body, but not a body in itself. Every single cell, strand of hair, finger, toe, tooth, and so on is of no use on its own but together, make a life-living, love-giving human being.

Wonderful, dear. You now understand a critical piece of my plan for you. You and I can do great things together, like feeding the homeless and handing out diapers, but we can do colossal things together when we do them in unity with the rest of my body.

"Thank you, Lord, for this weekend. Something tells me there was more to it than your wanting me to have a relaxing and spiritual time, though. You are preparing me for something, aren't you?"

Yes, indeed!

"I am ready, Jesus. Lead the way."

DATE 39
Pamper Lake Highlands Event

Since my Walk to Emmaus weekend with Jesus a week ago, my eyes are open to how much I have been missing out on by not having friendships. I haven't figured out how to engage with others consistently yet, but I definitely want to. I am starting to see how we all make up different parts of the body and how important it is to be close to people as we journey through life.

I enjoyed spending some time with D'Lane the other day. I was taken aback when, during our visit, she teared up and said, "Caren, I love you and have missed you. I am happy you are here, and I really hope you stick around this time." I never dreamed that any of my old friends liked me enough to miss me, much less loved me! She must have seen something in me back then that I couldn't see myself. For the first time I realize I am not the only one I hurt when I pulled away from people. I feel sad that I hurt D'Lane's feelings, and I resolve not to run away from friendships again.

Jesus and I have spent more time together this week, and I am considering going to church to be around other believers.

There is one problem, though, which I tell Him about.

"Lord, I'd like to try church again, but I can't because I work a double shift on Sundays."

Do not worry. When the time is right, I will help you with that. Caren, we had a wonderful time at the retreat last weekend. Are you ready to take the next step of our journey? I would like to do another outreach project together.

I remember the diaper giveaway. "Sure, we can do something like that again."

I have something different in mind this time that involves you, me, and the body in your community. I want to do an outreach event that will lead to transforming lives.

An event? That sounds a lot more involved than setting up a table with my daughter and handing out diapers. I answer skeptically, "Umm . . . this is *me* you're talking about, Jesus."

Yes, it is.

"Look, Lord. People always help me, not the other way around. I don't have much money or education. I've made some bad decisions in the past and plenty of people in this close-knit Lake Highlands community are aware of them. I doubt they will take me seriously. More likely, they will gossip about me. I think it's best if I stay under the radar or reach out to a different community where nobody knows me. I simply don't have the resources or skills to pull off a community event."

You are correct. You cannot do this on your own. But with my help, you can. You can motivate an entire community to help us. But you must take one step at a time, knowing I will not leave you. Do you trust me?

"Yes, 100 percent! But . . . "

Caren, do you trust me?

I sigh. "Yes."

Then you know I would not ask you to do anything that is not in the best interest of all involved. You are ready to take the next step toward the calling I have for you.

"Okay, but you know I'm scatterbrained. I can barely organize my *day* let alone an entire event! And I don't have a platform. How can I rally an entire community?"

You and I will do this together. Do you remember the story of a man named Moses? I used him to lead the Israelites out of Egypt and into the promised land. Caren, <u>I do not call the equipped; I equip the called.</u> I will go before you and walk beside you. You can do this because I will give you the words to say and the strength you need, one step at a time. Have faith in me.

"Okay, Jesus, I trust you. Where do we begin?"

He asks me what community need I feel passionate about. My answer is diapers, of course. Many families are oppressed and have few resources. Parents can at least get help with food and shelter from government programs, but I know from experience that none of the programs provide diapers. You can't even use food stamps to buy diapers. The result is that parents have to keep their babies in the same diapers for longer than they are intended to be used, which causes painful diaper rashes. Most can't use cloth diapers because they have limited or no access to washing machines. When there is no money for diapers, their babies have to go without, soiling themselves, their clothes, beds, carpets, and the like.

"Surely if my community knew about this problem, they would help, wouldn't they?" I ask.

Yes, they would.

That's a nice thought. But . . . "How will distributing diapers transform lives?"

I like how you think. That part will come. First we create awareness. Then we create change. One step at a time.

***

Over the next five to six weeks, the Lord makes great things happen. He directs me to one person, who connects me to the next, and so on. I come up with "Pamper Lake Highlands" as the name of the event, and I learn with relief that my play on the word Pampers® does not break any laws. I secure a venue at the neighborhood rec center for June 14. A friend gets me a write-up in the local paper, and the article ends up informing and inspiring the community. As the word begins to spread, diaper donations begin trickling in. I don't have much storage space in my house, so a local realty company, Nathan Grace Real Estate, volunteers to collect and store them for me.

I am still unclear where this is headed. Sure, giving underprivileged folks a ton of diapers is amazing and meets an important short-term need. But a one-time gift of diapers doesn't solve the long-term problems associated with poverty.

Very insightful, Caren. You have hit upon our next step. To get there, you must begin to share some of our story.

"Our story?"

Yes, our story. Think about it. I have pursued you since you left me at age ten. Many people assisted me in my pursuit. Remember who you were when you moved to Texas twelve years ago. Reflect for a moment about how much you have learned and changed. Think about the men and women from Lake Highlands whom I placed in your life to help, love, support, and mentor you and your children.

At first I am in denial. But realization quickly dawns . . . how could I be so blind? This community supported me from day one. The mothers of my children's classmates befriended me. People at the church I attended befriended me. I became a better mom by watching others model good parenting, something

I had never witnessed before. D'Lane gave me the priceless gift of encouraging me to see a therapist. A few other friends helped me lose weight by getting up at 6:00 a.m. three times a week to walk around the high school track with me. I learned the importance of education, which led me to attend classes at the community college (some paid for by generous friends) and obtain my GED. This community literally helped rebuild me! And the whole time, I took everyone for granted. I assumed all who helped me did so to check off their good deeds for the week and feel better about themselves. I accepted their help almost begrudgingly, not liking the feeling of being a charity case. I saw their words and actions through the lens of my own twisted perception of humanity. I was so convinced I was unlovable that I didn't perceive their overtures as acts of love.

"Lord, I had it so wrong! Those people embraced me and my family. They were an example of the Church, letting you work through them to pursue us. I feel horrible!"

You were terribly wounded, dear. You could not even accept my love, so it is not surprising you were unable to accept love from my people.

"But how can I make amends now that I understand?"

Continue to walk with me. I am the great restorer, repairer, and re-deemer. It is time to use your story to demonstrate how, with my guidance, a community can help break the cycle of poverty. Share the key elements that worked for you.

What helped me? Being in a community of faith, even though I didn't "buy in" to all they were preaching. Counseling. Help with parenting skills. Education. Breaking free from addictive behavior. Learning to take better care of my body. Imagine if we could help provide these things for other oppressed people in the community! We could attract people with the gift of diapers and then offer them help in these areas. If the community gives downtrodden families the kind of help they gave me, those families have a chance of defeating abject poverty like I did!

"You are a genius, Jesus! I'm even more amazed to learn you've been walking beside me this entire time. I never realized that even when I refused to believe in you, you were busy loving me through an entire community!"

I am finally completely free from the prison of feeling unlovable. Words cannot adequately describe how exhilarating this is. I feel love and strength like I've never known before. I see life in a new light. Instead of feeling like a soiled, defeated, broken mess of a woman, I feel washed clean, built up, and redeemed. Jesus is not a myth. He is real! And I am honored to let Him use me for His purpose.

***

I write a letter to the community, sharing part of my story. I explain that I was raised in an abusive home, dropped out of high school, and entered the world with no life skills and no experience of love. I write that I had no self-worth. Weighing in at 275 pounds, I ended up in a homeless shelter with my little boy, who took his first steps there. I confess that my son went without clean diapers because I had no money. But then I describe how my life changed after moving here, how this community mentored me—how they took my hand and led my family across the bridge from an oppressed life to something greater. I assert that together we can do the same to bring others in our community out of poverty. Through various contacts, the letter finds its way into the hands of several school's communication volunteers who email it to hundreds of parents in the community. My story breathes new life into the campaign, and diapers and offers of help flood in.

Over the next three weeks, the momentum builds for the Pamper Lake Highlands event. I worry more than a few times. I fear that people will think the idea is silly or that I am a loony bin case. I'm afraid the event won't be successful, we won't receive enough diapers, we won't reach enough people in need, or that I'm not qualified to lead an event of this magnitude. Every time I doubt, the Lord reminds me of His power and love. He reminds me that He has chosen me to do this and that I am uniquely qualified to be His voice. He will do the rest. His assurance keep me going.

With the help of hundreds of people in the community, plans fall into place. I get a Pamper Lake Highlands logo designed with the tag line "We Are His Hands and Feet." Banners, yard signs, and table signs are printed. A native Spanish speaker translates for me so I can print in both English and Spanish. In addition to 15,000 diapers, 500 hot dogs, chips, and waters are donated. Some people bring tables. Others sponsor bounce houses. A few volunteer to man the tables where they will distribute diapers and encourage people to sign up for future English as a Second Language, parenting, nutrition, and GED classes. A few more volunteer to set up and clean up. We advertise by passing out flyers in low-income housing areas.

June 14 arrives. I am a nervous wreck at first, but all (well, most!) goes smoothly. The Pamper Lake Highlands event is a tremendous success. Approximately 175 people receive diapers, and most of them sign up for at least one class. The volunteers bring loads of energy and community spirit as they become more acutely aware of their neighbors' struggles. It becomes obvious that Jesus is seeking both volunteers and those in poverty, just as He sought me and my family. I meet two women and their children who have recently become homeless. I meet a woman who lost her five-month-old baby girl less than a month ago. She is grieving deeply, and today is the first time she has left her house since the tragedy. I am amazed watching the Lord work in all of these people's lives simultaneously.

Something else amazes me. I am overwhelmed and humbled by the way the Lord has taken what used to be my source of shame—my sinful, broken past—to help others. He told me He would, and I trusted it would happen, but hearing and believing something is vastly different than experiencing it firsthand. I am blown away.

When I get home from the event, I drop to my knees. "Jesus, thank you so much for teaching me and using me to help others. How amazing you are! The love you have for your people is so strong and deep, it is almost tangible. Your love is growing inside me, making me feel love for others like I've never experienced before. To think that almost a year ago I wanted to die! Thank you for healing me and giving me purpose. I love you!"

I love you, darling. Keep following me.

DATE 40
One-Year Anniversary

I feel frustrated and discontent this morning. The Pamper Lake Highlands event was almost two weeks ago, and nothing important has happened since. I have accepted and claimed my purpose as revealed to me by the Lord, but now I feel like He has left me hanging. I know that sounds silly, but I can't help feeling that perhaps He has lost interest in me or needs a break from me. I share my feelings with Stewart via text, and he responds, "Striving to be better is positive. But equally important is to celebrate the past and your progress. In addition to living and enjoying the present moment . . . " Stewart's advice makes sense, yet my disgruntled feelings continue.

I feel like I've been climbing out of a very deep hole for eighteen years, and while I'm proud of all I've accomplished and overcome in that time, I am weary of climbing. I want to reach my destination already! But I don't feel competent enough to fulfill my purpose yet, which indicates more climbing lies ahead. Not only that, but I also feel a little lost right now. Life is huge with many roads to choose from. How am I to choose the correct path? Between being a single mom of three children, working long hours as a waitress, and trying to prepare for this beautiful purpose I am supposed to fill, I am spread thin.

"Jesus, I need to spend time with you. I am feeling lost."

Caren, do you know what day it is? Look at the calendar.

My calendar tells me it is June 26, 2014. Exactly a year since my first date with the Lord. I almost took my own life that day, but I went paddle boarding with God instead.

"Today is our anniversary! You remembered, and I forgot!"

Of course I remember. It is a special day. One year ago you called out to my Father. Would you like to celebrate by paddle boarding again?

"Yes! I'd love to! Oh, Lord, I was beginning to think you left me."

Caren . . .

"I know. I should know better by now!"

He laughs at me. *You will learn.*

***

As we pull up to the lake, butterflies of excitement dance in my stomach. Confident this time, I rent a paddle board, drag it into the lake, and stand up immediately. I've got this! I glance toward the beautiful center part of the lake, but I head down the dingy stream to the right, where we paddled a year ago. The cute turtles and ducks make me smile. I am glad to see them. I am struck by how different I am from a year ago. I am completely present. I notice the beauty around me without effort. A year ago I was dissociated from the world. I lived in what I called my "mind's maze." I was so busy trying to break free of my labyrinth of hurtful thoughts and feelings that I couldn't pay attention to anything else. When God prodded me to look around the lake as I paddled last year, I remember feeling startled by all the colors, plant life, and animals. Noticing God's beauty is no longer foreign to me. What a different life I live now!

I look around again. I appreciate all I see, but I don't want to be here this time.

"Lord, why can't we go to the other side of the lake now?"

I never said you should not.

"Oh! I guess I assumed you wanted me to start over here."

You are funny, Caren. Sometimes you move so quickly that you forget to ask for direction.

I laugh. He's right! But actually I am glad I went this way first. Seeing this side of the lake is a great reminder of where I started. I was a truly broken woman then. I am so grateful to the Lord for building me into the person I am today.

I want you to know you are good enough, Caren. Your heart is pure and open, so you are teachable. I am in awe of the diligence and drive that brought you to this point in your life. I am proud of you.

"Thank you. That means everything to me."

Ready to go to the other side of the lake?

"More ready than you know . . . that is, if you weren't Jesus and didn't already know everything!"

I turn my board around and paddle quickly toward the deeper water. I glide under a bridge and am greeted by a breathtaking view of the lake. In the distance, the expansive body of water meets a blue sky peppered with white, fluffy clouds. A few sailboats and kayaks dot the water. The sun shines brightly. I begin to paddle even more quickly. I can't wait to get there! After a few minutes, I slow down. I wonder where I am rowing to. The lake is miles wide. I can't reach the skyline, and I can't reach the other side of the lake on a paddle board! I am amused at myself. I am finally in the middle of the beautiful lake—where I longed to be—and instead of enjoying it, I am paddling as fast as I can to get further out! I stop paddling altogether and allow myself to float for a while. The gentle waves of the clean water feel peaceful. I look down and notice hundreds of minnows of varying sizes surrounding my board. I enjoy watching them swim hither and thither, and I'm amazed at the way each type of minnow stays with its own school of fish.

Stewart's words from this morning come back to me. This experience demonstrates exactly what he was saying! I can look at the lake behind me and appreciate how far I have come, and I can look at the lake ahead of me and yearn to go farther, imagining what being closer to the skyline would be like, but I should also observe the beauty of the waters I am in right now, today. If I hadn't, I would have missed the cute little minnows zipping around. I would have missed how quiet and relaxing it is to float here.

The discontented feeling finally leaves me. I am going to enjoy my life for what it is today. I appreciate how much healthier I am, emotionally and spiritually. I will simply *be* once in a while. I will celebrate what I have now. Jesus is good for bringing me here to spend time with Him to celebrate our relationship.

"Thank you, Lord, for the unique confirmation of how far I have come, the pleasant and peaceful present, and the beauty that lies in my future. I am ready to relax and enjoy myself with you." I lie back on the paddle board, enjoying the feel of the waves and the warmth of the sun.

I like that idea. Enjoy this moment. There is no rush to get to the next. We will begin our next adventure in my perfect timing. For now, enjoy life as it is. We have much more work to do together. Be patient and follow my lead.

DATE 41
Lake House with Friends

Today's July heat is suffocating, even for Dallas, so Victoria and I readily accept D'Lane's invitation to come over and go swimming. Having friends again is nice, and the appreciation I feel for my friends is even nicer. I've spent more time with D'Lane lately. We even attend a Bible study together. D'Lane has changed spiritually since I knew her eleven years ago. She committed to sobriety from alcohol, and seeing her thrive brings me joy.

My daughter goes for a swim while D'Lane and I sunbathe on lounge chairs and chat. We talk about how much we love our Bible study. I tell her how much I like our teacher, Marsha Holmes. She seems wise and exudes the love of Jesus. I sense a depth of knowledge in her, and I suspect I've seen only a glimpse of what she has to offer. D'Lane looks thoughtful and says, "I'm not sure why, but I think you, Marsha, and I should spend a weekend together at her lake house sometime. I'll ask her and will get back to you by the end of the weekend."

The possibility of having "those types of friends" is excit-

ing—friends you are so comfortable with that you can spend
a weekend together talking, laughing, sharing meals, and the
like without feeling self-conscious. In the past, the thought of
sharing an entire weekend with my friends would have terrified
me. Spending even a few hours together was stressful because
I couldn't be myself. I believed I had to prove to my friends
that I was likable, so I constantly analyzed my words and actions. Thoughts like "I should try to make a joke right now" and
"I should clean their kitchen or cook them something to show
what a good friend I am" ran through my head regularly. Before
I added to a conversation, I'd scrutinize my words to make sure
I wouldn't sound stupid or offend anyone. I worried that I liked
my friends more than they liked me. If I could tell a friend truly
liked me, I feared that once she found out what I was really like,
she would lose interest. You can see why being with people was
so daunting to me. It was a lot of work!

***

When I get home from working my usual Saturday double-shift,
I listen to a voice message from D'Lane. Marsha wants us to
come to her lake house in two weeks! This gives me time to
arrange my work schedule, and since we'll be gone only Friday
and part of Saturday, Dae can watch Reggie and Victoria while
I'm gone. I am so excited.

"Thank you, Jesus! You must have orchestrated the timing
of this getaway so that it works out perfectly for me. I love that
you are giving me friends! I am still a bit nervous, though. Do
you think they'll notice my underdeveloped social skills?"

*You are welcome. Marsha and D'Lane are good friends for you, and
you are a good friend for them. Do not be afraid to tell them about being in*

solitude for years and not being used to true friendships. The purpose of the weekend is to bring you all together in fellowship, allowing you to share your stories about your lives before you drew close to me.

***

Friday morning arrives, and D'Lane and I drive to Marsha's lake house together. I drive D'Lane's car because she dislikes driving long distances, and the lake house is about an hour away. Her car doesn't have an automatic transmission. I haven't driven a stick in years, but she has confidence I can do it. She says, "It's like riding a bike. Once you know how, you don't forget."

We have a great time talking and laughing together the entire way. When we arrive in town, we stop at the local grocery store to buy food for the weekend, and then we stop at a rural fruit stand where farmers are selling fresh peaches and tomatoes. As D'Lane predicted, I had no problem driving on the highway, but I am having a little bit of difficulty driving on these country roads. As I drive up the sloped fruit stand driveway onto the street, the car stalls. We are halfway in the driveway and halfway in the street, and a car is approaching rapidly on my left. I freeze. D'Lane's calm voice snaps me out of my panic. "Just let off the brake, and you'll roll back down the hill." I follow her instructions, and the car eases backward as the oncoming car zooms past. My heart is beating so hard I think it might escape from my chest.

"D'Lane, I almost got us killed!"

She says with a smile, "You did fine. Let's get back on the road so we can get to the lake house."

I offer a silent prayer to the Lord. "Thank you for keeping us safe! And gosh, Lord, I really love D'Lane. Thank you for such a calm, understanding friend."

We arrive at the lake house, greeted by Marsha at the door. She hugs us and then gives us a tour. The house is pretty and spacious, and the outside view is stunning. An expansive back-yard meets the lake where a dock sits topped by a beautiful sun deck. Instead of feeling envy, I derive pleasure from seeing all the Lord has blessed Marsha and her family with.

The three of us throw on our swimsuits, grab rafts, and float on the water while we talk and share stories. D'Lane encourag-es me to tell Marsha about my journey with Christ and about the book I am writing. I'm scared and self-conscious at first, but thinking about how the Lord has redeemed me and wants to use our story to help others allows me to push away my fear. I instead feel eager to recount the miracles my children and I have experienced. D'Lane shares her equally incredible story about accepting and walking with Christ. Marsha does more listening than talking. I notice what a good listener she is—pres-ent, engaged, seemingly very interested—and I resolve to learn to do the same.

Hours pass in an instant. Eventually hunger brings us back inside. Together we prepare a delicious grilled salmon dinner, eat, and then head to the dock to watch the sun set. Marsha shares her story with us then, and I listen intently. I am thrilled to hear how Jesus has worked in these ladies' lives. It is fascinat-ing how He has used all of our pasts as stepping stones to pre-pare us for this fellowship with each other. Equally enthralling is the way in which each of us hears the Lord. Marsha hears Him mostly through His Word in the Bible. D'Lane hears Him speak through circumstances and through other people. I am reminded of what Jesus said to me on Valentine's Day. He interacts with each of us in a unique way that speaks to us best.

At 10:30 we decide to go to sleep so that we can get up early enough to see the sun rise tomorrow. I sink into my bed, supremely comfortable, whether from the quality of the mattress or from a long day of fellowship in the sun, or both. I have been talking silently to the Lord throughout the day, mostly thanking Him for the opportunity to be with other women who love Him. A few times I regressed to feeling slightly self-conscious and wondering what the women thought of me, but each time the Lord gently reminded me to stay in the present and be myself. I fall asleep basking in the glow of my newfound friendships. I have waited a long time for friends, and these ladies were worth the wait.

***

We awake at the crack of dawn. The sunrise is gorgeous. Marsha and D'Lane watch from lawn chairs in the backyard, but I climb up on the sun deck for a better view. It stands so high that I see only the water and the glow of the sun barely peeking above it. I take a picture and send it to Stewart, wishing the camera could capture the beauty of the moment. I want to share this experience with him, and I have a pang of longing, wishing he loved me as deeply as I love him. I want nothing more than for my sweet Stewart to know the Jesus I know. I want him to believe that the Lord truly answers prayer in wondrous ways. I hope that through witnessing my journey, Stewart will be inspired to draw closer to Jesus.

With a shake of my head, I put Stewart out of my mind and return to the present. I climb down and join the girls to watch the sun make the rest of its ascent. After breakfast we return to the lake to swim, float, and chat some more. The conversation is lighter today, and I relax into genuine camaraderie, abandoning all my insecurities. All too soon it is time to pack up and drive back to Dallas. I leave feeling refreshed and energized.

What an amazing weekend. For the first time in my adult life I was at ease being myself around others. God has changed my heart, my mind, and my soul. The proof is the vast difference between my past relationships and my relationships today. What joy! What freedom! What lightness of heart! I am no longer mired in worry about how others view me. Instead I take pride in being exactly who I am in Jesus Christ.

DATE 42
Five Days and a Minivan

Since the lake house weekend, my friendships with D'Lane and Marsha have strengthened. For the most part, I am able to genuinely engage with them without running away. The difference between my friendships now and my friendships before my solitude with the Lord is enormous. Being with friends is relaxing and enjoyable now, not an exhausting exercise in hiding how broken I am and analyzing what to do and say to make people like me. I love that I can be myself with my friends. I love the new me—a woman with integrity and purpose who is secure in herself. As I finish getting ready for a 1:00 lunch date with Marsha, I thank Jesus for all He has done in my life and especially for my new friendship with Marsha. I am looking forward to seeing her.

I brace myself for an unpleasant, sweltering ride as I climb into my van. At the beginning of summer, its air conditioning quit working again. That would be bad enough in the Dallas summer (102 degrees today), but my windows are still permanently stuck in the up position, except for those couple of inches on the driver's side, so I can't even roll them down to circulate the hot air. At each stoplight, I open my door briefly for a few seconds of relief.

Not surprisingly, my van failed inspection the last time I took it in to the shop. I don't have the money to make the necessary repairs, so my inspection tags are expired. Last week a police officer pulled me over and gave me a ticket I can't afford. I have been asking the Lord for months to provide me an affordable, dependable vehicle, but He keeps telling me to be patient. I know He loves me and provides for me, but asking me to be patient while my only mode of transportation is falling apart seems inappropriate. I can't figure out a solution to the problem. I don't have enough money to buy a used vehicle. My credit is shot from living irresponsibly in the past, thus any loan I'd be able to secure would come with a high interest rate. Even if I were to get a loan, the most I can afford to pay is $150 per month, which is unrealistically low for a car note. I can't imagine why the Lord wants me to continue driving around in this blazing hot van illegally, but I know of no other options, so all I can do is wait.

Marsha and I have a great time at lunch. We gab the whole time about a myriad of subjects, including our faith in the Lord. I thoroughly enjoy hearing about her relationship with Jesus because it is different than mine yet equal in magnitude. At one point I sense that the Lord wants me to tell Marsha about my car situation. Talking about it takes courage. This is the type of thing I hid from friends in the past for fear they would judge me harshly and peg me as being irresponsible. I buck up and tell her all about it. I even confess that my general manager told me to go to a seedy shop in Dallas that sells fake inspection stickers. I am conflicted. I don't want to break the law, but I am breaking the law whether I drive around with my real expired sticker or a fake up-to-date one. At least a fake sticker will prevent me from getting another ticket I can't afford. Marsha doesn't appear shocked or dismayed at my confession. Instead she thinks for a few seconds and suggests we both pray about it for three days.

"Why three days?" I ask her.

She smiles. "Well, Jesus was raised from the dead in three days. Surely He can solve a vehicle dilemma in three days!"

I love her confidence in the Lord! Seeing others trust Him like I trust Him lifts my spirits. Marsha and I pray together before leaving the restaurant. As I wait at a stoplight, sweating and letting in fresh air through my door, a horn honks. Marsha waves at me from the next lane to get my attention. She tells me by mouthing words and pantomiming that she is not going to use her car's air conditioning during our three days of prayer. I mouth, "Why?" and she responds, "Because Jesus told me not to!" Wow. I love it! Somebody else is doing something a little wacky simply because Jesus told her to!

I continue home as I talk to the Lord excitedly. "Wow, Jesus! What is happening here? You're talking directly to Marsha now too? She usually hears you speak to her through the Bible!"

Dear, this is our next date: Seventy-two hours of prayer.

"So we are sharing this date with Marsha? That's not how our dates usually work."

You are correct. It is time to bring others from the body of believers into our journey. Pray, have faith in me, and enjoy the experience.

When I reach home, I begin praying in earnest for the Lord to show me a solution to my van problem. I pray off and on throughout the rest of the day as I go about my usual business. I know that breaking the law is sinful, so I begin to wonder if the Lord wants me to stop using my car altogether, at least through these seventy-two hours of prayer. We live fairly close to most of the places we go—the children's schools, a grocery store, their friends' houses—so we could walk or find rides, I suppose. The real problem is that I work tomorrow night, so I would need to find a way to get to my restaurant in Highland Park. Perhaps I could take the DART train instead of driving.

I pick up the boys from football camp at the high school and tell them about my latest date with Jesus. I explain Marsha and I are praying about our situation for seventy-two hours and that I am contemplating not using the van during that time. They are horrified at the thought of walking everywhere in this heat. They try to talk me out of it.

I call DART when we reach home and learn that, because of construction, the DART route from the station near my house to Highland Park is currently an hour-and-a-half train ride. I also learn that the train stops running at 10:00 p.m. I work later than that, so the train is not a viable option after all.

***

I begin praying on Day Two as soon as I awake. Within the hour, D'Lane calls me. She has been out-of-town the last few days, helping a friend move her mother into a memory care facility near Austin. D'Lane tells me, "Now that my friend's mom can't drive, my friend's father has an extra vehicle. He is considering selling his minivan. I'm calling you because I have a strong feeling that the Lord wants me to purchase it for you and allow you to pay me back in installments that fit your budget. Her father isn't 100 percent sure he wants to sell it, so before I pursue buying it from him, I want to make sure you are interested."

My jaw drops. I am speechless. I get ahold of myself and ask D'Lane, "Did Marsha tell you about our seventy-two hours of prayer?"

She has no idea what I'm talking about. This is mind-boggling! I excitedly explain. I am so wound up that D'Lane asks me to slow down at one point. When I finally get the whole story out, she says, "Okay. You and Marsha keep praying, and I will join you. I think we should complete the seventy-two hours in case Jesus has something else in mind for you. If no other solution presents itself, and my friend's father decides to part with his minivan, then I will consider that confirmation that I am supposed to buy his van for you."

I hang up with D'Lane and immediately call Marsha. With sheer exhilaration, I share what happened. She is equally thrilled and believes we have received our answer, but agrees to complete the seventy-two hours of prayer just in case.

I hang up and think hard about what these two women are sacrificing for me. D'Lane is offering to loan me a large sum of money, trusting I will be able to pay her back eventually. Marsha is driving around in July Texas heat without air-conditioning, even though she has no logical reason whatsoever to suffer; she has plenty of money and a nice car. Both are praying relentlessly for a few days on my behalf. And why? Simply because Jesus asked them to. I am humbled. I thank Jesus for placing these women into my life and orchestrating this beautiful experience.

D'Lane, Marsha, and I continue to pray for the entire seventy-two hours. In the end we all agree that D'Lane's minivan connection is the Lord's solution. D'Lane returns to Dallas, and the following day she, her two daughters, Fiona and Sally, my daughter Victoria, and I drive to Austin together. My sons stay home, and I do not tell them where we are going. I want to surprise them. We have a blast on the three-hour drive. We play travel games, stop for dinner, and talk with each other as if we are one big happy family.

We pick up the van but do not head home right away. Instead we spend some time with the father of D'Lane's friend. Seeing how heartbroken he is about his wife's decline is emotionally draining, but he perks up a little as he tells us about his wife. He brings out photos of her and shows us her sewing room. I appreciate the nice visit. We load the children in the van, and I follow D'Lane back to Dallas. I can't possibly thank her enough, but I can be a consistent and loving friend in return.

We arrive home, and I bring the boys outside to show them what Jesus brought us. They are surprised and happy and want to celebrate. We all get in the van, put the air conditioning on full blast, and drive to get celebratory ice cream shakes. I am thrilled they were able to witness first-hand that Jesus answers prayer.

It is nearing midnight by the time I settle down after our long and miraculous day. I am exhausted but content as I crawl into bed and curl up with my pillow. "Jesus, you are incredible. Thank you for all the love I felt the last few days. I can't believe that only five days after starting our prayer fest, I have a new minivan! Thank you for taking care of me."

You are welcome, Caren. I gave you this date to provide you with a working vehicle, but just as importantly, to give you the experience of working with others in my name. Not only am I moving inside your heart, but I am also moving in the hearts of the people in the world around you. I want to build your faith in me and my people. The next steps of our journey require that you understand you are not to work alone. I will call the body to help you fulfill your purpose.

"Thank you! I know I don't deserve this kind of love, but I accept it. What you are telling me makes me nervous, but eager too. Continue to lead the way, Jesus. I love you and will follow you."

I think about how my past relationships were usually secret. Oftentimes nobody but the person I was friends with or dating and I knew about our relationship. Up until the last few months, I even kept my dates with the Lord mostly between us. As I fall asleep, I marvel at how much more rewarding it is to share my relationship with Jesus.

DATE 43
Redbox and Popcorn

In the three weeks since the Lord provided us a minivan, we have moved from our rental house to an apartment. Even though the landlords at the rental house are amazing, I desperately needed to move because I couldn't afford the rent anymore. I didn't think any apartment would accept me due to my poor credit, but with the Lord's help, I secured an affordable apartment a few miles away. D'Lane, Virginia's husband, Mike, and both families' children helped us move. Carrying all our belongings up three flights of stairs with no elevator was no easy task, but my friends helped me cheerfully. Once again I am humbled by their capacity for generosity. They are wonderful role models, and I am consciously trying to be as helpful to others as they are to me.

We settled into our apartment, which is quite nice, but I feel restless. My life consists mostly of working and taking care of the children. Money is too tight to do much outside of the house. I've been thinking about Stewart even more than usual, fantasizing about what it would be like to share a cozy home and family with him. I still long for the day he falls in love with me, so much so that sometimes I literally ache for him. Intellectually I know we are probably not meant to be together, but my heart doesn't want to let go of the fantasy.

I think one reason I'm dwelling on Stewart is that I am a little bored with my current "vanilla" life. There has been no excitement for a while. Life is standing still. The Lord said we would do great things together, but we aren't doing much of anything anymore. Sharing these kinds of feelings with the Lord has always helped before, so I give it a shot.

"Jesus, I don't want to offend you, but I am feeling nervous and antsy. Stewart doesn't reciprocate my love, I am stuck waitressing, and quite frankly, I am a little bored with this "goody two shoes" life. I know it sounds ungrateful because you took me out of my darkness, and my life is obviously much better than before. But now life feels monotonous! Do you want me to be content with this domestic, abstinent life from now on? Aren't we going to move forward onto the great things you said we will do together? Have you left me? Are you mad at me? Did you find someone better equipped to carry out your plan?"

Sweet, Caren. You are precious. I know where your insecurities stem from. I will help you work through your childhood issue.

I am a little offended. "Excuse me, are you saying I am acting like a *child*?"

Yes, like a seven-year-old child, to be exact. You were temporarily living with your father, and your mother promised to pick you up for the weekend. You were a good girl all week in anticipation. Finally, Saturday came, and you waited for your mom on the stairs, staring out the glass door. Every time a white car passed, your heart raced with excitement at the thought it might be her. She never came for you that weekend, though. In fact, she did not come for two years. Sweetheart, I am very, very sorry that happened to you.

Tears sting my eyes at the painful memory. "Lord, why bring up such an awful thing?"

To help you recognize that your reaction to your current circumstance is based on a negative past experience, not on what is truly happening today. I want you to work through the memory so it no longer has power over you.

"How do you expect me to feel, Lord?" I ask, hurt. "I've done everything you asked me to do, but you haven't spoken to me about your plan in over three weeks. You hold all the cards. I am dependent on you to tell me what my next move is, just like I was dependent on my mother to pick me up that day. I am growing weary and disheartened waiting for you as I did waiting for her. She devastated me by not keeping her promise. You promised that you have a special purpose for my life, and I can't bear the thought that you might go back on your promise and leave me to work as a waitress the rest of my life!"

I know, dear. Being severely let down at such a critical time in your emotional development makes trusting the word of others truly difficult. Stepping back and observing the reality of the past three weeks will help you. Think about it. Every day we have grown together. Every day you have gotten a step closer to where you need to be. You needed to get a few things in your life in order before taking on any more tasks.

I think about it, and realize I have been pretty busy with mundane, yet important, tasks lately. Of course there was getting the van. Then there was moving into a new apartment. The new school year started, and I had to register Victoria for second grade and Reggie for ninth grade—a big transition from junior high into high school—and buy the required school supplies. I helped Dae take the steps needed to make his dream of joining the United States Marines real. The Lord is right. I have been busy! If Jesus had asked me to work on the next big chapter in my life during these last few weeks, I wouldn't have had time to support my children in the way they needed.

Exactly. I have allowed you time to be present for your family—your first responsibility and most important calling.

Wow. I feel chastened. I am so busy focusing on my future calling that I overlooked the gift of my children and my calling of motherhood. Once again I have taken for granted the amazing things happening in my life right now.

"I am so sorry, Lord! How do you put up with me?"

Easy. I love you and know your heart, Caren. No matter how many times you stumble, you are always open to learning.

"Thank you. I am grateful you don't give up on me."

Would you like to have a date today? A movie named Noah *was released on DVD recently. Rent it from Redbox, pop some popcorn, get cozy on the couch, and we can watch a movie together.*

***

As Jesus told me, *Noah* was available at the nearby Redbox. I finish popping the popcorn and get comfy on the sofa. I briefly imagine what Jesus would look like if He were sitting next to me. I laugh at myself because I can't help but picture Him the way He is depicted in movies and pictures: olive skin tone, beautifully chiseled face, dark hair with a beard, a white robe, and sandals. Though I can't see Him or touch Him or know what He truly looked like, I find comfort in being with Him. When I am on a date with the Lord, I feel as if time stands still.

I can't remember the last time I've been excited to watch a movie, but I sure am now. I grab the remote and press play. I don't even fast-forward past the previews because I want this date to last as long as it can. The movie is clearly made for the big screen and includes scenes that are not in the Bible; however, I still enjoy being reminded of the story of Noah. God had a plan for Noah since his childhood. He chose him specifically to be a father and husband and to build an ark in preparation for a flood of epic proportions. Noah was obedient, so the Lord used him and his family for a mighty purpose. I have no doubt that had Noah refused the task asked of him, God would have accomplished His goal another way. But because Noah was open and teachable, he and his family were blessed. Noah had the honor of being the right man for the right job, so to speak, and the same holds true for Moses, Ruth, David, Paul, Martin Luther King, and many others.

Yes, Caren. I still use people to accomplish mighty tasks. All people on this earth have a purpose and can be used for great things if they let themselves. Great things come in many packages: parenting, being a student, mentoring, teaching, writing, singing, building an ark, setting a nation free. All purposes are equally important and not to be taken lightly.

I understand. I should take pride in all areas of my life, big and (seemingly) small. I need to recognize that everything happens in God's timing; I must trust Him and simply do as He asks, when He asks. I'm sure Noah struggled with fear and doubt. His neighbors and even his family must have thought he was crazy to build a boat in the middle of dry land. He needed a whole lot of faith and courage to carry out God's plan. I wonder if Noah ever worried that the Lord had abandoned him during his journey. If he did, he obviously overcame his worries because he finished building the ark. I'll remember this the next time Jesus calls me to do a task that doesn't make sense to me at the time.

"Thank you, Lord, for showing me a great movie. What a great visual of what you were trying to tell me earlier!"

You are welcome, Caren. Before our date ends, I want to address some-

thing you said before.

Uh oh. Is He going to scold me for being unappreciative? I ask hesitantly, "What is it, Lord?"

I would never replace you. Nobody is a better person to carry out the plans I have designed for your life.

I smile widely. "Thank you, Jesus. I am honored, and I love you."

DATE 44
Mickey D's and Forgiveness

I arrive home on a Saturday night after working a double shift, utterly exhausted. For the last month I have continued focusing on my family, waiting for the Lord's signal that I am ready to take the next step toward His plan for me. Nothing earth-shaking has happened, but I am excited about tomorrow. I told my boss I can no longer work on Sundays, and tomorrow is my first free Sunday!

I will miss my Sunday income, but I am not worried. I trust the Lord will provide for us financially throughout the week. My desire to start going to church again with the children drove my decision to talk to my boss. We haven't attended church as a family in many years, and I think going together now is more important than ever. Da'Shon leaves for the Marines in less than a year. I want him to be secure in his relationship with Jesus before he goes out into the world on his own. Reggie is in high school now, where he encounters more temptations to go astray. He struggles with not having his father in his life. I've been taking him to counseling, but the other day I caught him sneaking calls to his dad. When I forbade him to have contact with him—legally he is not supposed to—and asked him why he wants to talk to his dad after all his dad has done to him, he said with tears in his eyes, "He's my *dad*, Mom!" He feels like he is missing a part of himself, so perhaps he can find that missing piece in Jesus. Victoria already loves Jesus and has wanted our family to go to church with her for a while now. I am glad I can finally satisfy her desire, and I'm thrilled that the boys are perfectly willing, even happy, to go.

Victoria is the first to rise on Sunday morning and runs into my bedroom. "Wake up, Mommy. It's Sunday! We need to get ready for church!"

Boy, do I love her. I ask, "Did you wake your brothers?"

"No, Mom, they will ignore me. Will you wake them up? They'll listen to you."

"Sure, but come with me so I can tell those big boys that they better listen to you when you tell them it's time to wake up!"

She smiles and follows me, loving the idea of the boys' being ordered to listen to her.

We manage to get ready and out the door in time to arrive at Lake Highlands United Methodist Church, the church we attended several years ago, for 9:30 Sunday School. Victoria goes to the younger kids' class, the boys hang out in the coffee room with other teenagers, and I go to an adult class Marsha leads. I thoroughly enjoy learning the Bible from her. Then the children and I meet for the 10:45 contemporary service. The sermon is about forgiveness. The pastor does a wonderful job explaining how important it is. I leave in a good mood.

We return home, and I talk to the Lord as I prepare lunch. "Wow, Jesus! The church service was great today! I am really happy to be back. Church is an excellent place for fellowship with family and friends and for learning. I sure agree with Pastor Andy. Forgiveness does bring freedom—to both parties involved! I remember feeling as if a weight was lifted from my shoulders when I forgave my dad and my brother."

A few years ago, my dad called me and asked for my forgiveness. He admitted to being emotionally detached and not protecting me from my mother's craziness when I was young. And then last summer, God called me to make amends with my biological brother who sexually molested me as a child. After not speaking to him for many years, I called him and described what he had done and then explained that I do not blame him for the things he did to me because someone had to have been abusing him as well. He was too young to think of doing the things he did, so I told told him I forgive him. We both experienced tremendous relief and peace.

I am glad you went back to church as well, Caren. I like watching you interact with friends. You are doing an amazing job. I am proud of you.

"Thank you. You have worked wonders in my soul. I am an entirely new creation now!"

Speaking of forgiveness . . .

My hackles go up. I don't know why or how, but I sense what the Lord is about to say. "Lord, please don't go there. I know what you're about to say. I'm not ready for that!"

He asks with amusement in His voice, *Really? And what am I about to say?*

"You want me to forgive my ex-husband, don't you?"

Yep.

How can the Lord ask this of me? I hate Big Reggie! He hurt me and my children, he refused to love us, and he completely abandoned them. I can't stand him. The mere thought of him infuriates me!

Do you see what thinking about Big Reggie does to you? That is exactly why I ask you to forgive him. I want you to experience freedom from your hurt and rage. Only by forgiving him can you release yourself from the prison of hatred you are trapped in.

I can't accept the notion of forgiving him. He physically abused the children for crying out loud! When we were together, he was both emotionally and literally distant from me. I tried to make him love me for thirteen years, but he preferred hanging out with his buddies more than being at home with his family. In the four years since he left us, he hasn't bothered to take the state-mandated anger management classes required to legally visit the children. How can he walk away from them so easily? I wouldn't let anything stand in the way of seeing my babies. And I am angry that he left me with the sole responsibility of raising them.

"Lord, I don't like him, I don't understand him, and I don't want to forgive him."

I do not ask you to like or understand him. I simply ask that you look inside your heart and think about the reasons why forgiving him would benefit you, your children, and us.

I try to do what He asks. I know there are several good reasons to forgive Big Reggie. It would release me from my hatred, of course. It would also be good for the kids. I know from experience that children love their parents, no matter how badly the parents behave. My children must feel sad about losing their father, yet they rarely mention him to me. They know I hate him, so they are probably burying their feelings because they are afraid of upsetting me. I don't want to make their heartache worse by making them uncomfortable to talk to me about it. Plus, forgiving him would set a wonderful example for the children, showing them that all things are possible through the Lord.

"Okay, yes, there are many good reasons to forgive him, Lord. But how? Why does letting go of my hatred feel so impossible?"

You have spent a long time despising Big Reggie. You have held on to your anger for so long that bitterness now defines the relationship. Also, you rely on your anger to avoid feeling hurt. I want you to release all of your anger, resentment, and hurt to me. Doing so will bring us one step closer to our goal.

"But how, Lord? How?"

It is time for date forty-four, my love.

***

As the Lord instructs, I call Big Reggie after lunch. I tell him that God wants me to invite him to see the children. I make it clear that I'm resistant to the idea, but if he wants to see them, he can meet us at McDonald's in an hour. He agrees with surprise, pleasure, and a little bit of wariness in his voice.

I don't tell the kids what I am up to. I am afraid Dae or Victoria will resist going, and I know the Lord wants us all there. I tell them to get in the van for a surprise outing. We walk into McDonald's, and they immediately spot Big Reggie.

"Dad?" Reggie asks in happy disbelief. Dae looks surprised but not particularly angry, and Victoria looks ambivalent. Big Reggie approaches us with an ear-to-ear smile. He shakes Dae's hand and gives Reggie a bear hug. He hugs Victoria too, which she accepts, but she doesn't hug him back. I explain to the children that this surprise is the Lord's idea. Big Reggie treats the kids to drinks and shakes, and we sit down to visit.

I stay quiet for the most part and let them talk to each other. Big Reggie tells them repeatedly how much he loves and misses them. He keeps shaking his head while saying, "I just can't believe this. Today is the best day ever." Dae is polite but distant; Big Reggie is not his birth father, and they never had a true father-son relationship. Reggie, on the other hand, is clearly overjoyed to see his "Pops." Victoria looks pleased, but she calls him Big Reggie instead of Pops, and she hangs onto Dae more than usual.

As Big Reggie and the children catch up, I feel my anger evaporate, as if God flipped a switch in my brain. I look at Big Reggie, and instead of seeing an evil monster who ruined our lives, I see a vulnerable human being who made mistakes. I realize with wonder that by being obedient to the Lord, by accepting this date with Him, I have been instantly freed from the bondage of my hatred.

With forgiveness comes the awareness that I have been suffering more than I recognized. Subconsciously I have been carrying painful "what if's" inside me: What if my children blame me one day for their father's abandonment? What if they believe I am a wedge between them and a possible relationship with their father? I am now free from that burden. Whether or not Big Reggie rebuilds a relationship with his children is no longer my responsibility. He and the children can decide how to move forward from here, knowing I approve of any decision.

After about a half hour, everyone is ready to leave. As I drive home, I feel a new kind of closeness with the Lord, my children, and myself. The bond between us is even greater than before. I hide very few areas of my life from the Lord anymore. I feel great freedom, joy, and contentment in handing my life over to Jesus. And I am proud that I am pleasing in His eyes.

DATE 45
Another Picnic

Another month has passed, and the Lord and I are finally starting to move forward with His plans—building the Pamper Lake Highlands organization. Since the large community diaper give-away in June, I've wondered how to build a program that helps families in need on a regular basis. We have contact information for the people who signed up for future self-improvement classes, but we haven't done anything with it yet. I struggled all summer because I didn't think Jesus was moving things along quickly enough. Now I am starting to see progress.

I have no experience with nonprofits, other than benefitting from them when I lived in severe poverty. I know what works and what doesn't work. The Lord assures me my experience is what uniquely qualifies me for this role. I believe Him, but figuring out what to do is difficult with no education or experience. I am making progress slowly, with the Lord guiding me each step of the way.

Through friends of friends and God-designed "chance" encounters, I meet wonderful people in my community who are connected to local nonprofits and passionate about making a difference in the world. I meet with a few community leaders, like our local councilman Adam McGough, who express interest in facilitating contacts with people who will support and encourage me. Especially helpful is meeting Kathy Stewart, Executive Director of the Lake Highlands PID (Public Improvement District). Kathy explains in detail the next steps required to make Pamper Lake Highlands official, including getting incorporated and putting together a board of directors. Her kindness puts me at ease, leaving me feeling less overwhelmed. Kathy also organizes a meeting between her, the founder of a nonprofit that provides free after-school tutoring in local low-income apartment communities, and me. The meeting goes well, and the woman invites me to speak at her organization's next monthly crime watch meeting in the clubhouse of one of the apartments it services. She asks me to talk about Pamper Lake Highlands and give away diapers to some of the families there, and she suggests that I get information from anyone interested in participating in future programs.

The crime watch meeting is this evening. I feel nervous, eager, and thankful at the same time. We are another step closer to empowering needy families to improve their circumstances. In a burst of love, I say, "Jesus, I am so excited! I can't believe I'm about to speak in front of people who are living oppressed lives like I used to live. I get to tell them there is hope. We are building a program that can help them! Before I go, I want to feel as close to you as possible. Can we have a quick date?"

I would love to. What would you like to do?

"I am happy doing anything with you. Since I only have a couple of hours, how about I pick up a salad from a drive-through, and we go to White Rock Lake to have a picnic? I can leave right now, as is!"

***

When I arrive at the lake, I realize I forgot a blanket. The old sheet I keep in my trunk will have to do. I chuckle as I remember my fifth date with the Lord at this same spot. Our picnic included candles, crystal bowls, sparkling water, and a rose! God was good to pursue me in such a grand way. Now I understand that sitting on the ground He created, looking at the water He designed, seeing the animals He formed, and feeling the wind He makes is grand enough without any extra touches. But back then I was clueless about what was right before my eyes. God knew what I needed at the time, and He courted me accordingly!

I eat my salad and talk to Jesus. "Wow, what a perfect day for a picnic."

Yes it is, if I do say so myself.

I laugh at His joke. I love the Lord's sense of humor. I love everything about Him. He is the love of my life, everything I've dreamed of. He is the oxygen that sustains me. I am overcome with emotion.

"Jesus, this contentment is what I've longed for my whole life. You took a broken woman and made her whole with your perfect love. I am completely transformed, and I love the woman I've become. When I look in the mirror now, I see you shining through me. My shame is gone. I am honored that you desire to reside in a place once so soiled. You moved in with your power to cleanse and made my soul fit for a king. And now you are my partner in helping change others' lives. I love you."

I love you too, dear, and I love being loved by you. I have longed for you since your youth. I am proud of you and your willingness to partner together on this amazing journey.

"The thing that amazes me most is how you completely trust me. You could hold grudges about my past, but instead you give me a remarkable opportunity join Him, as He leads others out of oppression!"

You have made that possible by opening your heart to me and being obedient. I reward you for your faithfulness, just as I reward many others for theirs.

I still think it is incredible. The Lord's love cannot be compared to human love. I begin to think about the upcoming meeting. Yesterday I gave a presentation in my speech class at the community college, and I did a horrible job—stammering and pausing as I tried to remember what to say next. The embarrassing experience makes me doubly nervous about speaking tonight.

Remember to let me speak through you, Caren, the Lord reassures me. *Do not focus on the obstacles you face. If you instead trust that I will give you the tools you need to fulfill your calling, you will exceed what you think is possible for yourself.*

I let go of my worry, finish my salad, and look around. Little honey bees buzz from clover to clover. They are cute as they go about doing what God created them to do. October is still rather warm in Dallas. The bees are probably collecting as much pollen and nectar as possible before the cold weather arrives. I lie back on my sheet and close my eyes for a few minutes, absorbing the warmth of the sun and feeling the wind on my face. I have never felt as safe as I do walking with Jesus.

Caren, seeing you like this brings me great joy. I am pleased to have been the one to lift your chin and wipe away your tears. You are finally treating yourself the way you deserve.

"Thank you, Jesus. Thank you!"

***

As the Lord promised, my presentation on Pamper Lake Highlands goes smoothly. My enthusiasm about the program sparks a lot of excitement and curiosity. I distribute twenty-five diaper gift bags and get the names of several women who express interest in participating in future Pamper Lake Highlands classes. I don't know what will happen next—when we'll start the classes, or if any of the women will show up. The only thing I do know is that this is the start of something amazing.

DATE 46
Four Hours in a Storage Unit

Things have been moving right along with Pamper Lake Highlands since my presentation last month. Recently the Lake Highlands Area Early Childhood PTA (LHAECPTA) selected us as its fall/winter service project. Its members collected over 3,500 diapers for our organization! Seeing my community invest in empowering families to improve their lives is encouraging. LHAECPTA also donated six large storage containers, which came at the perfect time. When we had the Pamper Lake Highlands diaper giveaway in June, I rented a storage unit for all the donations, signs, banners, and other event supplies. I know the Lord is a God of order, but you'd never believe it by looking at that cluttered space! Organizing it will be a huge job. The Lord knows that organization and administration are not my spiritual gifts, but I believe He would like me to take proper care of the beautiful gifts of diapers we've received. Perhaps one of my friends will help me.

I call several of my contacts and girlfriends, but nobody is available to help me today. I want to take the day off and relax, but I feel the Lord tugging at my spirit. He wants me to go to the storage unit.

"Okay, Lord. I know you want me to go, but I can't find any helpers today. I can't do that big of an organization project on my own."

I know, dear. That is why I want to go together. This will be our next date—you, me, and thousands of diapers. papers

Well, when He puts it that way, how can I resist? The unit is in dire need of a system that enables us to easily access any size diapers we need. Plus, we need to store the diapers properly so they are not damaged. Even though it's an overwhelming task, I want to do it. "Okay, Lord. I appreciate the community for being generous and trusting me with their donations. The diapers were given in love, and they deserve to be treated with care."

I like your mindset. Do not worry. We will have fun together!

"I know we will. I love that anything we do together brings me joy." I laugh when I realize I am now looking forward to sorting, bagging, and labeling thousands of diapers, a job I was dreading moments ago. "Lord, if that doesn't show I am smitten with you, I don't know what does!"

I head to the storage unit, leaving my phone at home. I don't want any interruptions. When I open the door to the unit, I am taken aback by the sheer number of diapers. Gratitude overwhelms me. So many people took the time to drive to a store, select the size and brand of diapers they thought we could use, and buy them for families in need using their hard-earned money. What a beautiful picture!

"Lord, thank you for trusting me with this task. I offer you the hands you have given me and the mind you have blessed me with to start organizing this unit with you today. Please bless these diapers and the precious, innocent babies who will wear them. Please protect the children, Jesus, as we walk beside their parents on their journey from a life of oppression to a life of prosperity with you."

Thank you, Caren. Your words are beautiful. You are changing into the woman I created you to be. This makes me proud.

"It is all your doing, Jesus! You gave me a new heart and mind. I think differently than I did in the past. I now have empathy and gratitude. I feel true joy from helping others. I don't deserve any of this, but you gave it to me anyway because you love me. What a gift! Thank you for using me as a vessel to help these families. Thank you for using my past experience for this calling. Thank you for pursuing me and bringing me to this very moment. You are the love of my life."

You are welcome. I rejoice when you use your heart, hands, and mind for the good of my people. Your entire life's journey has made you the woman you are today. Every. Single. Step. Your experiences make you relatable to others who struggle in a life of darkness. Your determination is inspiring. You are faithful, and I will continue to use you if you let me.

His words delight me, and I am ready to tackle our project. However, the Lord tells me He first wants to paint a vibrant picture that will fill my heart with more passion and strength for the next steps of our journey. I close my eyes and listen.

Imagine your mother as a tiny baby. Her parents did not know me. They knew only the oppression of the generations before, thus they raised her in the same way they were raised. Now imagine if instead someone had come into her parent's lives and taught them about me. What if someone had helped them discover their potential? Imagine how different your mother's life would have been. She would have witnessed my transforming love and power by watching her parents walk beside me. She would have grown up knowing my love, and she would have become a more loving and effective mother to you. Imagine the kind of childhood you would have had with a mother who possessed my love in her heart. She would have parented you very differently than the way she did.

With tears in my eyes I reply, "My life would have been drastically different. I would have learned what love looks like. I would have known you earlier. I could have made better decisions for my life and saved years of heartache and pain."

Thinking in these terms fuels my passion for Pamper Lake Highlands. I now fully understand that targeting parents with babies not only helps the parents break out of poverty but also helps break the cycle of oppression. If we can help these parents, we can prevent them from passing on poverty and brokenness to another generation. Genius!

I also better understand the importance of my role in Pamper Lake Highlands. My personal experience of the many factors contributing to oppression—ignorance, abuse, fear, addiction—makes me keenly passionate and understanding of others going through similar experiences. And because I personally experienced Jesus' miraculous healing and restoration, I can sincerely teach others about His love. I can encourage them to accept Jesus and be restored as well. I can show them that breaking the cycle of poverty and passing down a legacy of love to their children is possible.

Exactly, Caren. But it is important you know that my goal is not to heal only those living in poverty. People of all social classes suffer spiritual oppression and brokenness. The reason I have asked you to write a book about our experiences is to pursue a broad spectrum of people. This is what I do. The bigger the mess, the more I clean up!

"I understand, Lord. Thank you for healing me, thus giving my children a chance at knowing a life with you. I am proud of the woman I am becoming with your help."

I roll up my sleeves and begin sorting diapers by size and

placing them neatly into bins. Four hours pass in the blink of an eye. I am amazed at how much the Lord and I accomplished. Not only does the storage unit look much better, but my vision for the future is also much clearer. I leave with a sense of accomplishment and anticipation about where the Lord will lead me next.

DATE 47
Time to Eat

I stand staring at the contents of my refrigerator, going through my options. The holidays are over, and I have put on about ten pounds. I hate myself for gaining weight every year! I *know* the best tactics for maintaining my weight over the holidays, but by the time the new year rolls around, my eating is usually out of control. My choices today must take me a step closer to losing these ten pounds, in addition to the fifteen I already needed to lose before the holidays. If I eat an apple and a salad I won't feel guilty, but the chips and cheese are much more enticing. I decide to compromise. I will eat only three chips and a pinch of cheese, and then I'll eat a salad and half an apple.

I open the bag of chips and cut a small piece of cheese. They are both delicious, and I immediately crave more. Well, the chips I selected were really small, I reason—the equivalent of one big chip. I can have a few more. And the piece of cheese was tiny too. I've done a good job counting calories today, so it won't hurt to have another small piece.

I look around to make sure I am alone. I always tell the

children to make a plate of food and sit down when they eat, so I certainly don't want them to see me eating at the counter with the fridge open. I know that sounds hypocritical, but I am starving, and I will be sure to sit down after I make my salad.

I pop the additional chips and cheese into my mouth. They taste so good! I eat a few more. I wish I could eat as much as I wanted without gaining weight. I suppose I could eat more and get rid of the calories by throwing up afterwards. I've already eaten more than I originally intended anyway. I eat a few more chips and slice more cheese, looking over my shoulder to make sure the children cannot see me. A few minutes later, I snap out of a daze of sorts. The entire bag of chips and block of cheese is gone. What have I done? Shame engulfs me. I promised the Lord and myself that I would never again binge and purge. I have come too far in my healing to resort to this type of behavior!

I am too ashamed to ask for Jesus' help with this. I know what I can do. The other day I watched a documentary on a forty-day fast in which you consume only puréed fruits and vegetables. It sounded really effective in detoxing the body. I can do the fast, reset my system so that I don't crave unhealthy foods anymore, lose the twenty-five pounds, and then ask Jesus to help me from there. I have some vague misgivings, but I push them aside. I am determined to get myself under control so I can approach Jesus about my eating problem in a healthier, less shameful state.

***

The first three days of the fast have been difficult. I have headaches, and I am extremely grumpy. I am proud of myself for sticking with it, though. I've read that if I can get past the first week, the rest will be easy sailing.

***

I have made it through two weeks of drinking puréed fruit, vegetables, and nuts for all of my meals. Only twenty-six more days to go! I've turned down several requests for lunch meetings and asked for coffee meetings instead. Explaining to others what I am doing would be tricky. I'd rather not put myself in that predicament. I am focused on getting control of my appetite. If I can do this, I might be free of my food cravings once and for all.

***

I am on Day Twenty of my fast. People at work and church have started noticing my weight loss. I love the way that feels! Their compliments give me strength to continue. My goal weight is 140 pounds. If I continue to lose weight at the same pace throughout the remainder of the fast, I will weigh just under 140 pounds at the end of the forty days. That sounds perfect because I am sure I will put on a few pounds when I start eating solid foods again. I feel a shiver of anticipation at the thought of being my ideal weight again.

***

I have fasted for thirty days now, during which I have spent time with the Lord but deliberately dodged His efforts to talk to me about my diet. I plan to go to Him eventually, but I want to reach my goal weight first. This morning the scale read 150 pounds. Yes! Ten more days of fasting should be enough time to lose ten more pounds. And if I removed all fats from my smoothies, like nuts and avocados, I would be even hungrier than I have been, but I would lose weight more quickly. As soon as I have the thought, I realize how fanatical I sound. I hear the Lord try talking to me again, and this time I open my heart and listen.

Caren, what are you doing?

Like a child caught in the act of misbehaving, I hang my head in shame. The truth of my dieting madness the last thirty days washes over me. Drinking all of my food, severely limiting the variety of food I eat, and keeping myself in a state of constant hunger is abnormal and not sustainable. I have modeled unhealthy eating behavior to my children. I have tried to hide my actions from Jesus. I've rationalized my choice to starve myself for a month, but deep down I've known that pursuing this path is wrong. I imagine this is how Adam and Eve felt in the Garden of Eden when they were caught eating the forbidden fruit.

A spark of defensiveness rises through my shame. "Well, what do you want me to do, Lord?" I ask angrily. "It's not my fault I have issues with food! My mother passed her eating disorders onto me. I don't know any other way, and . . . "

Caren.

He does not need to say more. I get it. I am an adult and make my own decisions now. By purposely ignoring Him about this issue, I chose to act in sin.

Yes, you did ignore me and chose to handle the problem without my guidance, and I allowed you to. I knew you would eventually recognize how out-of-control you were and come to me. Caren, I agree that your mother gave you unhealthy messages about food and weight when you were a child. I do not discount the effect her disordered eating had on you. But you know me now, and you know you can turn everything over to me. I will help you persevere.

"I knew if I came to you, you would not support the forty-day fast, and I wanted the weight gone more than anything. I feel silly. Of course when I resume normal eating, I will most likely regain every pound I lost, maybe even more since I did not lose the weight gradually. And that will make me feel helpless and out-of-control yet again, which will make me want to continue hiding from you . . . "

That is exactly how all sin works. It tries to hold you captive. Only with my help does sin lose its hold.

I am painfully aware of how right He is. I was caught firmly in the web of sin for the last thirty days. But I have no idea where to go from here. I don't know what a healthy relationship with food looks like. I have no idea how God intends for us to eat. He urges me to look in the Bible for guidance.

"I will, but the Bible is a big book. Can you be a little more specific as to which passages I should read? Should I search the Internet for help?"

You can search for food and appetite-related scripture, but do not read other people's opinions on the matter. Read the scriptures yourself and look for those that speak to you personally.

***

I've researched the Bible for a couple of days, and I believe I have the answers the Lord wanted me to find. Many scriptures contain useful information, but a few speak to me more loudly than the rest.

I first looked for information about what people ate during biblical times and discovered these three scriptures:

Everything that lives and moves about will be food for

*you. Just as I gave you the green plants, I now give you
everything* (Genesis 9:3).

*Have you any food here? And they gave him a piece of
a broiled fish, and of a honeycomb. And he took it, and
did eat before them* (Luke 24:41-43).

*And God said, "Behold, I have given you every plant
yielding seed that is on the face of all the earth, and
every tree with seed in its fruit. You shall have them
for food. And to every beast of the earth and to every
bird of the heavens and to everything that creeps on the
earth, everything that has the breath of life, I have given
every green plant for food." And it was so* (Genesis
1:29-30).

I interpret these scriptures to mean that God welcomes me
to eat what He created for man to eat: fruits, vegetables, seeds,
nuts, grains, fish, and meat. I do not believe He requires me
to eat all of these things, but He offers them as options. For
example, I don't care for meat from mammals, so I can decline
chicken, beef, pork, and the like. I love fish, so I am welcome to
eat tuna, salmon, trout, and so on.

My other takeaway from these scriptures is that eating foods
made by God is safe. The scriptures refer to the food *God* gives
us, the food *He* created. I think I should avoid "man-made"
or processed food. I should steer clear of foods modified with
chemicals, pesticides, artificial colors, and artificial flavors.

I then looked for scriptures that address overeating. I found:

So, whether you eat or drink, or whatever you do, do all

to the glory of God (1 Corinthians 10:31).

*Or do you not know that your body is a temple of the
Holy Spirit within you, whom you have from God? You
are not your own, for you were bought with a price. So
glorify God in your body* (1 Corinthians 6:19-20).

*It is not good to eat much honey, nor is it glorious to seek
one's own glory* (Proverbs 25:27).

*Their end is destruction, their god is their belly, and they
glory in their shame, with minds set on earthly things*
(Philippians 3:19).

I know the Lord provides food for us to heal and nourish
our bodies. Hunger pains are a signal to eat, but I rarely eat
because I am hungry. Instead, I eat to fill a void, comfort a pain,
celebrate an event, and prevent myself from feeling uncomfortable emotions. When I overeat, I feel ill and gain excess weight,
which is harmful to my body. When I operate from the other
side of my eating disorder, either starving myself or inducing
vomiting immediately after eating, I harm my body as well. I
should not intentionally harm myself if my body is a temple the
Holy Spirit lives within.

Finally, I researched how to handle temptation in moments
of weakness because understanding what I should do is very
different from being able to actually do it. Much of the time I
am a slave to my cravings for food. I have tried for years to free
myself from the hold food has over me. I have been successful
for certain periods of time, but I always return to my demons. I
have proved to myself that I cannot truly conquer my addiction

on my own. Three scriptures clearly address this issue:

> *But he said to me, "My grace is sufficient for you, for my power is made perfect in weakness." Therefore I will boast all the more gladly about my weaknesses, so that Christ's power may rest on me. For when I am weak, then I am strong* (2 Corinthians 12:9-1).

> *Do you not know that your bodies are temples of the Holy Spirit, who is in you, whom you have received from God? You are not your own* (1 Corinthians 6:19).

> *No temptation has overtaken you except what is common to mankind. And God is faithful; he will not let you be tempted beyond what you can bear. But when you are tempted, he will also provide a way out so that you can endure it* (1 Corinthians 10:13-14).

I must freely admit I have no power over my addiction. I must accept that my body is to be maintained for God's glory, not used to satisfy my greed. And when I am faced with temptation, I should trust God to get me through it.

I present to the Lord all I have learned through His word over the last few days. He replies approvingly. *Very good, dear. Eat what my Father created for you to consume. Fresh fruits and vegetables, nuts, grains, clean fish, natural cheeses and meat, honey, and oils are all good options. Tune in to your body's signals. When you feel the pang of true hunger, that whisper or grumble in your belly, feed your body. When your belly is comfortably full, stop eating. Do not eat to the point of discomfort. Do not use mindless eating as a way to ignore your feelings. When you are stressed, sad, angry, or bored, turn to me and the loved ones in your life. When you are happy, celebrate with me and those you love. I want you to fully experience life, with all the emotions it brings. Eat with me and your family as a way to nourish your bodies.*

I feel tremendous relief from learning from Christ and His teachings that I can be free from my appetite. Christ can free me from the pain and shame surrounding overeating. He wants me to enjoy the gift of food in a healthy way. He implores me to turn to Him when I struggle with the urge to overeat.

I can't wait to go grocery shopping and begin implementing this new approach to food! I am not naïve. I know I will stumble as I learn to use Christ's way. I do not expect instant perfection, but I understand what is required to conquer this addiction.

DATE 48
My Soul Provider

Since that November day in the storage unit when the Lord gave me a clearer vision for the Pamper Lake Highlands ministry, many wonderful things have happened. First and foremost, Jesus helped us establish a board of directors and become incorporated. As of December 29, 2015, Pamper Lake Highlands is an official 501(c)(3) nonprofit organization!

Since then, the Lord has been putting together a concrete plan for the ministry. (Ministry! I am humbled even saying the word. I still find it hard to believe that Jesus is using *me* for ministry.) We now have a clear mission: to provide resources and programs that will help needy families rebuild their lives.

We have determined that one important piece of the ministry is to provide Bible study classes, or perhaps a women's ministry, to encourage women to develop a closer relationship to the Lord through fellowship and His Word. I don't know how the Lord will reach the women who attend, but I know He has a plan, so as long as we put this piece into action, He will do the rest. Jesus asks that we not try to force Him on anyone. He simply wants the organization to provide a venue in which He can reach people. Making it clear that the Lord is the foundation of the organization, even in the IRS nonprofit filing, is vital.

A second component of the ministry is providing education classes. Because many of the needy families in our community are Hispanic immigrants, the Lord wants us to focus initially on teaching English as a Second Language (ESL). Jesus provided avenues that led us to partner with LIFT (Literacy Instruction for Texas), an established nonprofit, which will be a valuable resource in making our program successful. The ESL classes will include free curriculum-based childcare so that mothers with pre-school-aged children can attend. We want the program to be a loving place where oppressed and isolated women and children become empowered through connections with others while learning their community's primary language. While the mothers learn English, we will prepare their children for elementary school. Many children of non-English-speaking parents start kindergarten developmentally behind because of the language barrier, lack of experience in classroom settings, and limited exposure to American social customs. The Lord wants Pamper Lake Highlands to bridge the language and social gap for these children.

A third piece of the ministry is to provide a parenting program. Once again, Jesus went to work putting a partnership into play. A church friend, Diana Lawson, heard that the Lord and I are building a nonprofit ministry. Because her daughter works at the Methodist Children's Home, she knows they partner with various organizations to provide a nurturing parenting program. Diana asked me if I had considered including a parenting program in our ministry. She was surprised and excited when I informed her that Jesus already told me we needed such a program and that He just used her to help make it happen! Methodist Children's Home agreed to provide its trained facilitators to teach the classes. They will help families break unhealthy cycles. So many mothers mean well and desire a closer relationship with their children but only know how to parent in the way they were taught. Our classes will encourage more positive communication between the mothers and children who attend, identify the successful parenting methods the mothers are using, and teach new strategies to replace the unsuccessful methods of their past.

The fourth and fifth parts of the ministry are Christian counselors and addiction recovery programs. Both are essential anti-oppression tools to implement down the road, but the Lord wants us to first work on the other three pieces.

I love how the vision for the organization has come together, but I struggle with how to turn the vision into a working ministry. February is halfway over, and the Lord said the programs should start in September. There are hundreds of loose ends. The potential partners the Lord provided can only become our partners if we find a facility for the classes. We need $7,500 for the LIFT partnership to cover materials and their services. We must find all of our own volunteers. We need to raise money to pay for childcare workers, supplies, and the myriad of other things it takes to run a program of this nature. I cannot personally fund the programs, I don't know how to raise money, I know of no facility we can operate from, and I have no skills in recruiting volunteers. On top of all those obstacles, I have limited time in which to work on the organization. I have to work to pay the bills and take care of my own family. I take my concerns to the Lord.

"Lord, I am ready for you to share with me how your vision

is to come about. I now know what the ministry will look like, but I don't know how I can ever put it together, let alone by September."

Slow down, dear. I hear a lot of "I's." Like everything else up to this point, I will do what needs to be done through you and others. Building Pamper Lake Highlands over the next several months is our next date. I will strengthen and provide for you, your family, and this ministry in miraculous ways.

"But how will I have time to work with you on such a big project? My free hours are stretched thin as it is. Don't get me wrong, Jesus. I am thrilled to do this with you. It just seems . . . well, impossible!"

I think you know better than to use the word impossible when it concerns me, no?

"I know, I know. But where do I start?"

Remember, I am calling you to be a missionary. You need to ask my people for help.

"Ask your people? You mean you want me to ask people for money?" I am slightly panicked at the thought. Asking for money is out of my comfort zone, to say the least.

Yes, ask for money, prayers, volunteers, a facility, diapers. You must rely on my people for many things going forward.

"Ugh. People will think I am a bother. They will cringe when they see me coming!"

Trust in me. Be obedient and share our story with others, as well as the vision I have given you. You will have to become more vulnerable, which is not easy. Do not rely on your own understanding. Trust that if you lean on me, I will provide everything you need.

I believe what the Lord says and understand what a beautiful thing He is promising. But I've never been more afraid of anything in my life! I will try my hardest to do as He asks.

***

Today I celebrate the end of my seven-month date with Jesus because today marks the first day that Pamper Lake Highlands is a fully operating organization. We began ministering to forty-five women and twenty-two children via two ESL classes on this twenty-first day of September 2015. On Friday our parenting classes begin. My heart brims with joy.

The journey getting to this point was filled with ups and downs. I attended countless meetings. I heard a lot of "yes's" and almost as many "no's." I experienced incredible joy at times, and I shed many tears at times. I got upset at Jesus more than once along the way because it was "too hard." But when I remembered to lean on Him, He lovingly showed me why things weren't going smoothly; every time, the problem was that I had fallen back into my insecurities and tried to take things into my own hands. When I resumed leaning on Him, He provided what we needed. He often closed one door only to open another.

An amazing part of the journey was quitting my waitressing job on May 1 to become a full-time missionary. Obeying Jesus' call to give up a steady income to live on fundraising instead took a giant leap of faith, but I have not regretted it. Jesus is now my sole provider, or as I like to say, my "soul" provider.

We operate out of a little church the Lord led me to named Forest Meadow Baptist. The pastor and his loving congregation allow us to use their facilities during the weekdays at no cost to our ministry. We have access to two adult classrooms and three children's classrooms. We are indeed partnering with LIFT, thanks to a huge donation from the amazing Lake Highlands Women's League. Members of my church, people from the Lake Highlands community, and many friends provide everything else we need to run the ministry. They volunteer as teachers, they donate their time, and they donate their financial resources.

This has been one of the longest, most challenging, and most rewarding dates I've had with the Lord. Jesus' Word is truth, and I am happier than I could have ever imagined that I have given my life to Him.

DATE 49
California Love

With Pamper Lake Highlands in full swing, I suppose I should be completely content, but Da'Shon has been weighing on my mind lately. One of God's blessings this past summer was Dae's graduating high school in June and being accepted to Marine boot camp in San Diego, California, in July. Seeing his classmates and him graduate was one of the proudest moments of my life. Some of the seniors wore cords on their robes indicating various academic achievements. When Dae walked across the stage to receive his diploma, I thought to myself, "If only there were cords for all the things you had to overcome and all the things you had to be responsible for!" The day he graduates from the twelve-week boot camp and becomes a United States Marine will be an even prouder moment. Yet, with my joy comes deep sadness.

I was not prepared for the emotions that came when Dae left home. Our family has never been a traditional family. I was a single mother for most of my son's life. He never knew his father. Even though he had a stepfather the few years I was married, Big Reggie was mostly absent. Like most single mothers, I worked long hours. I relied on Da'Shon to be the "man of the house" at too young of an age, so he was the male figure and role model to his younger siblings the majority of his life. He had to be responsible for not just his own life and academics, but for his brother's and sister's as well. He babysat them, helped them with homework and projects, cooked them dinner, gave his little sister baths, and tucked her in and read her bedtime stories. He played referee when Victoria and Reggie fought and made sure the house was clean before I got home from work. He filled so very many roles in our home with no male role model, and somehow, he rarely caused trouble. He refused to become a statistic.

Since the Lord began healing me two years ago, Da'Shon and I have gotten much closer. He knows I love him, but my heart is riddled with guilt and regret. You see, I was hard on my sweet boy because I needed him to be responsible, but I needed him to be responsible because *I* had been so *irresponsible*. I lived recklessly. Because I was sexually active with a man I hardly knew and got pregnant, Dae carries the pain of missing a father figure. As if that weren't enough, I did it again. I got pregnant by another man who didn't love me and was not father material, and Dae had to pick up the slack. He didn't have the mother he deserved either because through most of his life, I was too exhausted from work or depressed to parent him the way he deserved. My sweet boy did not have a true childhood because of my choices.

The Lord has forgiven me for my mistakes, and I am thankful. But forgiving sin does not erase the consequence of that sin. As much as I try not to wallow in shame, I feel the painful consequence of my choices. I mourn that I didn't spend more time with Da'Shon. I regret that when I did spend time with him, I was so busy "making a responsible man out of him" that I failed to tell him how proud I was of him. When he was sad or in pain, I brushed him off, saying things like, "You are fine. Quit crying." I grieve that I did not allow him to be a little boy, and now that I am emotionally and spiritually well enough to be a better mother to him, he is gone.

I have been depressed, crying, and overeating the last several weeks. I know I can go to the Lord with my burden—He and I have worked on this before—but I've been resisting. I think a part of me wants to feel this way as a punishment. Subconsciously I think I deserve to feel shame, and the more I overeat, the more shame I feel. Today I am finally ready to lay my heartache at the feet of my loving Jesus.

"Please help me, Lord."

Oh, Caren. I know you are hurting. I understand the pain you feel. You made poor decisions without me in your life, and your son bore the weight of many of them. However, like I have done for you, I will use all your son's experiences to develop him into the man I created him to be. Thank you for choosing to give me your grief. I want to be the one that comforts you and wipes away your tears. I love you.

"I hurt your little boy, Lord. My life choices robbed him of his childhood. Please forgive me."

You are forgiven. I came to absorb sin. Through me, your wrongs can be made right. Though Dae had a difficult childhood, I was there with him, loving him and protecting him. I gave him the strength he needed to fulfill the roles he needed to. Through this, our boy's character is much stronger and more loving. Da'Shon had the childhood he had, and I loved him the whole way through.

"Thank you for that, Jesus. Thank you. In all of his letters, Dae writes that he wants to make me proud. He already makes me proud! How will he ever believe he is good enough exactly as he is?"

Simple—tell him. In these final five weeks of boot camp, write him letters telling him everything you wish you had told him before he left. Remember, Caren, you loved your son the best you knew how at the time, and you worked hard to become a better person for your children. He noticed your determination, and he felt your love. Never doubt that.

Relief and gratitude wash over me. I feel much better. I think about how many letters I can write in five weeks. I would love to see him graduate from boot camp with the children by my side, but I can't afford plane tickets to San Diego. I ask, "Jesus, will you make seeing Dae graduate on October 19th possible?"

I would love to. Will you do me the honor of going to San Diego with me and your family for our second-to-last date? I will provide what you need to have an amazing vacation there.

Of course I agree wholeheartedly. Then I sit down and write my son a letter. I share with him all the reasons I am proud of him. I acknowledge all he did that made raising our family as a single mom possible. I want to empower him. I'd like him to see that a little boy was capable of being an incredible role model and inspiration to his entire family—including me—through the Lord's strength.

Interestingly, his response to my letter says he knows how much I love him. He is happy to hear that he makes me proud. He shares that he looks forward to venturing out into the world as a man. He finds strength in his faith and keeps himself focused by reading the scriptures his girlfriend and I send daily. The most gratifying thing he tells me is that he wouldn't change his past if he could because it made him who he is today. Figuring that out for myself took years; I'm glad he is many steps ahead of me in self-awareness. I begin to feel brighter about our past and look forward to my San Diego date with Jesus and my family.

***

The Lord has worked wonders in the last several weeks. First He placed the suggestion to purchase my round-trip flight on the hearts of my dear friend Lori and her husband, Kirk. Lori is one of my past friends who welcomed me back with open arms when I emerged from solitude. This latest generosity is just one example of the love and support she and Kirk have given my family.

Five weeks before the trip, the Lord helped fifteen-year-old Reggie get his first job. So I charged his round-trip ticket, and he received his first two paychecks just in time to reimburse me.

Finally, Victoria had the idea of raising money for her airfare with a bake sale. A ton of friends from church and the community came to support her, resulting in a total profit of exactly four dollars more than the cost of her ticket.

Then, a few days ago, I learned that my brother Matt, and his beautiful wife, Lori, my once roommate and best friend all through high school, are flying to San Diego to celebrate with us! I am so excited to celebrate this together with them! Lori was always such an amazing friend and even though Matt isn't my biological brother, he has always loved me like he was. As always, the Lord came through for me using His body of believers to make my dream of seeing Da'Shon graduate come true, and now I get to do this with my brother and dear friend Lori.

And now, in thirty-five minutes, my children and I will board a plane to San Diego, and we are staying for five days and four nights! I sit in the airport waiting for our flight to board, feeling grateful. "Jesus, I can't believe I am about to take the first flight of my entire life and for such an incredible reason! I will see Dae graduate from Marine boot camp. I'll experience the ocean with my children for the first time, *and* we get to see Matt and Lori! Lord, thank you for each person who had a part in making this trip happen."

You are welcome. Enjoy yourself and revel in the love that your friends showered on you to make this possible.

I have a desire that I am a little nervous to bring to the Lord. But I want to share everything with Him, even things He might not approve of, so I ask, "Jesus, can we see Stewart while we're there? He lives in San Diego after all. He said he would try to make time to see us, and you made it happen once before, so I thought maybe . . . please, Lord? I really care for him and would love to see him this weekend."

I think I can arrange that as well, but I want you to enjoy time with your family, celebrate the occasion we are here for, and then we will discuss visiting Stewart. Deal?

I readily agree to stay in the present moment, and I promise that seeing Stewart will simply be an added bonus to an amazing trip, not the highlight.

***

The last four days have flown by. Matt and Lori head back to Ohio this morning, and we head back to Dallas tomorrow. I will miss them both and look forward to seeing them and their three children next winter. I am so grateful we had this time together. I loved hearing Lori's laugh again, she has such a gentle and giving way about her. Experiencing this time with them was such a gift. I am deeply touched by how much love they both shared with us.

Between the thrilling plane ride here, the moving graduation ceremony, and the family bonding, this trip has been amazing. Our hotel is in historic Old Town San Diego, within walking distance of many fun activities. For the most part, though, we have simply enjoyed hanging out together.

We have eaten in many restaurants, and Matt and Lor treated us to most of our meals. They are both so generous and allowed Dae to choose the cuisine each night, to make up for twelve weeks of eating cafeteria-style boot camp food. He ate to his heart's content and made us laugh with hilarious boot camp stories. A particularly fun evening was the night we went to a delicious, upscale sushi restaurant. Dae dared Reggie to take the "wasabi ginger challenge." If Reggie could eat an entire ball of wasabi and ginger, Dae would give him $100. The rest of us belly laughed as Reggie gave it his best try. He managed to get a few good chomps in before his gag reflex got the best of him!

Another highlight of this trip has been marveling at how much Dae has changed. He has always been a sweet boy, but he used to be easily irritated with his family, especially in public. He thought I was too affectionate and too picky. He considered Reggie too loud and obnoxious, and he got tired of Victoria's being clingy. This week, though, none of that seems to bother him. He appears to enjoy our quirks, welcomes hugs and affection from his family, and laughs at Reggie's over-the-top gestures and jokes. He looks as if he is soaking up this time with us and his precious girlfriend, Yaneth. He is open about loving and missing us, and he tells us he couldn't have asked for a better family to be a part of. After the guilty regrets I struggled with this summer, hearing that makes my heart sing.

Shortly after Matt and Lori leave to catch their 8 a.m. flight, I receive a text from Stewart inviting us to brunch. I eagerly accept, and we agree to meet at 11:00 at the Hotel del Coronado, a luxury beachside resort. We haven't visited the ocean yet, so the hotel is a perfect location. As I shower, my excitement bubbles over. "Lord, are you serious? Thank you so much! I have longed to see Stewart again for over two years. I can't wait to see his face and hear his voice."

I quickly tamp down my excitement. I must steer clear of falling into a fantasy. This is simply a friend meeting a friend for brunch. I secretly worry that if I get too excited, the Lord might take the moment from me. I know Jesus is not vengeful, but I also know, deep down, that He doesn't support my feelings for Stewart. He clearly approves of Stewart's being my friend because He has allowed me to see him, and Stewart has been nothing but kind and appropriate these last few years. The problem is, I have tried to make our relationship more than it is, and my feelings for him are a mess. I sense that before our fifty dates are over, Jesus wants to address this with me. I don't want to think about it, though. If I give my feelings for Stewart to the Lord, I might have to give up my fantasy, and where will that leave me? Feeling unwanted? I shake off my thoughts, put a smile on my face, and get ready for a fun day.

***

Our Uber driver drops us off at the front of Hotel del Coronado. The grand Victorian style resort is magnificent! I catch myself almost running to the path that leads to the ocean. We pass the yogurt shop and are faced with the most breathtaking sight I've ever seen: the ocean in all its magnificence. What a vast amount of water! I smell its salty scent and hear its mighty crashing waves. "Kids!" I yell. "Do you *see* this?"

Reggie replies wittily, "Nah, Ma. You're the only one who can see the miles of ocean in front of us."

I laugh. "Don't be a punk, dear. This is the most beautiful thing I have ever seen!"

Dae grins and pipes in, "You're so cute, Ma."

After a few more minutes admiring the view, we continue down the path and find a perfect spot on the deck. I text Stewart where to find us. I am lousy at giving directions, so it takes him a few minutes, but then he is there, just as tall and beautiful as I remember. I want to run to him, but I restrain myself. I can't act that way in front of the children or risk scaring Stewart off. Instead I stand up casually, smile, and wave him over. When he reaches us, I give him a quick hug and introduce him to the children. The kids know about my friendship with Stewart, and they probably sense I like him a lot, but they do not know I pine for him like I do.

Brunch is delicious and fun. Stewart puts the kids at ease with his laidback manner and dry sense of humor. We all enjoy the food, laugh, and share stories. Stewart banters with the kids, giving Reggie a hard time when they show him the video of his wasabi challenge. We ask for the check, and I realize with a jolt that our time together is coming to an end. Stewart has a 1:00 appointment. How I love this man! It breaks my heart that he doesn't want anything more between us. I've spent hours upon hours picturing a life with him, and my feelings are appropriate in that fantasy. But I know they are silly and have no basis in reality. I pull myself to the present moment so I can enjoy his company before he leaves. I think to myself, "Life is perfect at this moment. I am with the people I love the most, the ocean is beautiful, the weather is hot, the sky is crystal clear, and I am celebrating my son's amazing accomplishment with Jesus, my children, and the man I adore."

The server gives us the check, and Stewart hands her his card. Dae, Yaneth, and I had planned to split the tab, but Stewart beats us to it. His generosity is another reason I admire him. We walk up the path toward the hotel. Stewart and I pull a few steps ahead of the children. He bumps me playfully, saying, "Well, I met the kids!" I laugh and shoot back, "And you're just as tall as ever!"

Dae and Reggie shake his hand, Yaneth and Victoria give him a hug, and finally he and I give each other a friendly hug. I thank him for brunch, and he heads to the parking lot. I don't let the children see a change in my demeanor, but I feel the same anguish I did when I said goodbye to him at Scruffy Duffies so long ago. I long to run after him and invite him to spend the day at the beach with us. I have to remind myself that this trip is about spending time with Dae before he is sent for more training, not about Stewart. I also remind myself that the Lord allowed me a few hours with Stewart, and I want to show Him I can be satisfied with His gift.

We spend the rest of the afternoon on the beach. Victoria and I collect seashells as souvenirs. Yaneth and the boys play in the ocean. We have frozen yogurt before returning to our hotel. I text Stewart and invite him to visit us again before we leave tomorrow, but he has other plans tonight. I am slightly disappointed, but I focus on how nice the Lord was to give me an ocean brunch with him.

The next day, the children and I explore San Diego for several hours before our late afternoon flight. As I sit quietly staring out the plane window, the magnitude of the Lord's gift settles over me. This vacation was like nothing I've experienced before. I love Jesus so much! As the plane takes off, though, my heart drops. I feel as if I am leaving a piece of my heart in California. I know I need to do something about my feelings for Stewart. A knot forms in the pit of my stomach, and tears roll down my cheek.

"I know, Lord," I say. "I know."

DATE 50
Freedom and Restoration

November has rolled around, and the weather is starting to cool. Victoria and I are sitting on my bed when I am suddenly overcome by an unusual feeling. I long for my mother to crochet me a blanket like she used to do when we were kids. The thought comes from out of nowhere. I tell Victoria, and she replies innocently, "Maybe you should call her and ask her to make one for you."

I haven't spoken to my mother in years. My children know this, and they know about my childhood, so her suggestion is as odd as my thought. I reply noncommittally, "Maybe."

Intellectually I have forgiven my mom, but the wall around my heart is still high and strong. I forgave her for how she treated me; I am even thankful for everything she did because it led to my being the woman I am today. I wish her well and hope she finds peace with Jesus as I have, but she lives in Ohio, and I have no desire to be in a relationship with her. I accepted her as a Facebook friend a couple of years ago, and I've seen a lot of her posts—many about Jesus—but I do not communicate with her.

She is simply my birth mom. I no longer need a "real" mom.

And now comes this strange desire: I want a blankie from my mommy! Why? I can buy a blanket from a store. The answer is obvious and terrifying. I desire a piece of my mother. But it's not like I want her back in my life. I just want something made by her. This urge could not be of my own doing. I suspect a certain Someone is stirring things up.

"Jesus, what are you up to? I don't want a relationship with my mom. I've been completely fine staying away from her, so why do I suddenly feel this way?"

Darling, it is time to open your heart to your mother. All I request is that you ask her to make you a blanket, nothing more.

"So you put the desire for one of her blankets in my heart? I thought you gave us free will. Isn't that cheating? You make me feel something I don't want to feel, and I can't ignore it because now I really, really want a freakin' blanket? Ugh! Thanks a lot, Lord. Now what?"

Listen to sweet Victoria. Call your mother and ask her to make you a blanket.

"Fine, I'll do it. But not right now. Maybe later today."
Your choice.

***

The house is settling down for bedtime. Victoria and I are lying on my bed about to read a book together when I feel the Lord prodding my heart.

Is it later enough for you?

I get nervous, and my thoughts race. I don't even have my mother's phone number. But that's a silly excuse. My grandmother has had the same phone number since before I can remember, and she keeps in contact with my mom. But I haven't called my grandmother in a couple of years, so calling her out of the blue feels awkward too. Maybe Victoria should call her.

"Hey, babe," I ask her. "Do you want to call your great grandmother?"

"Sure, mom. What should I say?"

"You can just tell her hello," I say nonchalantly.

Victoria agrees. I know my tactic is a bit deceptive, but I am afraid to call my grandmother on my own. This way I can test the waters. I'm sure she'll be happy to hear from her great granddaughter, and as they talk I can muster my courage to ask for my mother's phone number.

I dial the number and hand the phone to Victoria. I can hear my grandmother's voice say "Hello?" faintly on the other end.

"Hi, Great Grandma. This is Victoria."

"Who?"

"Victoria, Caren's daughter," she answers.

I hear Grandma. "Caren, is that you?"

Victoria giggles and says more loudly. "No, Great Grandma. This is Victoria, Caren's *daughter*. Your great granddaughter!"

"Victoria!" Grandma cries. I listen with excitement. "Well! Hello, honey! How are you? I haven't heard your voice since you were a little bitty girl. How have you been? Golly, you sound so beautiful, like such a big girl!"

Victoria is all smiles now. "Thank you, Great Grandma. I'm nine years old. How old are you?"

I listen as they chat, waiting for the right moment to ask for the phone. Then I hear Grandma say something unexpected. "Victoria, your grandma just walked in the door." She directs her voice away from the receiver and says, "Hey, Laura.

Your granddaughter, Victoria, is on the phone!" Then back to Victoria: "Do you want to talk to your grandma?"

Victoria looks at me for approval. I shake my head yes. Now I am really nervous, but excited at the same time because it dawns on me that my decision to live without my mother deprived my children of a grandmother. My heart opens to the possibility of my daughter having a relationship with her grandma. The only problem is that I am not prepared to talk to my mom today. I feel too vulnerable. I had barely gotten up my nerve to talk to my grandma.

They greet each other warmly and begin to talk. After a few minutes I whisper, "Ask your grandma to make you a blanket." I am being childish, but I don't care. When Victoria asks for the blanket, the pressure I've been feeling is alleviated.

"Certainly!" Grandma responds. "What color blanket do you want?"

"Umm, I like turquoise and green."

"A dark green or lime green? I think turquoise and lime would look beautiful together."

I've never known Victoria to favor lime green, but she agrees enthusiastically. I realize my body is tense, and I'm clutching my hands together tightly. I take a deep breath, in and out. I give myself a silent pep talk. Everything is fine. All is going smoothly.

My head snaps up at Victoria's next words. "I love you too, Grandma. Yes, Mommy is right here. Sure, I'll hand her the phone."

Like a squirrel dodging a speeding car, my thoughts scuttle and freeze. I'm not ready for this! What do I say? Jesus tricked me! He knew my mom was going to my grandma's house at this time. That's why He nudged me when He did! I groan. Victoria hands me the phone, whispers, "Mom, she's waiting," and watches me with anticipation.

Well, I don't know what is about to happen, but I trust Jesus and think He is brilliant to have me do this in front of Victoria. My little girl can witness firsthand what a powerful and good God we serve. I say shakily, "Hello?"

"Caren, it is so good to hear your voice. I've been praying for this for a long time, honey. This is the best birthday present Jesus could have given me."

I look at my calendar. November 12. Today is the eve of my mother's birthday. I tell the Lord silently, "Aren't you clever!"

The conversation is surprisingly unstilted. We talk for about twenty minutes. I learn that she is moving to a new house in Parma, Ohio. She sings in her church choir and has found peace and grace in Jesus. I finally ask her my question. Will she make me a soft pink and cream blanket? She says nothing would please her more. She passes the phone to my grandma, and we chat for a few minutes as well. I don't know why I stopped calling Grandma a few years ago, but she doesn't hold a grudge. She is thrilled to hear from us. She puts my mother back on the phone, and we say our goodbyes. Before we hang up, my mom says, "Caren, this is a wonderful birthday gift. Thank you for calling and letting me talk to my granddaughter. I love you, sweetheart, and I am proud of the woman you've become."

I reply in kind. "Thank you, Mom. Happy birthday. I love you too."

***

I have wrestled with the possibility of having a relationship with my mother since the Lord provided an inroad a month ago. I am glad I spoke to her, and there is no longer a wall between us.

I am especially happy that my children are starting to have a little bit of contact with their grandmother. I've exchanged a few brief texts with my mom since our conversation, but nothing meaningful. I'm sure the Lord wants more, but I can't imagine having a real relationship with her after all that has happened. More importantly, she has never acknowledged what she did to me, nor apologized.

Today is December 15. I am headed to a three-day personal growth seminar called The Landmark Forum. Stewart recommended it for Reggie to help him with integrity and a few issues he has been struggling with. Reggie went last month and had a powerful, positive experience. He realized that his struggles stem from not having a personal relationship with his father. He decided to move in with Big Reggie to build a bond with him before graduating high school and making his way in the world. I did not want to let my boy go, but after much prayer, I believe Reggie's living with his father is the Lord's will, so I stepped aside.

Because of Reggie's positive experience, I am attending The Forum too. My goal is to get over my fear of fundraising for Pamper Lake Highlands. I've had plenty of therapy, and I'm on an amazing journey with Jesus, but I still struggle with self-esteem and worthiness issues now and then. I believe the Lord thinks this weekend will help me.

The Forum is amazing. I learn how to overcome many of my fundraising insecurities, as I desired. But the Lord is also using this weekend to heal my heart regarding my mother. I've been reminded that my past is simply the stories I tell myself, and I am the one who assigns meaning to those stories. I've been encouraged to stop focusing on labeling my mother's actions as right or wrong and instead acknowledge what she did and didn't do, let it go, and focus on who she is now. My mother has periodically tagged me in posts and messaged me on Facebook for a couple of years now, but I've chosen to ignore her. I realize my refusal to engage is a way to protect myself, punish her, and be the one in control. I want an apology from her—I have been downright self-righteous in my belief that I deserve one—but I have rejected her attempts to reach out to me.

I am finally ready to let go of the past and live in today. I am ready to entertain a relationship with the person she is now and see how it goes. Isn't that what I ask of the Lord? If Christ can forgive me for all my sins, even aborting His child, then surely I can forgive my mother. She was a broken woman who lived in a broken world and did broken things. But Jesus wiped her slate clean. Who am I to reject her because she was once soiled? I will not withhold my love from her any more. I will give her the grace that Christ has given me.

When I return home, I call my mom and ask for her forgiveness. I admit that I have deliberately robbed her of my love and a relationship with her grandchildren and me. By opening this door for her, I have given her the safe space she needed to be vulnerable. She begins to weep. She asks for my forgiveness and gives me the apology I've waited for my entire life.

Later that night on Facebook, I see a video of her singing in her church choir. My hearts fills with joy and pride that she is sharing her voice, rejoicing in the Lord. I am reminded of the parents I met at Terilli's on our eighteenth date, how pride for their daughter shone in their faces. This is how I feel now! How wonderful to feel "daughterly love" for the first time in my life.

***

Victoria is at a friend's birthday party this Saturday evening. Today is February 13, the day before Valentine's Day. I don't have a sweetheart, so I decide to take myself to dinner at Terilli's for a little "me time." *Trust In You* by Lauren Daigle plays on my car radio as I drive to the restaurant. It reminds me of my journey with the Lord. As the song ends, I am compelled to tell Him how much I love Him.

"Jesus, you are so good to me. I know I am difficult to deal with at times. Thanks for not giving up on me."

Seeing you happy and whole is worth every bit of difficulty! I am glad you allowed me to heal the broken areas of your life. There is only one area you have not let me help you with. Caren, do you trust in me with your whole heart?

I know what He is getting at, and I don't like it. I love Stewart, and I want to believe that someday he will return my feelings, and we will live happily ever after. I've held this dream tightly, close to my chest, and have refused to give it to the Lord. He wants to take it from me, though, and I feel like a child being robbed of her security blanket.

"You have it wrong, Lord," I say defensively. "Stewart might love me someday. Millions of friendships turn into love affairs. Maybe being honest with him about my feelings will spark something he doesn't even realize is there. He has changed toward me a little already. I can tell by his words. He respects me and thinks I'm amazing. If I wait a little longer and try a little harder, eventually . . . "

Sweet Caren. Can you not see that I want to free you from your quest to be "good enough?" You are already good enough for me, and you are good enough for you. You do not need anybody else's affections to validate your worthiness. Do you remember what Dr. Tom told you?

He is referring to a previous therapist whose office I was

crying in about four years ago. Immediately after Big Reggie left me, I became involved with a man who, like all the other men I've dated, was completely unavailable. Even though I didn't like him that much at first, I found myself obsessed with him after he stood me up. He began to treat me poorly, yet I continued to pursue him. The more he rejected me and mistreated me, the more I wanted him to love me. I told Dr. Tom, "I don't really want to be with him, so why do I want him to love me so badly? He is unavailable, unkind, and doesn't care about me. Why do I keep doing this to myself? When will I stop?" His reply was simultaneously simple and complex. "You will stop when you quit trying to make your mother love you."

I guess Jesus is saying that I am repeating my pattern of chasing unavailable men, but Stewart is different than the men I've tried to win over in the past. He is kind and helpful and does not take advantage of me. I've confided in him for four years, sharing all my concerns, my past, my dreams, and my fears, and he does not judge me. He is quick to give advice or to just listen . . . but I have to admit, Stewart doesn't share himself with me. I long for more of him, but he makes it clear he wants only friendship from me.

"But I love him, Lord."

I understand, but the way you love him is not what I want for you.

"I need to at least tell him how I feel, to give him a chance to consider loving me in the same way!"

I don't wait for a response. I will take the matter into my own hands. I pull into the nearest gas station, park my car, and text Stewart. I tell him that I love him, and when I imagine my soulmate, he is the one I think of. I confess that I've felt this way since I've known him, and I hope that one day he will reciprocate my feelings.

There! I did it! I finally told him the truth of my heart. Now all I can do is wait. I pull back onto the road and continue toward Terilli's. Five minutes later, my text chimes. My throat tightens, and my heart races. I am terrified to read his reply. At the next red light, I pull out my phone to read his response: "I don't see that for us." And then: "I don't mean to hurt you, but I believe I have been very consistent over the years about how I feel."

I am shattered and begin to sob. I have to pull over again. I regress to asking myself, between sobs, the same questions that used to plague me. What is wrong with me? Why can't he love me? What was the point of changing so much if I am still unlovable? I succumb to my emotions for a while until I calm down enough to hear Jesus consoling me. But I don't want to be consoled. My sadness turns into anger in a flash.

"I don't want your pity, Jesus. This is your fault. Why didn't you make Stewart love me? You could have changed his heart like you changed mine. You know I want nothing more than for him to love me. I've been good. I've done everything you've asked. I gave up everything to follow you, but you still won't let me have Stewart! Why? Please?"

I know you are hurting, Caren. Let it out. I can take it.

"No, no, NO! Stop with all the loving stuff. I'm mad at you, and I don't want to be calmed down. Why can't Stewart love me? I cherish him. I am clean and good and wholesome now. Aren't I finally worth loving?"

I love you, and your worth is immeasurable. Work through your feelings, dear. I will be here when you are ready.

After crying for another half hour, I finally pull myself together enough to turn the car around and head home. I am mad at myself. I could have enjoyed a nice meal and live jazz at Terilli's, but instead I opened Pandora's box on the side of the road.

Now that I am calmer, I am not as angry at the Lord. I know intellectually that giving up Stewart is part of the freedom Jesus wants for me, but my heart and emotions have to catch up. I face the truth. Subconsciously—well, maybe not so subconsciously, but I tried hiding my thoughts from the Lord—I have expected my last date with the Lord to include a "surprise" happy ending with Stewart as my soul mate and forever partner. I believed that once I was fully in love with Jesus and did everything He asked of me, He would then change Stewart's heart. I even perceived my abstinence as a gift I could one day give Stewart. Of course, I also hoped that God would heal my heart and mind and give me a purpose for my life in our fifty-date journey—all of which indeed has happened—but I hoped I'd get the boy as well. And instead, Jesus is taking the boy out of our story before we even finish our last chapter.

I think back on my dating history. I've never been on a "real" date in my entire life—not even with my ex-husband! Sure, men have taken me to dinner, but not to get to know me better. They made it all too clear that there were strings attached, usually involving a motel room or the back seat of a car. I expected so little for myself that I allowed men to mistreat me, and as a result, I am forty years old and have never been properly dated by anyone but the Lord.

The time Stewart and I went to see the movie *Prometheus* is the closest I've come to having a date. We had recently become friends, but as we left the theater, I said, "Do you know this is the first real date I have ever had?" He gently corrected me. "This isn't a date. This is two friends going to a movie together." Even so, when he pulled up to my house, said goodnight, and waited for me to leave without hinting at anything "else," I was genuinely confused. I blurted out the most honest, unfiltered thing I could have said: "This is weird. I'm not used to not being treated like a whore." Stewart's face registered shock. His reply was simple. "Does that upset you?" I stammered, "Never mind! Please, forget what I said," and ran from the car as quickly as I could, embarrassed that I had been so blunt.

Boy, what a mess of a fantasy I've constructed since then. My blindness to the truth is painful to acknowledge. I have cried enough, though. I pull myself together to pick up Victoria from her friend's house.

***

Victoria and I go to church this morning, and I am able to soften my heart a little toward Jesus. I am still upset that He shattered my Stewart dream once and for all last night, but I love Jesus very much and know He is the reason for all that is good and pure in my life. Letting go of my anger is hard for me, though, so I am not ready to make amends with Him today.

After church I text Stewart and ask if we can talk. He says he will call me tomorrow at noon. I put a smile on my face for Victoria's sake and get through the day as normally as possible. We grocery shop, cook, eat dinner, do our nails together, and watch TV, but I feel ill and carry a deep sadness in my heart.

***

I eagerly wrap up the Monday morning Pamper Lake Highlands ESL program. Classes end at 11:00, but the church doesn't clear out until 11:30. I want to be at my house when

Stewart calls. On one hand, I dread the conversation, but on the other, I long to talk to him about what happened. He is a kind and understanding man. One of the reasons I love him is that he is the only man other than the Lord who has let me have a voice in our relationship.

Right on time, the phone rings. I answer nervously. "Hello?"

Stewart's voice sounds cheerful. "Hey! How's your morning?" We briefly exchange niceties before I cut to the chase.

"So . . . I am really struggling."

"Let's talk about that," he says in a softer tone of voice.

I share everything I've been thinking and feeling since Saturday night. I tell him I know my fantasy isn't fair to him, and that I realize that our relationship isn't even a real relationship. He interrupts me.

"Don't say that. Our relationship is our relationship. It may be different from other relationships, but it is just as valid. Do you cherish our friendship?"

"Of course I do, Stewart. That's why I don't know how to let you go."

"Do you have to let me go? Can the friendship we have be good enough for you?" he asks.

"I don't know. I constantly long for more of you. I want you to call me and share the highlights of your day."

Stewart sighs. "That's not my personality, Caren. Do you think I chat about myself to everyone else I know, just not with you?"

Now that he mentions it, I guess I have assumed he keeps me and only me at arm's length.

"I don't know," I say.

"Well, I don't. That's just not what I do. Can I be good enough for you as I am?"

It's my turn to sigh. "Stewart, obviously I think you're good enough. I've chosen to remain your friend all these years even though you don't love me like I love you, even though you don't call me or visit me."

He explains, "I don't call or visit because I don't want to confuse you. I know you struggle with your feelings for me, so I don't want to lead you on. Just because I don't have romantic feelings for you doesn't mean I don't genuinely care about you. I think our friendship is worth keeping, if you are open to it."

Well, I can't get him to join me on the "love" side of the fence. Lord knows I've tried. Perhaps I can figure out a way to join him on the friendship side. I say, "I do cherish our friendship. I'll give it a try, but you'll have to be patient with me as I work through my emotions. Thanks for taking the time to talk to me."

"You're welcome. Thanks for answering my call."

We hang up, and I release the tears I've been holding back. I don't want to lose Stewart's friendship, but I love him too much to be content with no hope for something more. Dammit, I didn't think things would turn out this way. I'm still angry at Jesus. I can't seem to quit blaming Him for breaking my heart, even though I know it is of my own doing.

***

I've been grieving since my phone call with Stewart yesterday. I have finally accepted the truth. There has never been any hope of a romantic relationship between Stewart and me. I used his unexpected kindness and decency to justify a romantic fantasy. I clung to that fantasy despite years of evidence that it was improbable. Part of me wants to hide from the new light of truth.

The fantasy is easier. But the rest of me is relieved that I am one step closer to the Lord's plan for me. I take a hot bubble bath to relax. My tears come again, and I finally relent and let Jesus in.

I cry and splash my hands onto my legs angrily. "It isn't fair, Lord! I love him so much, yet he won't love me in return. I would have loved him beautifully if he had let me. You don't understand how horrible this feels!"

I know exactly how loving someone who refuses to give you their whole heart feels, Caren. I feel the same way every single day with my beloved people. I felt the same way when I pursued you all those years. My heart breaks for my people. I have the remedy to all their problems. I am the truth and the light, but so many refuse to accept me.

I am stopped short. I feel the Lord's anguish so strongly that it is almost palpable. I never thought of how He must feel, rejected repeatedly. Now I cry for Him, for the burden He bears. How many times did I alone push Him away? I shut Him out of my life and my heart time and time again, but He refused to give up on me. And there is a whole world of people just like me. I feel deep sadness for what I have done, what mankind has done, rejecting Jesus' perfect love for us.

Caren, will you allow me to be enough for you? Will you trust I have plans for you and will fulfill your dreams, even dreams you are not yet aware of? I will always listen to you and never judge you. You are perfect to me. I want your whole heart, even the spot you have reserved for Stewart.

I have sudden clarity that my feelings for Stewart serve no higher purpose. I've kept him in the part of my heart I've reserved all my life for feeling "not good enough." Dr. Tom was right. When I was a child, I tried to be good enough for my parents to notice and love me. I continued trying to be good enough for every male in my adult life. I tried to be good enough for my friends. I realize with a start that I have not experienced a single day in my entire life without a longing for acceptance and adoration from someone who won't give it to me. Perhaps I persisted in pursuing Stewart because I was clinging to a familiar feeling, albeit a twisted one. I realize that though I let the Lord change my heart in so many ways during forty-nine dates over almost three years, I held on to feeling not good enough for Stewart. I refused to let the Lord be enough for me.

That's why Jesus wants me to let go of loving Stewart! Christ has healed the little girl in me who longed for her mommy to love her. I no longer need to replay the same scenario. If I let Jesus remove the Stewart fantasy from that spot in my heart, He can heal it once and for all and fill it with His perfect love.

My sweet Jesus sacrificed His life for me. He is there when I need Him, whether I want Him or not. He has the answers to everything I long for. With an upturned face streaming with tears, I cry, "Jesus, I am so sorry for rejecting you. I am sorry I resisted letting you be enough for me. I am ready now. Please, Lord. Take this ache and fill my heart with your love instead. I know this won't be the last time I resist giving my life to you completely, but never give up on me. I always understand eventually."

An incredible feeling of peace bathes me.

Caren. Thank you for finally surrendering all of yourself to me. I can now tell you that these last four months have been one long, progressive date. I did not tell you before because your heart was so set against forgiving your mother and letting go of Stewart. If you had known our fiftieth date was for that purpose, you would have been devastated and even more resistant than you already were, and you would not have entered into it with the right mindset. But now you understand, our final date was finding complete freedom and restoration.

My mouth drops. Our fifty dates are over? Today, February

15, 2015, is the end of our fifty dates?

Yes, my love, but do not worry. Though our fifty dates are complete, we are not finished with each other. Not by a long shot! Our journey is a long and amazing one and I have great plans for us. Now we have really begun . . .

Acknowledgments

My dear and precious Jesus . . . thank you for your constant pursuit of me. My life is rich and filled with beauty and purpose. Your grace is never failing. I am beyond honored that you would take this journey with me and use our story for kingdom work. I don't deserve this kind of love, but I am so happy I get to receive it! I choose you. You are my deepest love, my favorite friend, and my dearest companion, and I want to do forever with you.

My dear children, Mommy loves you each so much. Thank you for being patient with me while I tried to figure life out. You were each the reason for my fight every day and the reason I didn't give up. There has been no greater gift from the Lord than you children. I am honored to be your mom. I'm so proud of each of you for the wonderful people you are. Da'Shon, you are such a magnificent young man. You are responsible, loving, and kind, and the glue that held our home together. You will be an amazing husband and father one day. Reggie, you have the potential to be an incredible leader one day! Son, you're so fun, charismatic, and very talented. The Lord will use you to do great things. Just continue to seek Him and listen to His direction—the places He will lead you are going to be quite an adventure, I'm sure of it. My little princess, Victoria, you were born to be a missionary. Your heart is so beautiful; you love and empathize in a way I could only dream of. You seek to see and be near the unnoticed; this is a special gift from the Lord, and I am so honored you are my missionary partner. Yaneth, I may not be your birth mom, but you are just like a daughter to me. Our family is so very blessed by your presence. Your heart is beautiful, and you are one of the most selfless, generous, and kind people I have ever met. Thank you for loving our family like you do. Yaneth Lopez, you are my Ruth, and I cherish the gift the Lord has given me through you.

This book would not have been possible without my dear father and loving stepmother, Sally. You both introduced me to Christ as a little girl. I believe it was because of the seed you planted that I knew to call out to Father God in my darkest days. Thank you, and I love you both so much.

Mom, you gave me life, you chose to keep me, and you did the best you knew how. Look at the beauty the Lord made from our pasts! My life would not have been what it was without you, and I wouldn't change a day of our time together growing up, as each experience brought me to where I am today. I am so thankful the Lord restored our relationship; He is so wonderful. Thank you, Mom. I love you.

Grandma, thank you for having the best lap and bosom a little girl could rest in! "Hold on to your Girdle, Myrtle"—This is gonna be one heck of a ride!

Matthew, thank you for believing in me all these years. We came from different parents, but I have always called you my "real brother" because you have always loved me as your little sister. You've been so generous, protected me, and never did me harm. Zach, Liv, and Lexi, your Aunt Caren thinks you are each so amazing! Your Mommy will live on through each of you, and I know you will make her proud.

Audrey Steinle—Wow, where do I begin? I could write an entire book on how a Christian therapist should be because of who you were EVERY. SINGLE. WEEK . . . for two and a half years! You were so kind and patient. You never judged, always listened, and gently showed me what it looks like to love a sister in Christ. Thank you for being faithful to the Lord's call on your life. God used your obedience to help Him do a complete deliverance. I can't wait to see what He has planned for us to do in the future—get your passport ready, friend!

Thank you to my friend and talented content editor, Tracy Hundley. When the Lord called me to write this book, my rebuttal was, "But I'm not a writer, and I didn't even finish high school." His reply: Just write, and I will provide everyone and everything needed to turn this into our book. And then He provided you. You called me and said, "I think God is asking me to help you or your ministry. Can you tell me a few of your needs?" All I did was mention the book, and you knew! Thank you for your gifts and talents, for pushing me to write better, and for filling in the gaps where I fell short. You took your time and dedicated your gifts so I could get to the next step. Everything you touched, you improved. You edited in such a beautiful way that I never lost my voice. You are so talented, and I can't wait to work together on the next book!

Lori Beth Lemmon, the same goes to you. Thank you for all of your support and encouragement on this journey. When I came to you, I only had a few "dates" under my belt—this book was just a call the Lord had given and some brief notes, but you believed in it. You spent hours on and off the phone helping me put together the book proposal. The Lord used that proposal to breathe life into the concept, and then He used it to lead me to Fedd Books . . .

Whitney, Lauren, Jessica, Erin, and the whole Fedd Books team, thank you for believing in this book. It is such a unique piece of work, and I know the Lord called your office to work together to do what it would take to get this into the hands of our amazing readers. Whitney, I sent you the proposal, and you took the time to read it and then ask the whole editorial team to look at it as well. Thank you for believing in the concept—even when it was in the "I said, God said, I said, God said" form—and for encouraging me to keep writing. I'm so excited to see what the Lord does with this book because of the Fedd Books' touch!

To my dear friends and generous investing partners, Natalie and Mike Boyle, Marsha and Craig Holmes, D'Lane and Bill Maselunas, Elizabeth and Russel May, and Lori and Kirk Mc-Gregor, thank you. Thank you for walking by faith and believing in the beautiful things the Lord will do by putting this book into the hands of its readers. Thank you for believing in me! Each of you brings something so special to my life. I love you all so much and cherish you, your love, and your support.

To the rest of my dear family and friends and the Lake Highlands community, thank you! There are so many people who played a part in this journey, past and present. I don't know how I could begin to mention one name and have room for each of you. But I do know my heart is so thankful to you all. My children and I have new lives now! We no longer live in poverty or under oppression, and we owe that to many of you. The Lord used each of you strategically to help us. Thank you for teaching us a new way of life.